Sexuality in
Close Relationships

SEXUALITY IN CLOSE RELATIONSHIPS

Edited by
KATHLEEN MCKINNEY
SUSAN SPRECHER
Illinois State University

LEA LAWRENCE ERLBAUM ASSOCIATES, PUBLISHERS
1991   Hillsdale, New Jersey   Hove and London

Lawrence Erlbaum Associates, Inc., Publishers
365 Broadway
Hillsdale, New Jersey 07642

Library of Congress Cataloging–in–Publication Data
Sexuality in close relationships / edited by Kathleen McKinney, Susan Sprecher
    p.   cm.
Includes bibliographical references and index.
ISBN 0–8058–0719–5
1. Sex. 2. Sex (Psychology) 3. Interpersonal relations. 4. Sex customs—United States.
I. McKinney, Kathleen. II. Sprecher, Susan, 1955– .
HQ21.S4765 1991   91–3458
                                                                    CIP

Printed in the United States of America
10 9 8 7 6 5 4 3

Contents

Editors' and Contributors' Biographies

Kathleen McKinney, editor, received her Ph.D. in 1982 from the University of Wisconsin–Madison and is professor in the Department of Sociology, Anthropology and Social Work at Illinois State University. Her areas of specialization include social psychology, sex roles, and human sexuality. McKinney is involved in research on sexual harassment, contraceptive attitudes and behaviors, and sexual standards. She has publications in these areas and on teaching in several book chapters and journals. McKinney is co-editor (with Susan Sprecher) of *Human Sexuality: The Societal and Interpersonal Context* (Norwood, NJ: Ablex, 1989).

Susan Sprecher, editor, is currently an associate professor in the Department of Sociology, Antropology and Social Work at Illinois State University. She received her Ph.D. from the University of Wisconsin–Madison in 1985. She is a co-author (with Elaine Hatfield) of a book on physical attractiveness and a co-editor (with Kathleen McKinney) of a book on the societal and interpersonal context of human sexuality. She has also published several articles and chapters on such topics as equity and exchange, self-disclosure, sexual standards, and determinants of relationship breakups.

Arthur Aron received his Ph.D. in social psychology from the University of Toronto in 1970; his dissertation was a series of experimental studies on romantic attraction. Since then he has held positions at the University of Paris (Laboratoire de psychologie sociale), the University of British Columbia, Maharishi International University, California Graduate School of Family Psychology, and Santa Clara University. He is now at the University of California at Santa Cruz. His current research focuses on exploring the implications of the self-expansion model of motivation in close relationships. Specific current research includes the cognitive structure of closeness, the effects of falling in love on self-concept, and motivational factors in unrequited love.

Elaine Aron completed her graduate training at York University in clinical and personality psychology. She has subsequently held a variety of positions involving research, counseling and the training of counselors. She has taught at Maharishi International University, Chapman College, and Santa Clara University. Currently she is a lecturer in psychology at the University of California at Santa Cruz. She is a coauthor of *Love as Expansion of the Self: Understanding Attraction and Satisfaction* (Hemisphere, 1986) and *The Heart of Social Psychology* (Lexington, 1989). In addition to studies of close relationships and love, she has published research on creativity, emotions, and consciousness and meditation. In addition to her academic interests, her first novel was published last year, and she is the author or coauthor of several nonfiction books.

Robert G. Bringle received his Ph.D. in 1974 in social psychology at the University of Massachusetts-Amherst. He is currently an associate professor of psychology at Purdue University at Indianapolis. His areas of research interest include jealousy and close relationships, evaluation of social and health programs, cognitive development, and the social psychology of aging. Recent publications include an article in the *Journal of Social and Personal Relationships* and chapters in several edited volumes in the areas of jealousy and close relationships.

Bram P. Buunk is a professor of social psychology at the State University of Groningen, the Netherlands. He received his Ph.D. from the University of Utrecht in 1980. Buunk has published over 100 scholarly articles, mainly in the areas of close relationships and organizational behavior. In addition, he has authored or edited eight books. He is also the associate editor of *Gedrag en Gezondheid,* the Dutch health psychology journal.

F. Scott Christopher received his Ph.D. from Oregon State University in 1982 in human development and family studies. He was a member of the faculty at the University of Nevada–Reno before joining the Department of Family Resources and Human Development at Arizona State University in 1986, where he is currently an associate professor. His main research focus has been on premarital sexuality, with an emphasis on how sexual involvement relates to relationship development.

William R. Cupach received his Ph.D. in communication arts and sciences from the University of Southern California in 1981. He is currently associate professor of communication at Illinois State University. His recent research focuses on how communication is used to manage problematic situations, such as interpersonal conflict, social predicaments, and relational disengagement. He co-authored the *Handbook of Interpersonal Competence Research* (with B. Spitzberg) (New York: Springer-Verlag, 1989)

John D. DeLamater is a professor of sociology at the University of Wisconsin–Madison. He received his Ph.D. in social psychology at the University of Michigan in 1969. His interests include human sexuality and social controls of individual behavior. His current research includes work on the determinants of contraceptive use and choice of method by single women, and the sexual transmission of HIV/AIDS. He is author or co-author of two books—including a textbook entitled *Social Psychology*—(San Diego, CA: Harcourt Brace Jovanovich, 1990) and numerous articles.

Steve Duck received his Ph.D. at Sheffield, United Kingdom, and is currently Daniel and Amy Starch Research Professor in Communication Studies at the University of Iowa and founder and editor of the *Journal of Social and Personal Relationships*. He has been active in the field of research in personal relationships, founding the International Network on Personal Relationships (known as the Iowa Network) and two series of international conferences on personal relationships. He edited the *Handbook of Personal Relationships* (New York: Wiley, 1988) and has written or edited over 20 books, including *Relating to Others* (Belmont, CA: Dorsey/Brooks/Cole 1988) and *Human Relationships* (Beverly Hills, CA: Sage. in press)

Steven W. Gangestad received his Ph.D. from the University of Minnesota in 1986, specializing in social/personality psychology. He currently is an assistant professor of psychology at the University of New Mexico. His areas of research interest include evolutionary psychology, biological foundations of personality, and interpersonal relations. He has authored several empirical articles focusing on evolutionary and biological approaches to understanding personality and relationships.

Mary F. Goggins is currently a graduate student in clinical psychology at the University of Kansas. Her areas of interest include the attribution process of acquaintance rape victims, the effects of acquaintance rape on victims' physical health, and differences in consequences for acquaintance and stranger rape victims.

John H. Harvey received his Ph.D. in social psychology in 1971 at the University of Missouri–Columbia and is a professor in the Department of Psychology at the University of Iowa. His major focus is on attribution theory, especially as applied to dynamics in close relationships. He has authored or edited many books, including co-editor (with W. Ickes and R. Kidd) of the three-volume *New Directions in Attribution* series (Hillsdale, NJ; Erlbaum, 1976, 1978, 1981), co-author (with Weary) of *Perspectives on Attributional Processes* (WC Brown), co-author (with H. Kelley and others) of *Close Relationships* (New York: 1983 Freeman). He was also founding editor of the *Journal of Social and Clinical Psychology*.

Jayme Jones received her M.A. in clinical psychology from the University of Kansas in 1990. She is currently a graduate student in the clinical psychology program at the University of Kansas. Her research interests include sexual violence, physical violence, child abuse, and women's issues. She is also interested in education and prevention programs in these areas. Her therapeutic interests include crisis intervention, grief counseling, and issues facing survivors of sexual and physical violence.

Lawrence A. Kurdek received his Ph.D. in developmental psychology from the University of Illinois in 1976. He is currently a professor at Wright State University. His research interests include social-cognitive development, the effects of divorce and remarriage on parents and children, and the development of relationship quality in homosexual and heterosexual couples.

Sandra Metts received her Ph.D. in communication research from the University of Iowa in 1983. She is currently an associate professor in the Department of Communication at Illinois State University. Her recent publications have been concerned with the strategic use of communication in face-threatening situations such as relationship disengagement, sexual rejection, and being discovered deceiving one's partner.

Charlene L. Muehlenhard received her Ph.D. in psychology in 1981 from the University of Wisconsin–Madison, after a clinical internship at the University of Mississippi Medical Center/VA Consortium. She began her career on the faculty at Texas A & M University. She is now at the University of Kansas, where she holds a joint appointment in psychology and women's studies. Her research is on sexual coercion, especially on the interface of sexual coercion, the social construction of gender, and the social construction of sexuality.

Terri L. Orbuch received her Ph.D. in 1988 at the University of Wisconsin–Madison and is an assistant professor in the Department of Sociology at the University of Michigan. Her major research interests include relationship loss, account making in response to severe stress, sexuality, and symbolic interactionism. She has been co-author (with Harvey and Weber) of *Interpersonal Accounts: A Social Psychological Perspective* (Oxford: Basil Blackwell, 1990), editor of *Relationship Loss: Theoretical Perspectives* (New York: Springer-Verlag, 1991), and co-editor of *Attribution, Accounts and Close Relationships* New York: Springer-Verlag, 1991).

Mark W. Roosa received his Ph.D. from Michigan State University in 1980. Since that time he has been at Arizona State University, where he is now an associate professor in the Department of Family Resources and Human Development. His research interests include adolescent sexuality, pregnancy, and parenting and the impact of parental alcoholism on children.

Arthur Satterfield is currently a graduate student in clinical psychology at the University of Kansas. His areas of interest are sex roles, intimate relationships, sexual harassment, and human sexuality. He recently published a co-authored article on sexual harassment in *Journal of Interpersonal Violence*.

Jeffry A. Simpson received his Ph.D. from the University of Minnesota in 1986 specializing in social/personality psychology. He currently is an assistant professor of psychology at Texas A & M University. His areas of research interest include interpersonal relations, personality and social behavior, and evolutionary psychology. He has authored several empirical articles focusing on the relation between personality and processes underlying the initiation and dissolution of romantic relationships.

Sexuality in
Close Relationships

Introduction

Kathleen McKinney
Susan Sprecher
Illinois State University

For several years we have been researching and teaching human sexuality and close relationships. Recently, some of our research has dealt with the interface between these two areas (e.g., sexual standards for different relationship stages, sexual harassment, the influence of sexual behavior on perceptions of and attraction toward others, sexual aspects of dating relationships, and effects of AIDS on close relationships). We decided to edit this volume because no previous book exists that focuses on the interface between the two related fields of human sexuality and close relationships. This volume represents our second effort to provide a book on sexuality that has a sociological and social psychological viewpoint (see also *Human Sexuality: The Societal and Interpersonal Context,* Norwood, NJ, Ablex, 1989).

In this introduction, we will discuss the research areas of both sexuality and close relationships. This discussion will begin with definitions of the constructs *sexuality* and *close relationships.* Second, we briefly cover the history and status of the areas including key journals, conferences, and professional organizations. Next, we point out recent work that attempts to bridge the two areas. Fourth, we provide an overview of the volume (purpose, audience), and finally, we offer a brief summary description of each chapter in this volume.

DEFINITIONS OF "SEXUALITY" AND "CLOSE RELATIONSHIPS"

We have titled this book *Sexuality in Close Relationships.* What do we mean by *sexuality* and *close relationships,* and what is their connection? There are several

1

definitions of sexuality offered in the literature (see Aron and Aron this volume). We prefer the sociological definition offered by Reiss (1989). He defines sexuality as "the erotic arousal and genital responses resulting from following the shared sexual scripts of that society" (p. 6). Sexual scripts indicate the with whom, where, when, how, and why the erotic arousal and genital responses may occur. For example, our society encourages sexual behavior (e.g., sexual intercourse) within the institution of marriage or another close relationship and in a private location. Although this book is about erotic arousal and genital responses, it is also about a lot more. We use *sexuality* very generally to refer to sexual behaviors, arousal, and responses, as well as to sexual attitudes, desires, and communication.

Although we use the term *close relationships* in the title, the relationships could also have been described as personal, interpersonal, significant, intimate, meaningful, loving, or committed. In fact, the various contributors to this volume use all of these adjectives and others to describe the type of relationship in which sexuality usually occurs. Our choice of close relationships is based on our observation that relationship investigators are increasingly focusing on the concept of relationship closeness or using the phrase *close relationships* (see, e.g., Berscheid, Snyder, & Omoto, 1989; Clark & Reis, 1988; Kelley et al., 1983).

Kelley et al. (1983) define a close relationship as having a high degree of interdependence. They write that

> A high degree of interdependence between two people is revealed in four properties of their interconnected activities: (1) the individuals have *frequent* impact on each other; (2) the degree of impact per each occurrence is *strong;* (3) the impact involves *diverse* kinds of activities for each person; and (4) all of these properties characterize the interconnected activity series for a relatively long *duration* of time. (p. 13)

Most of us are interdependent (and thus close) with several people—parents, friends, siblings, children, and a romantic partner.

Sexual behavior and/or sexual desire do not occur in all close relationships, nor is a close relationship necessary for having sex. Most people in our society, however, experience most of their erotic arousal and orgasms in relationships that have varying degrees of closeness. That is, while two people are involved sexually, they usually interact *frequently,* engage in several *activities* together (and not just sex), *influence* each other's behaviors, decisions, goals, and so forth. This interdependence is *long term* rather than short duration. The result is that the sexual aspect of the close relationship is intertwined with several other aspects of the relationship—such as communication, love, and emotions. Some of the chapters in the volume focus on the intertwining of sexuality and relationship characteristics.

SEXUALITY, CLOSE RELATIONSHIPS:
TWO DISTINCT RESEARCH AREAS?

Historically, research in the area of human sexuality has had a physiological or clinical viewpoint. The emphasis has been on sexual response and sexual problems (e.g., Masters & Johnson, 1966, 1970). Social scientists (psychologists and sociologists) added to this literature but often focused on sexual deviance. Notable exceptions to this early literature are the Kinsey, Pomeroy, & Martin (1948, 1953) studies and the work of Mead (1935), which focus more broadly on sexuality and have a social and cultural viewpoint.

Recent work has become more diverse in terms of topic areas and involves researchers in several disciplines including sociology, social psychology, psychology, communication, family studies, and anthropology. Several journals exist in the field including *Journal of Sex Research, Archives of Sexual Behavior, Homosexuality,* and *Psychology of Human Sexuality.* Research on sexuality is also published in journals in related fields (e.g., *Journal of Marriage and the Family* and *Sex Roles*). The Society for the Scientific Study of Sex is an interdisciplinary professional organization that sponsors a large annual conference and a newsletter. Two other major organizations in the area are the Sex Information and Education Council of the United States (SIECUS) and the American Association of Sex Educators, Counselors and Therapists (AASECT). Other organizations (American Sociological Association, American Psychological Association, National Council on Family Relations) have sections on sexuality. The journals, organizations, meetings, and involvement of respected researchers in the field of sexuality research have increased the legitimacy of this area.

The study of close relationships has also grown tremendously in the past decade. Sex, love, conflict, relationship maintenance, relationship termination, and several other diverse topics related to close or personal relationships have become the focus of research by scholars in several related fields, including psychology, social psychology, sociology, communication, and family studies. Before this recent upsurge in interdisciplinary work on the study of close relationships, the topic was studied in a limited way. Family sociologists studied the marital relationship and the family, but primarily as social institutions. Social psychologists studied interpersonal attraction, or why people initially like others, but tended not to investigate what happened after the two people liked each other enough to begin dating.

Beginning in the 1980s, several edited volumes and textbooks devoted to the study of close relationships were published. In 1983, the *Journal of Social and Personal Relationships* was created. Furthermore, articles on close relationships have been published in several other journals including *Journal of Personality and Social Psychology, Social Psychology Quarterly, Journal of Clinical and Social Psychology,* and *Journal of Marriage and the Family.* Two international societies whose membership consists of scholars devoted to the study of close relationships now exist. These are the International Society for the Study of Personal Relationships (ISSPR) and the International Network of Personal Relationships (INPR). Together, these societies offer a conference each year, workshops, awards for distinguished scholarship, several newsletters, directories of scholars in the relationship field, and a sense of network with other scholars with similar interests.

RECENT INTERFACE
BETWEEN THESE TWO AREAS

Although recognizing that sexual behavior often occurs in a close relationship, researchers in the area of sexuality have traditionally ignored the relationship and examined the *individual's* sexuality. Often this individual-level analysis is warranted for the topics that have been examined. For example, sexual response cycles are experienced by individuals, not dyads. Atypical or aberrant sexual behavior (e.g., transvestism, voyeurism, exhibitionism) is most often individual behavior. An enumeration of the range and extent of sexual outlets is obtained from individuals who provide information across several relationships through a lifetime. In other words, because an individual's sexuality is not limited to one current, close relationship, it is appropriate to ignore the relationship itself for many research questions in the area of sexuality.

Similarly, those who study close relationships are not always interested in the sexual aspect of the relationship. In fact, researchers on close relationships have been more interested in general topics on the relationship that are only indirectly related to sexuality, including love, relationship satisfaction, power, equity, and communication. Because these dimensions of the relationship are not manifested only or primarily in the sexual area of the relationship, it makes sense to examine these variables more generally.

Increasingly, however, researchers have focused on sexual behaviors, desires, or attitudes within a specific, close relationship. The research questions that have been examined include: How often do couples engage in sexual behaviors and what types? What are the different pathways to sexual involvement? How is sexual intimacy or sexual satisfaction related to other aspects of the relationship, such as relationship satisfaction, conflict, and love? How do couples communicate their sexual needs, desires, and dislikes? What is sexual jealousy, and what are its effects on the relationship? Is there sexual coercion in close relationships, and what are its causes and consequences? Researchers (including ourselves) have also been interested in people's attitudes about what is appropriate sexual behavior in close relationships at different stages. The research that has addressed these and many other questions is reviewed in this volume. We hope that this book will help generate additional research ideas on the topic of sexuality in close relationships.

OVERVIEW OF THE VOLUME

This volume contains nine original chapters related to sexuality in close relationships written by respected international researchers. These researchers represent several disciplines including psychology, social psychology, sociology, communication, and family studies. They are influential scholars in either close relationships or sexuality, and most of them have done work in the interface between these two areas.

Because we intend to cover sexuality in the context of close relationships, the primary perspective of this book is social psychological. The chapters focus on topics such as methodological issues in studying close relationships; the reciprocal influence of personality, love, jealousy, and other emotions with sexuality in close relationships; sexual aspects of homosexual close relationships; sexual coercion in close relationships; and sexual communication and decision making in close relationships. In addition, there is an afterword by well-known relationship researcher and editor of the *Journal of Social and Personal Relationships,* Steve Duck.

This volume is aimed at a fairly wide audience. The coverage, language, and difficulty level are suitable for advanced undergraduate students, graduate students, faculty, and other professionals. The book is of interest to individuals in social psychology, psychology, sociology, communication, family studies, and women's studies. We believe the volume could be used as a major source in courses on close relationships, sexuality, or male-female relationships; as a supplementary source in courses on marriage and the family, sex roles, and gender; and as a resource for those who teach, research, or do clinical work in the areas of human sexuality or close relationships.

OVERVIEW OF EACH CHAPTER

Chapter 1, "Methodological and Conceptual Issues in the Study of Sexuality in Close Relationships," is written by Terri Orbuch and John Harvey, who argue that sexuality is, primarily, a social process. They present a fourfold conceptual scheme to summarize the types of methodologies used in sexuality research. In addition, Orbuch and Harvey have three major goals in their chapter: (a) to examine the previous research and methods in the study of sexuality in general, (b) to discuss types of research on sexuality in the close relationship, and (c) to offer new directions of research in the study of sexuality and close relationships.

"Love and Sexuality" is the topic of chapter 2 written by Arthur and Elaine Aron. They cover the interface between love and sexuality, drawing on theoretical and empirical work of their own and other scholars. They begin with a discussion of definitions and typologies of love and a definition of sexuality. Next, the Arons offer an organizing framework that classifies prior work in terms of the emphasis given to love versus sexuality, and they use this framework to present the theories and research on the relationship between love and sexuality. In addition, they briefly cover data (primarily survey research with college students) on what members of our culture think about love and sexuality. Finally, they present models that view the relationship between sexuality and love as a result of a third factor, including a brief presentation of their "Self-Expansion Model."

The chapter by John DeLamater, entitled "Emotions and Sexuality" (chapter 3), tackles a relatively new and limited area of research. He begins with definitions of emotions and sexuality. The chapter continues with three major sections: (a) a discussion of emotion as an antecedent to sexuality, (b) consideration of emotions as a component of sexual behavior, and (c) coverage of material looking at emotion as a consequence of sexuality. DeLamater concludes with a brief discussion of jealousy.

Chapter 4 covers the literature on "Personality and Sexuality: Empirical Relations and an Integrative Theoretical Model." Jeff Simpson and Steve Gangestad wrote this chapter, which emphasizes the notion that individual differences, including personality, influence our sexual attitudes and behaviors. First, they review some of the personality dimensions that underlie sexuality. Next, they present some of their own related research, including the Sociosexual Orientation Inventory they have created. Past research and models on markers of sociosexuality, and extraversion and lack of constraint are reviewed. Finally, they discuss an evolutionary framework, including their own model, which helps make sense of the relationship between individual differences and sociosexuality.

"Sexuality and Communication in Close Relationships" is the title of chapter 5, written by William Cupach and Sandra Metts. They begin by reviewing research on the importance of communication in sexual relationships. An intriguing discussion of sexuality in cross-sex friendships follows. The third and fourth sections of the chapter look at the role of communication in the involvement and perceptions of dating and developed sexual relationships, respectively. Subtopics include communication and the initiation, resistance, and meaning of sexual behavior in those relationships.

Scott Christopher and Mark Roosa cover the large amount of literature on "Factors Affecting Sexual Decisions in the Premarital Relationships of Adolescents and Young Adults" in chapter 6. They emphasize the importance of separating discussions of research based on school-age samples from that of college-age samples, and the chapter is structured in this manner. Their review is organized by looking at these two age groups and focusing on research and theories that cover the role of individual factors, social environment factors, and relationship factors as influences on sexual decision making. They conclude with a discussion of future theoretical and methodological directions.

Chapter 7 is entitled "Extradyadic Relationships and Sexual Jealousy." This chapter was written by Robert Bringle and Bram Buunk. These authors discuss different views, types, definitions, and outcomes of jealousy. They focus on theory and research on the relationship between jealousy and extradyadic relationships for both "traditional" (dating, marriage) and "nontraditional" (open marriages, swinging) relationships.

The chapter on "Sexual Violence and Coercion in Close Relationships" (chapter 8) was written by Charlene Muehlenhard and several graduate students (Mary Goggins, Jayme Jones, & Arthur Satterfield). They discuss sexual coercion of males and females in heterosexual and homosexual relationships. Their focus is on sexual coercion in dating and marital relationships. Sexual coercion is broadly defined and includes various forms of sexual activity and different types of coercion (physical force, verbal force, threats, manipulation, power differences). The authors review research on the prevalence, causes, and consequences of sexual coercion in close relationships.

Larry Kurdek wrote the final chapter (chapter 9) on "Sexuality in Homosexual and Heterosexual Couples." Kurdek compares homosexual and heterosexual couples in terms of sexuality. He begins with a discussion of the importance of studying homosexual couples and some of the unique features of such relationships. He then reviews prior research comparing homosexual and heterosexual couples. Kurdek's chapter draws extensively from his own recent study of both partners in gay, lesbian, and heterosexual unmarried and heterosexual married couples. Couple types and partners within couples were compared on a variety of measures of sexuality including sexual satisfaction, the importance of new sexual techniques, beliefs regarding sexual perfection, and the importance of sexual fidelity.

Finally, Steve Duck offers an insightful afterword for the volume entitled "Couples and Coupling," which includes critical comments about and an integration of the material in the volume. Duck focuses on the neglected issue of "everyday talk" and the importance of "process" in sexuality and close relationship research.

ACKNOWLEDGMENTS

We gratefully acknowledge the assistance and input of several people who contributed in various ways to this volume. First, we thank Illinois State University for some of the resources that helped make this book possible. Second, we thank the contributors to the volume for the quality chapters and prompt response to deadlines. Third, we thank the staff at Lawrence Erlbaum Associates for their expertise in the publishing aspects of this project. Finally, we want to acknowledge our families for their patience and support during the tenure of this project.

REFERENCES

Berscheid, E., Snyder, M., & Omoto, A. M. (1989). The relationship closeness inventory: Assessing the closeness of interpersonal relationships. *Journal of Personality and Social Psychology, 57*, 792–807.

Clark, M. S., & Reis, H. (1988). Interpersonal processes in close relationships. *Annual Review of Psychology, 39*, 609–672.

Kelley, H. H., Berscheid, E., Christensen, A., Harvey, J. H., Huston, T. L., Levinger, G., McClintock, E., Peplau, L. A., & Peterson, D. R. (1983). Analyzing close relationships. In H. H. Kelley et al. (Eds.), *Close Relationships* (pp. 20–67). San Francisco: Freeman.

Kinsey, A. C., Pomeroy, W. B., & Martin, C. E. (1948). *Sexual behavior in the human male.* Philadelphia: Saunders.

Kinsey, A. C., Pomeroy, W. B., & Martin, C. E. (1953). *Sexual behavior in the human female.* Philadelphia: Saunders.

Masters, W. H., & Johnson, V. E. (1966). *Human sexual response.* Boston: Little, Brown.

Masters, W. H., & Johnson, V. E. (1970). *Human sexual inadequacy.* Boston: Little, Brown.

Mead, M. (1935). *Sex and temperament in three primitive societies.* New York: Morrow.

Reiss, I. (1989). Society and sexuality: A sociological theory. In K. McKinney & S. Sprecher (Eds.), *Human sexuality: The societal and interpersonal context* (pp. 3–29). Norwood, NJ: Ablex.

1

Methodological and Conceptual Issues in the Study of Sexuality in Close Relationships

Terri L. Orbuch
University of Michigan

John H. Harvey
University of Iowa

INTRODUCTION

During the 1980s, several books, articles, and chapters evaluated methodological and conceptual issues concerned with the study of sexuality (e.g., Callero & Howard, 1989; Green & Wiener, 1980; Jayne, 1986; a special issue of the *Journal of Sex Research* [Vol. 22, No. 1, 1986]; Weinstein, 1984). Compared to previous discussions, however, this chapter focuses on research and methodological issues arising from the study of sexuality in *close relationships*. Little research and theoretical emphasis have been given to the study of sexuality *within* close relationships. In most studies of sexuality, the relationship is implicit in the examination of the issue, yet relevant relationship aspects are not actually documented. In addition, few studies go beyond the individual as the unit of analysis.

In a poignant essay examining the social construction of sexuality, Weeks (1986) stated that sexual relations are but a form of social relations; sexuality is a product of the social environment around us. An implicit assumption in Weeks' essay, and a major theme of this chapter, is that in its most meaningful form sexuality is but another social process, much like other social and relational processes. Allport (1968) defined the study of social-psychological processes as "the attempt to understand and explain how the thought, feeling, and behavior of individuals are influenced by the real, imagined, or implied presence of others" (p. 3). Given the breadth of this definition, one may be hard pressed to imagine

9

many instances of human behavior that do not have these features or implications (Harvey, Burgess, & Orbuch, in press). Nevertheless, one notes that the majority of sexual behavior also conforms to this definition of social processes. Most sexual activity occurs in interaction with others, whether that be real, imagined, or implied. Even those sexual activities that are conducted without the presence of others (e.g., masturbation) are usually influenced by the implied or imagined presence of others (e.g., through fantasy, erotica, or pornography). Thus, in this chapter the general emphasis in analyzing methodological and conceptual issues in the study of sexuality within close relationships is on the full social-psychological dynamics of this process.

If we define sexuality as but another social process, then the question becomes: If the key component of sexuality is that of relating closely to another human, how is the scientific study of sexuality any different from the study of other social or relational processes in general? Are there issues unique to the study of sexuality that do not arise in the study of other social phenomena? In examining these questions, the goals of this chapter are threefold. First, previous research and methods in the study of sexuality *in general* are examined. The first section addresses the interdisciplinary nature of the study of sexuality, an organization of the methods used to study sexuality, and the implications sexuality research and its inherent methodological issues have for research on sexuality in close relationships. Second, the chapter focuses on relevant research in the area. Lastly, after reviewing the relevant literature, we offer new directions of research in the study of sexuality and address specific issues that need to be delineated. In addition, we suggest that, where relevant, the concept of close relationships be given greater attention in research on sexuality.

RESEARCH ON SEXUALITY IN GENERAL

Interdisciplinary Topic of Study

By briefly discussing the backgrounds of scholars who have chosen to study the topic of sexuality, we can develop a broader picture of the interdisciplinary nature of work on human sexuality. Further, the disciplinary and theoretical approach a researcher chooses in studying a phenomenon will greatly influence the type of methodology chosen in the relevant empirical work.

It is not surprising to find that scholars from a wide array of disciplines in the behavioral sciences (e.g., sociology, psychology, communication, anthropology, family studies) have studied the topic of sexuality. Reiss (1982, 1983), Moser (1983), and others have debated the issue of whether established disciplines are better able to investigate sexuality than any new discipline (sexology). Although it is not the aim of this chapter to speak to that debate, the overarching discipline of sexology should be quite helpful and fertile to the extent that it can provide integrative analysis across these disciplines.

Anytime a phenomenon is studied by scholars trained in diverse disciplines, the knowledge gained by this approach has both advantages and disadvantages to the topic as a whole. A major benefit of an interdisciplinary approach to human sexuality is that different angles of the same phenomenon (sexuality) are being examined by experts who are adept and trained at studying their own piece of the pie. Scholars in different fields also can bring to the interdisciplinary dialogue an array of theoretical and methodological approaches. Further, they may be able to provide more constructive feedback to their colleagues in other disciplines because: (a) they can view the others' work without the fundamental biases and assumptive systems of logic inherent in the field in question, and (b) they may be less threatened by the potential success of endeavors by scholars in other fields. Finally, such interdisciplinary foci may be truer to the nature and breadth of most complex human phenomena such as sexuality.

This hybrid approach, however, has disadvantages for the area of sexuality research as well. As Jayne (1986) suggests, "communication difficulties are generated by this diversity, constituting a further challenge to researchers who seek to transcend what has gone before" (p. 4). In other words, along with a specific language of talking about sexuality, researchers from different disciplines also bring to the study of sexuality different methods, statistical analyses, and interpretations of the phenomenon. These differences can create obstacles when researchers try to talk to or learn from one another. In addition, keeping track of developments in any one discipline can be imposing, and that fact may be enhanced exponentially for interdisciplinary work. In sum, human sexuality is being studied by scholars who are trained in various disciplines and who conduct research that often employs different methodological designs. As will be seen, this fact becomes one methodological issue in the study of human sexuality in general and sexuality within close relationships.

Organization of the Methods in Sexuality Research

Table 1.1 presents an organization of the types of research methods for use in studying sexuality. This matrix (adopted from Olson's, 1977, analysis for close relationships) is a 2 × 2 matrix, organized according to the variables of type of data (subjective data are reports of inner feelings and attitudes, whereas objective data are reports of observed events or behaviors) and the reporter's frame of reference (the insider reference is from the participant, and the outsider reference is from someone observing the participant). The matrix suggests three types of report data: subjective data collected from the respondent about thoughts and feelings (insider-subjective); data collected from the respondent about personal behavior (insider-objective); and data collected from an outsider such as a friend about the target person's feelings, attitudes, thoughts, and subjective experience in general (outsider-subjective). The matrix shows only one type of objective, nonreport data: physiological and/or behavioral observation (outsider-objective).

TABLE 1.1
Four Types of Research Methods for Studying Sexuality Within Close Relationships

	Type of Data	
	Subjective	*Objective*
Reporter's Frame of Reference		
Insider	Self-report methods (e.g., attitudes toward oral sex, masturbation)	Behavioral self-report methods (e.g., frequency of intercourse)
Outsider	Observer subjective reports (e.g., report of how meaningful sexual experience is to one member of dyad)	(Physiological and/or behavioral methods (e.g., physiological measure of arousal, observation of kissing and foreplay)

Note. Adapted from "Insiders' and Outsiders' Views of Relationships" by D. H. Olson, 1977. In G. Levinger and H. L. Raush (Eds.), *Close Relationships*, Amherst: University of Massachusetts Press.

The types of approaches used to study sexuality and close relationships have almost exclusively been those of self-report of subjective experience (insider-subjective data) and self-report of behavior (insider-objective data). These approaches parallel the first and second quadrants of Table 1.1. Unfortunately, the third quadrant (outsider-subjective data), concerning reports by outsiders, has few entries at this juncture for sexuality within close relationships. In addition, because of ethical issues, few if any behavioral/physiological studies that examine sexuality within close relationships have been carried out to date (quadrant 4, objective-outsider data). Below we review relevant literature for each of the four quadrants pertaining to Table 1.1. We wish to point out, however, that future research in the area of sexuality within close relationships might give more attention both to behavioral self-reports (which conceivably could be verified by outside observers) and to observer-subjective reports from a variety of close others.

As noted, research in the area of sexuality has been quite heavily influenced by the report methodology, generally involving self-report only (both self-report subjective experiences typified in quadrant 1 and self-report of behavior exemplified in quadrant 2). Self-administered questionnaires, interviews, and behavioral records or diaries are typical modes of administrations in these self-report approaches. Using these first two types of approaches, researchers have accumulated a comprehensive body of data that has explored and examined sexual scales. These scales have measured sexual attitudes (e.g., Athanasiou & Sarkin, 1988; Eysenck, 1988; Fisher & Hall, 1988; Hendrick, Hendrick, Slapion-Foote, & Foote, 1985; McCabe & Collins, 1983; Mahoney, 1988; Valois & Ory, 1988), emotions (Smeaton & Byrne, 1988), and sexual behaviors and experience (Bentler, 1988; Brady & Levitt, 1988; Cowart-Steckler & Pollack, 1988;

Zuckerman, 1988). (For a comprehensive look at sexuality-related measures, see Davis, Yarber, & Davis, 1988.)

Furthermore, within these first two quadrants of Table 1.1, researchers have also attempted to describe factors such as anxiety (Janda, 1988; Leary & Dobbins, 1983), sex guilt (Mosher, 1988), locus of control (Catania, McDermott, & Wood, 1984), and issues of self-monitoring and self-focus (Fichten, Libman, Takefman, & Brender, 1988), which might inhibit or promote sexual behavior. Studies in this genre either ask individuals to self-report how certain factors affect the sexuality in their relationships or ask subjects to self-report their sexual behaviors along with measuring the specific factors. This research does not intend to link the specific factor to sexuality in the course of a relationship or to other relational factors, yet this assumption can implicitly be made.

The typical methodological technique used in the third quadrant of Table 1.1 (outsider-subjective) is the person-perception design. These studies (Damrosch, 1982; Istvan & Griffitt, 1980; McKinney, Sprecher, & Orbuch, 1987; Sprecher, McKinney, & Orbuch, 1987; Williams & Jacoby, 1989) examine how others might react to individuals with certain sexual histories, behaviors, or contraceptive usage. Respondents might be asked to report how attracted they are to a target individual because of observed characteristics or on the subjective states of this target individual. Nevertheless, these designs provide insight about the way people perceive others based on their sexually relevant features. Although such studies do not involve investigation of sexual interaction, per se, they may have strong implications for how perception and interaction will be related. Person-perception scholars have often argued for the value of this paradigm because of the link between perception and action (e.g., Darley & Fazio, 1980). Presumably, our perceptions of others influence our behavior toward them and members of their group, but such perceptions may influence us also in terms of self-perception along similar dimensions and plans for related behavior. The person-perception paradigm has been a traditional type of approach for social psychologists interested in how people form impressions of others, including prominent work on prejudice and discrimination. Given the discrimination based on sexual preference or perceptions of sexual inclinations that often occur in this society, the person-perception type of design deserves greater attention among scholars of human sexuality.

Finally, as previously stated, because of ethical issues, few physiological/behavioral studies for close relationships have been carried out to date. (The Masters & Johnson, 1966, behavioral/clinical study with couples would be one exception.) Several studies have assessed sexual physiology and response arousal to certain stimuli (e.g., erotica) through the use of instruments designed to measure physiological responses (for a review, see Bohlen, 1983). However, thus far these studies are less relevant to the overall thesis of this chapter because they do not directly link sexual physiology to the social and relational processes of sexuality.

RESEARCH SPECIFICALLY AIMED
AT INVESTIGATING SEXUALITY
AND CLOSE RELATIONSHIPS

Extensive research has aimed at investigating sexual processes that are both functional and dysfunctional to the close relationship. The assumption in these studies is that a form of sexuality is somehow dysfunctional or functional to "normal" relational functioning. For example, topics extensively examined are sexual aggression in relationships (see Mosher & Anderson, 1986; Pirog-Good & Stets, 1989; and Muehlenhard, Goggins, Jones, & Satterfield, this volume), communication about sexuality (see Tavris & Sadd, 1978; and Cupach & Metts, this volume), and the association between sexual satisfaction and relationship satisfaction (see Pinney, Gerrard, & Denney, 1987; Reiss & Lee, 1988, and De-Lamater, this volume).

These studies address the close relationship more directly than the studies cited in the previous section, oftentimes measuring how the relationship is affected by a form of sexuality or how sexuality is affected by the type of relationship. Nevertheless, the relational and sexual processes are not typically measured from a dyadic perspective. That is, even in these studies, reports from both members of the couple are rarely measured, and instead, sexuality within close relationships is still assessed by data collected from only one member of the couple.

Although there are exceptions (such as Christopher & Cate, 1985; Peplau, Rubin, & Hill, 1977), few studies have taken a dyadic approach to the study of sexuality within close relationships or have examined the direct association between sexual processes and other processes within a relationship. One such exception is a study by Christopher and Cate (1985), which assessed the development of sexually oriented behaviors within premarital dating relationships, as well as the association between these behaviors and other relational qualities, such as love, conflict, ambivalence, and maintenance behaviors. Christopher and Cate (1985) have data on both individuals in the couple, and they have empirically measured the association between dynamics within a relationship and the pathway of sexual development within that relationship. As more empirical studies are done in this fashion, one can begin to understand the broader framework within which sexuality develops in a relationship, how this development is associated to other relational processes, how both members of the couple assess the same sexual or relational process, and how this dyadic perspective is consequential to the outcome (i.e., development, maintenance, enhancement, conflict) in a relationship.

Special Problems in Investigating Sexuality
Within Close Relationships

Discussions of methodological issues that arise in research on sexuality typically focus on problems of biased population samples (Brecher & Brecher, 1986;

Morokoff, 1986) and response biases (Catania, McDermott, & Pollack, 1986; DeLamater & MacCorquodale, 1975; Johnson & DeLamater, 1976). These issues are important to this chapter as well because they are relevant in the examination of methodological issues in the study of sexuality in close relationships. Nevertheless, the study of sexuality within close relationships is imposing because of still other methodological obstacles that pertain to the unique or special nature of this type of data and the necessary procedures to obtain such data. Some of these obstacles are described below.

Obtaining sexuality data within close relationships constitutes an especially delicate proposition because of ethical issues and questions about self-presentation, distortion, embarrassment, and articulateness among research participants in reporting on relevant activities. Sexuality in this sphere not only is a private and very personal activity, but its perceived success to the dyad may be consequential to the maintenance and enhancement of the close relationship. Thus, the investigator has a special burden to avoid sexual matters in the relationship that when exposed impede on the relationship's maintenance or development. As an illustration, a study may probe wives' complaints about husbands' behavior (e.g., Madden & Janoff-Bulman, 1983) and may thus focus on sexual matters. A wife, in turn, may inform the investigator that she is dissatisfied with the husband's sensitivity regarding her sexual needs. Although the investigator may assume that the wife will not divulge her responses to the husband, the husband may be curious and solicitous of such information. Of course, if the wife communicated such information to the husband—and for the first time—it is likely that he may blame the study/investigator for causing the wife's concerns. He may feel that she would not entertain such concerns if the investigator had not "put them in her head" or dug around until they inadvertently surfaced (note that this logic is not uncommon among the spouses of therapy clients when the spouses begin to believe that the therapy is causing a rift in the relationship). Similarly, it is also likely that such information will promote positive communication between the two individuals about sexuality in their relationship. Regardless of whether a positive or negative outcome arises, the investigator should be aware that studying sexuality within close relationships may in fact change or influence the phenomenon at hand.

How does the investigator address such a potential peril in studying sexuality in close relationships? There are a number of possibilities to consider. One approach is to know as well as possible the nature of the close relationships under study, including their a priori levels of satisfaction and conflict. An investigator who does not anticipate studying conflicted relationships should try to include only research participants whose relationships are strong and can withstand some probing of delicate matters. On the other hand, if one cannot readily discern conflict beforehand, then a more general, cautionary approach is in order. Here the investigator may alert the participants about the possibility of conflict emerging from the study if they are not careful in treating it as a confidential communication. The investigator also may note the availability of counseling support for those who begin to have second thoughts when the study begins or for those who terminate the study when problems develop. The idea of linking research in this area to the possibility of counseling seems to be quite sensible and has been discussed in previous analyses of relationship methodology issues (e.g., Rubin & Mitchell, 1976).

Returning to our methodological organization in Table 1.1, we noted that research methods in the area of sexuality and close relationships most often involve report data and usually self-report data. Certainly, as with other types of relationship questions, it will be helpful if a variety of types of report data are emphasized. With regard to sexuality, there has been little if any work on others' reports of the target person's subjective experience (except work focusing on both members of a dyad) and too little work on others' report or self-report of behavior. What about so-called outsider-objective data in this area? It is unlikely that, on ethical grounds, a couple's intimate sexual activity could be extensively explored via psychophysiological measures or behaviorally via television or observers. There has been a small amount of informative work deriving from measurement of psychophysiological variables in married couples. This work was aimed at examining how such variables may be related to conflict and maintenance of relationships (e.g., Levenson & Gottman, 1983), and it suggests that sexuality in this context also could be explored via psychophysiological measures. However, in the main, investigators are not likely to develop an ethical way to observe the most intimate and natural forms of sexual behaviors in close relationships. Thus, our reliance upon report data is great, and report strategies, therefore, require careful analysis.

There are several hazards of research focusing on report data, as has been well described in the relationship field (e.g., Harvey, Hendrick, & Tucker, 1988). For sexuality data, these hazards are even more prominent and are discussed in the following list:

1. Research participants may distort aspects of their report of sexual activity and experience because of cognitive (e.g., memorial difficulty such as loss of recall of detail) or motivational factors (e.g., embarrassment about the possibility that their sexual behavior/experience is nonnormative or implies inadequacy or other negative traits).

2. Research participants may distort aspects of their report in order to try to present themselves in a certain light to the investigators. This issue is related to the motivational distortion noted above, but it may be special to the nature of the investigator. For example, males reporting to females about sexuality (or females to males) may be especially likely to try to report on behavior and experience that they think the others would find acceptable.

3. Research evidence strongly suggests that women are much more articulate about their close relationships than are men (and/or open to discussion of their

relationships; see Harvey, 1987, for a general discussion of such possibilities); hence, participants' articulateness may play a role in the collection of report data. This issue may be problematic across gender when questionnaire/interview items relate to *aggregate* feelings as might be found in one's answer to the question "How satisfied are you with your sexual experience in this relationship?" Individuals may be able to be relatively articulate about their satisfaction and yet may have a rather complex view that in no precise way gets reflected in a response to such a general item.

4. Relatedly, a research participant may not be able to understand a research question in the way intended by the designers of the study. This problem may stem from inadequate literacy, the overly general aggregate-type questions, or even different levels of understanding in the population regarding the meaning of questions about sexuality. For example, in a study of college students' reports of sexual activity and attitudes, Berger and Wenger (1973) found considerable confusion about the meaning of "loss of virginity." In this study, 41% of the students stated that female virginity was lost if the women self-stimulated to orgasm.

5. Research participants indeed may not fully understand the internal states (cognitive, emotional, and motivational processes) that guide their behavior and thus may not provide informative responses to probes that focus on their understanding of such processes.

It has been argued by Bem (1972) and most forcefully by Nisbett and Wilson (1977) that people often attempt to infer their internal states with the use of a conscious, verbal, explanatory system. This verbal system involves conscious attempts to estimate one's feelings independently of cognitive processes mediating behavior. This position can be best understood by making a distinction between conscious attempts to examine one's thoughts and feelings, and cognitive processes that typically do not occur in consciousness. As Nisbett and Wilson argued, many cognitive processes appear to be unavailable to conscious scrutiny. When asked to report these processes, people are unable to examine them directly. They often rely on a conscious explanatory system. For example, the type of sexual behavior that occurs within a relationship may be a reflection of unarticulated (or unrecognizable) hostility or distrust between the partners. However, when asked to report on their sexual behavior, these individuals do not have access to these cognitive processes, and instead may perceive the sexual behavior as enjoyable and reciprocal in nature. Although this problem is an imposing one for investigators, it is not insurmountable given careful research techniques, nor necessarily fatal if it exists to some extent in all report data.

"To some extent" is a key part of the rebuttal to Nisbett and Wilson. There have been some research and accompanying commentary suggesting that Nisbett and Wilson's position is too extreme. Indeed, people do have some access to causal, cognitive processes (Smith & Miller, 1978). Further, some have argued that Nisbett and Wilson's position is virtually unfalsifiable because it relies on statistical null effects to try to make a case for people's lack of access to their own cognitive processes. Perhaps a more reasonable line of inquiry concerns how much access people have under different conditions.

IMPORTANT PERSPECTIVES ON WHAT IS LACKING IN THE RESEARCH

By emphasizing the breadth of interaction/experience in sexuality in close relationships, a number of new methodological directions seem indicated. Most importantly, longitudinal research is needed that attempts to triangulate across people's thoughts, feelings, and behavior and thereby provide more comprehensive information about how sexuality and close relationships are coordinated. A design that may be fruitful is interaction record/diary reporting, which asks respondents to record interaction and personal reactions to events as these situations occur on a daily basis. This technique might be used not only to probe descriptions of sexual interaction, but also to study how people feel about such interaction, as it has implications for personal relationships. For example, will young persons beginning to date report that sexual experiences are associated with relational desires, expectations, and hopes? Further, in long-term relationships, are fluctuations in frequency of sex associated with conflict, happiness, trust and so on? Will such linkages of feeling, thought, and hope differ across age groups (e.g., persons in mid-life versus elderly resuming dating after divorce or death of a spouse), cohort groups (e.g., persons in mid-life in the 1960s versus those in mid-life in the 1990s), and gender? These later questions are informative regarding the linkage between sexual experiences and relational processes. They also point to the need and importance of conducting longitudinal research on the topic of sexuality in close relationships.

A methodological approach that has been used effectively is that of the Rochester Interaction Record. Nezlek, Wheeler, and Reis (1983) developed this technique to sample daily behavioral self-report by persons engaged in such activities as dating, schoolwork, interaction with friends, and discussions with parents. This approach might be used by investigators examining relational qualities and their relationship to sexuality experiences. A similar approach has been used by Csikszentmihalyi (1982), who also has employed a beeping device to signal respondents to report thoughts and feelings at certain times during their daily lives. These approaches may well prove to be too intrusive as one moves toward the arena of sexuality in close relationships, but their model may inspire investigators regarding how to study simultaneously aspects of sexual activity and relationship dynamics.

Methodologically, research must also attempt to assess *directly* the nature of sexuality within close relationships. In doing so, we propose that researchers go beyond the individual as the unit of analysis in their studies and collect data from both partners of a couple. Plus, researchers need to use appropriate statistical methods to analyze these dyadic data. Although it is not the aim of this chapter to discuss appropriate statistical analyses for dyadic data, the reader is referred to Kenny (1988), who stated that traditional mainstream statistical methods, such as analysis of variance, are inadequate for the study of interpersonal relations. Researchers who study two-person relationships and use these traditional methods often run into problems because the methods inappropriately impute causal linkages of influence on interaction. Kenny discussed two suitable approaches for the study of two-person relationships: "One can either study many dyads (a comparative study) or intensively study a single or a few dyads over time (a time-series design)" (p. 58). Because most sexual activity occurs in interaction with others, and thus a two-person relationship is defined, future research should give greater attention to this dyadic approach.

In addition, research should also assess the *meaning* of sexuality within close relationships in order to get a better understanding of its relevance to the nature of close relationships. New methodological directions are required to assess the association and nature of sexuality within close relationships, yet at the same time, researchers also need to examine the personal meaning of these sexual experiences to the individuals involved in the close relationships. How do individuals characterize and explain the presence or absence of sexuality within their relationships? Do researchers attribute a specific meaning to sexuality within a close relationship that might be different from the meaning for the individuals who are being studied? Further, do partners in a relationship attribute different meanings to the same sexual event/process? In answering these questions, it is recommended that the concept to be used should be the "account," defined as people's explanations presented in storylike form for past actions and events that include characterizations of self and key others in plots. Much of our work (e.g., Harvey, Agostinelli, & Weber, 1989; Harvey, Orbuch, & Weber, in press; Weber, Harvey, & Stanley, 1987) has explored more generally how individuals develop meaning and cope with stressful events in their lives through the account-making process. We wish to note that the same conceptual framework can be applied to the study of sexuality within close relationships; researchers can begin to use the account-making process as a vehicle to study the meaning individuals attach to their sexuality within close relationships.

The major advantage of the accounts conception in studying sexuality is an emphasis upon people's relatively *naturalistic* and *full* presentations or disclosures about matters of significance in their lives. We believe that such types of presentations are especially important as a goal for the scholar interested in an understanding of people's sexual attitudes and behaviors *within the context* of their close relationships.

Lastly, an implicit assumption in research on the topic of sexuality is the *development* or incorporation of sexuality within an individual (for research on sexuality in general) or within a close relationship (for research on sexuality within close relationships in particular). This emphasis on the development of sexuality parallels general close relationship research that was conducted in the 1960s and 1970s. Although there are exceptions (such as Hill, Rubin, & Peplau, 1976), close relationship research during that period of time concentrated on topics related to relationship formation (law of attraction, mate selection, early development), and topics of relationship maintenance (quality, satisfaction, adjustment, stability). These topics were emphasized in great detail, to the exclusion of topics related to relationship dissolution. Relationship dissolution has become a topic of concern in the relationship field only in the past decade or so.

Researchers need to begin to view sexuality within a broader theoretical framework of relational processes and begin to emphasize: (a) how sexuality is connected to all stages of a relationship (e.g., How does sexuality *maintain* a relationship? What are the consequences of the *loss* of sexuality within a relationship—either because of choice or because of necessity such as medical reasons—for other relationship dynamics? How does a relationship cope with the *loss* of sexuality?), and (b) what the implications a close relationship loss has for an individual's sexual identity, and thus self-identity. Given the proposition that sexuality is a private and very personal activity and that its perceived success has consequences for the dyad, it should also follow that the perceived absence of the activity may have significant effects on the dyad and for the individual's sexual and self-identity.

SUMMARY

Most of the relevant literature in the area of sexuality implicitly investigates sexuality within close relationships, yet the measurement of the relationship per se is often lacking in the empirical investigation. Hence, we drew extensively from the literature examining sexuality in general, and presented a methodological organization of the research, following the work of Olson (1977). This organizational table is a useful way to evaluate current research as well as to define methodological approaches that are lacking. New directions for future research (both methodologically and conceptually oriented) in the study of sexuality within close relationships were also addressed.

Although in its most meaningful form the sexual relation/process is yet another social relation/process, research must also begin to address the question of how the study of sexuality is different from the study of any other social or relational process. First, individuals may feel that sexuality is the most intimate area of behavior in their lives. Hence, they may be reluctant to report these behaviors to investigators, who are strangers. The personal nature of these data may create obstacles for the researcher, who wants to access this information and build an accumulation of knowledge on the topic.

On a related note, individuals are perhaps most vulnerable regarding this topic in terms of their ability and the normativeness of the activity involved. Accordingly, the disclosure of sexual information may be particularly sensitive to threats of self-esteem, thereby inducing greater self-presentation biases and distortion of report. In addition, individuals are perhaps most ignorant in this area regarding relevant cognitive processes (even more so than dating/relating). Thus, Nisbett and Wilson's (1977) thesis regarding one's knowledge of one's own cognitive processes associated with behavior may especially hold true in the area of sexuality. In sum, by evaluating how the study of sexuality may be different from the study of other social processes, one begins to understand the larger context within which the behavior exists.

REFERENCES

Allport, G. W. (1968). The historical background of modern social psychology. In E. Lindzey & E. Aronson (Eds.), *The handbook of social psychology* 2nd ed., pp. 1–80. Reading, MA: Addison-Wesley.

Athanasiou, R., & Sarkin, R. (1988). Sexual attitudes and behavior. In C. M. Davis, W. L. Yarber, & S. L. Davis (Eds.), *Sexuality related measures: A compendium* (p. 28). Lake Mills, IA: Graphic Publishing Company.

Bem, D. J. (1972). Self-perception theory. In L. Berkowitz (Ed.), *Advances in experimental social psychology* (Vol. 6, pp. 1–62). New York: Academic Press.

Bentler, P. M. (1988). Male and female sexual behavior. In C. M. Davis, W. L. Yarber, & S. L. Davis (Eds.), *Sexuality related measures: A compendium* (p. 90). Lake Mills, IA: Graphic Publishing Company.

Berger, D. G., & Wenger, M. G. (1973). The ideology of virginity. *Journal of Marriage and the Family, 35,* 666–676.

Bohlen, J. G. (1983). State of the science in sexual physiological research. In C. M. Davis (Ed.), *Challenges in sexual science.* Lake Mills, IA: Society for the Study of Sex.

Brady, J. P., & Levitt, E. E. (1988). Sex experience inventory. In C. M. Davis, W. L. Yarber, & S. L. Davis (Eds.), *Sexuality related measures: A compendium* (p. 90). Lake Mills, IA: Graphic Publishing Company.

Brecher, E. M., & Brecher, J. (1986). Extracting valid sexological findings from severely flawed and biased population samples. *Journal of Sex Research, 22,* 6–20.

Callero, P. L., & Howard, J. A. (1989). Biases of the scientific discourse on human sexuality: Toward a sociology of sexuality. In K. McKinney and S. Sprecher, *Human sexuality: The societal and interpersonal context* (pp. 425–437). Norwood, NJ: Ablex Publishing Co.

Catania, J. A., McDermott, L. J., & Pollack, L. M. (1986). Questionnaire response bias and face-to-face interview sample bias in sexuality research. *Journal of Sex Research, 22,* 55–72.

Catania, J. A., McDermott, L. J., & Wood, J. A. (1984). Assessment of locus of control: Situational specificity in the sexual context. *Journal of Sex Research, 20,* 310–324.

Cowart-Steckler, D., & Pollack, R. H. (1988). The Cowart-Steckler scale of sexual experience. In C. M. Davis, W. L. Yarber, & S. L. Davis (Eds.), *Sexuality related measures: A compendium* (pp. 91–91). Lake Mills, IA: Graphic Publishing Company.

Christopher, F. S., & Cate, R. M. (1985). Premarital sexual pathways and relationship development. *Journal of Social and Personal Relationships, 2,* 271–288.

Csikszentmihalyi, M. (1982). Toward a psychology of optimal experience. In L. Wheeler (Ed.), *Review of Personality and Social Psychology, 3,* 13–26. Beverly Hills: Sage.

Damrosch, S. P. (1982). Nursing students' attitudes toward sexually active older persons. *Nursing Research, 31,* 252–255.

Darley, J. M., & Fazio, R. H. (1980). Expectancy confirmation process arising in the social interaction sequence. *American Psychologist, 35,* 867–881.

Davis, C. M., Yarber, W. L., & Davis, S. L. (Eds.) (1988). *Sexuality related measures: A compendium.* Lake Mills, IA: Graphic Publishing Company.

DeLamater, J., & MacCorquodale, P. (1975). The effects of interview schedule variations on reported sexual behavior. *Sociological Methods and Research, 4,* 215–236.

Eysenck, H. J. (1988). The Eysenck inventory of attitudes to sex. In C. M. Davis, W. L. Yarber, & S. L. Davis (Eds.), *Sexuality related measures: A compendium* (pp. 28–34). Lake Mills, IA: Graphic Publishing Company.

Fichten, C. S., Libman, E., Takefman, J., & Brender, W. (1988). Self-monitoring and self-focus in erectile dysfunction. *Journal of Sex and Marital Therapy, 14,* 120–128.

Fisher, T. D., & Hall, R. G. (1988). A scale for the comparison of the sexual attitudes of adolescents and their parents. *Journal of Sex Research, 24,* 90–100.

Green, R., & Wiener, J. (1980). *Methodology in sex research.* Rockville, MD: National Institute of Mental Health, U.S. Department of Health, U.S. Department of Health and Human Services.

Harvey, J. H. (1987). Attributions in close relationships: Research and theoretical developments. *Journal of Social and Clinical Psychology, 5,* 420–434.

Harvey, J. H., Agostinelli, G., & Weber, A. L. (1989). Account-making and the formation of expectations about close relationships. *Review of Personality and Social Psychology, 10,* 39–62.

Harvey, J. H., Burgess, M. L., & Orbuch, T. L. (in press). History and theories of social psychology: Their relevance to behavior therapy. In P. R. Martin (Ed.), *Handbook of behavior therapy and psychological science.* Elmsford, NY: Pergamon Press.

Harvey, J. H., Hendrick, S. S., & Tucker, K. (1988). Self-report methods in studying personal relationships. In S. W. Duck, *Handbook of Personal Relationships* (pp. 99–113). Chicester, England: Wiley.

Harvey, J. H., Orbuch, T. L., & Weber, A. L. (1990). A social psychological model of account-making in response to severe stress. *Journal of Language and Social Psychology, 9,* 191–207.

Hendrick, S., Hendrick, C., Slapion-Foote, M. J., & Foote, F. H. (1985). Gender differences in sexual attitudes. *Journal of Personality and Social Psychology, 48,* 1630–1642.

Hill, C. T., Rubin, Z., & Peplau, L. A. (1976). Break-ups before marriage: The end of 103 affairs. *Journal of Social Issues, 32,* 147–167.

Istvan, J., & Griffitt, W. (1980). Effects of sexual experience on dating desirability: An experimental study. *Journal of Marriage and the Family, 42,* 377–385.

Janda, L. H. (1988). The sex anxiety inventory. In C. M. Davis, W. L. Yarber, & S. L. Davis (Eds.), *Sexuality related measures: A compendium* (pp. 19–20). Lake Mills, IA: Graphic Publishing Company.

Jayne, C. E. (1986). Methodology in sex research in 1986: An editor's commentary. *Journal of Sex Research, 22,* 1–5.

Johnson, W. T., & DeLamater, J. D. (1976). Response effects in sex surveys. *Public Opinion Quarterly, 40,* 165–181.

Kenny, D. A. (1988). The analysis of data from two-person relationships. In S. W. Duck, *Handbook of personal relationships* (pp. 57–77). Chicester, England: Wiley.

Leary, M. R., & Dobbins, S. E. (1983). Social anxiety, sexual behavior, and contraceptive use. *Journal of Personality and Social Psychology, 45,* 1347–1354.

Levenson, R. W., & Gottman, J. M. (1983). Marital interaction: Physiological linkage and affective exchange. *Journal of Personality and Social Psychology, 45,* 587–597.

Madden, M. E., & Janoff-Bulman, R. (1983). Blame, control, and marital satisfaction. *Journal of Marriage and the Family, 44,* 663–674.

Mahoney, E. R. (1988). Sexual behaviors and attitudes. In C. M. Davis, W. L. Yarber, & S. L. Davis (Eds.), *Sexuality related measures: A compendium* (p. 38). Lake Mills, IA: Graphic Publishing Company.

Masters, W. H., & Johnson, V. E. (1966). *Human sexual response*. Boston: Little, Brown.

McCabe, M. P., & Collins, J. K. (1983). The sexual and affectional attitudes and experiences of Australian adolescents during dating: the effects of age, church attendance, type of school, and socioeconomic class. *Archives of Sexual Behavior, 12*, 525–539.

McKinney, K., Sprecher, S., & Orbuch, T. L. (1987). A person perception experiment examining the effects of contraceptive behavior on first impressions. *Basic and Applied Social Psychology, 8*, 235–248.

Morokoff, P. J. (1986). Volunteer bias in the psychophysiological study of female sexuality. *Journal of Sex Research, 22*, 35–51.

Moser, C. (1983). A response to Reiss, "trouble in paradise." *Journal of Sex Research, 19*, 192–195.

Mosher, D. L. (1988). Multiple indicators of subjective sexual arousal. In C. M. Davis, W. L. Yarber, & S. L. Davis (Eds.), *Sexuality related measures: A compendium* (pp. 25–27). Lake Mills, IA: Graphic Publishing Company.

Mosher, D. L., & Anderson, R. D. (1986). Macho personality, sexual aggression, and reactions to guided imagery of realistic rape. *Journal of Research in Personality, 20*(2), 77–94.

Nisbett, R. E., & Wilson, T. D. (1977). Telling more than we can know: Verbal reports on mental processes. *Psychological Review, 84*, 231–259.

Nezlek, J., Wheeler, L., & Reis, H. T. (1983). Studies of social participation. In H. T. Reis (Ed.), *Naturalistic approaches to studying social interaction* (p. 57–73). San Francisco: Jossey-Bass.

Olson, D. H. (1977). Insiders' and outsiders' views of relationships. In G. Levinger & H. L. Raush (Eds.), *Close relationships* (pp. 112–135). Amherst: University of Massachusetts Press.

Peplau, L. A., Rubin, Z., & Hill, C. T. (1977). Sexual intimacy in dating relationships. *Journal of Social Issues, 33*, 86–109.

Pirog-Good, M. A., & Stets, J. E. (1989). *Violence in dating relationships*. New York: Praeger.

Pinney, E. M., Gerrard, N., & Denney, N. W. (1987). The Pinney sexual satisfaction inventory. *Journal of Sex Research, 23*, 233–251.

Reiss, I. L. (1982). Trouble in paradise: The current status of sexual science. *Journal of Sex Research, 18*, 97–113.

Reiss, I. L. (1983). Paradise regained? a reply to Moser. *Journal of Sex Research, 19*, 195–197.

Reiss, I. L., & Lee, G. R. (1988). *Family systems in America* (4th ed.). New York: Holt, Rinehart & Winston.

Rubin, Z., & Mitchell, C. (1976). Couples research as couples counseling: Some unintended effects of studying close relationship. *American Psychologist, 31*, 17–25.

Smeaton, G., & Byrne, D. (1988). The feelings scale: Positive and negative affective responses. In C. M. Davis, W. L. Yarber, & S. L. Davis (Eds.), *Sexuality related measures: A compendium* (pp. 88–89). Lake Mills, IA: Graphic Publishing Co.

Smith, E. R., & Miller, F. D. (1978). Limits on perception of cognitive processes: A reply to Nisbett and Wilson. *Psychological Review, 4*, 335–362.

Sprecher, S., McKinney, K., & Orbuch, T. L. (1987). Has the double standard disappeared? An experimental test. *Social Psychology Quarterly, 50*, 24–31.

Tavris, C., & Sadd, S. (1978). *The Redbook report on female sexuality*. New York: Dell.

Valois, R. F., & Ory, J. C. (1988). The Valois sexual attitudes scale. In C. M. Davis, W. L. Yarber, & S. L. Davis (Eds.), *Sexuality related measures: A compendium* (pp. 43–44). Lake Mills, IA: Graphic Publishing Company.

Weber, A. L., Harvey, J. H., & Stanley, M. A. (1987). The nature and motivations of accounts for failed relationships. In R. Burnett, P. McGhee, and D. C. Clarke (Eds.), *Accounting for relationships*. (pp. 114–133). London: Methuen.

Weeks, J. (1986). *Sexuality*. Chichester, England: Ellis Horwood Limited.

Weinstein, S. A. (1984). Social realities and measurement in the scientific study of sex. *Journal of Sex Research, 20,* 217–224.

Williams, J. D., & Jacoby, A. P. (1989). The effects of premarital heterosexual and homosexual experience on dating and marriage desirability. *Journal of Marriage and the Family, 51,* 489–497.

Zuckerman, M. (1988). Human sexuality questionnaire. In C. M. Davis, W. L. Yarber, & S. L. Davis (Eds.), *Sexuality related measures: A compendium* (pp. 92–98). Lake Mills, IA: Graphic Publishing Company.

2 Love and Sexuality

Arthur Aron
Elaine N. Aron
University of California, Santa Cruz

LOVE AND SEXUALITY

Love and sexuality are intimately connected in our culture and in our culture's social science.[1] This chapter examines these connections, first by defining love and sexuality, then by reviewing the theories and data on their relationship as well as the research on attitudes about their association, and finally by suggesting a connection between the two that arises from their being aspects of an underlying unity.

DEFINITIONS OF LOVE AND SEXUALITY

First, what do we mean by love? There is now a fair amount of systematic work on love, yet as Shaver and Hazan (1988) have noted, most researchers and theorists have side-stepped defining it. Instead, they have identified different categories of love (e.g., Berscheid & Walster, 1978), styles of love (Hazan & Shaver, 1987; C. Hendrick & Hendrick, 1986; Lee, 1977), loving versus liking (Davis & Todd, 1982; Rubin, 1970), or attitudes toward love (e.g., Sprecher &

---

[1]We have limited our discussion to the Western cultural context because most of the data (and theories based on those data) were gathered in this culture. Whether conclusions based on such information apply more universally is an issue beyond the scope of this chapter. Also, in light of space limitations we have taken a rather general approach and have not attempted to examine what are no doubt important variations in the pattern of the relation of love and sexuality across gender, sexual orientation, ethnic identity, social class, and so forth.

Metts, 1989). Operationalizations have variously emphasized behaviors, such as hugging and kissing or sharing (e.g., Swensen, 1961); cognitions, such as the pattern of characteristics people attribute to love (e.g., Fehr, 1988); emotions (e.g., Shaver, Schwartz, Kirson, & O'Connor, 1987); or cultural scenarios, such as love at first sight (e.g., Averill & Boothroyd, 1977).

In all of these approaches, however, the focus has been on categories, styles, attitudes, behaviors, and so forth, *about* a desired close relationship with a particular other person. That is, the point in common is that love has to do with wanting to be intimate with some individual. In light of this commonality, in our own work on love (e.g., Aron & Aron, 1986) we have emphasized the motivational side of love, with its goal of closeness with a specific other. Of course, whatever elements are emphasized, love clearly involves all of the various aspects taken together in some organized way.

Thus, we propose the following working definition: *Love is the constellation of behaviors, cognitions, and emotions associated with a desire to enter or maintain a close relationship with a specific other person.* For present purposes any of the available definitions of *close relationship* will be sufficient—for example, Kelley et al.'s (1983) behavioral interdependence (closeness as individuals having a high degree of mutual influence on each other's decisions, behaviors, and perceived outcomes), Clark and Mills' (1979) communal pattern of resource exchange (closeness as making decisions based on each other's needs rather than keeping track of rewards and efforts as in an exchange or equity situation), or Aron, Aron, Tudor, and Nelson's (1991) including other in the self (closeness as a cognitive merging of self and other so that other's outcomes, resources, perspectives, and so on, are perceived as one's own). We would also note that this working definition of love is neutral with regard to whether love is based on cultural scripts about who should fall in love when and how; possible genetically programmed action patterns, such as males perhaps preferring young, healthy women and women preferring older men with adequate resources; learning, such as certain persons having become more strongly associated with sexual reinforcement; or whatever. (Nor does it constrain any particular view regarding love categories, styles, or attitudes.)

Shaver and Hazan (1988), in considering love to be an emotion, used a definition of emotion that was similarly inclusive and also placed an emphasis on motivation-like factors. They defined emotions as "patterned action tendencies evoked by appraisals of events or situations in relation to concerns (needs, goals, values, desires)" (p. 475). However, we prefer to emphasize motivation directly because of its theoretical usefulness (Aron & Aron, 1986), because it is more inclusive than the emotion category (Shaver & Hazan, 1988, acknowledge that love is *both* an emotion and a predisposition to have an emotion), and because Rousar (1990) found that, when people were asked to describe the feelings aroused when they experienced love, joy, anger, fear, or sadness, a far wider range of emotional terms were checked for love, suggesting that it at least is not a unitary emotion in the same manner as these others.

And what is sexuality? As in the case of love, most researchers and writers on the topic have avoided definitions. Reiss (1986b) searched 20 human sexuality textbooks and found only 5 contained definitions of their topic, each quite different. Our own search through the literature yielded a similar paucity and a similar range. Some see human sexual behavior and motivation as "not biological but rather social and cultural phenomena" (Kon, 1987, p. 257). Or in Reiss' (1986b) words, sexuality "consists of those scripts shared by a group that are supposed to lead to erotic arousal and in turn to produce genital response" (p. 21). Others adhere to the biological understanding of sexuality as "first and foremost a mechanism by means of which species reproduce themselves" (Beach, 1977, p. 3). More typically, the definition falls somewhere in between, such as that of Strong and DeVault (1988), who described sexual behavior as "characterized by conscious physiological/erotic arousal (such as desire) and that may also be accompanied by physiological arousal . . . or activity" (p. G-9).

However, the core elements in most definitions seem to be physiological sexual arousal and sexual desire. Thus, we will use the following working definition: *Sexuality is the constellation of sensations, emotions, and cognitions that an individual associates with physiological sexual arousal and that generally gives rise to sexual desire and/or behavior.* Although this definition is structurally more complex than that of the definition of love, it also emphasizes a motivational element (sexual desire). This definition is also neutral with regard to how sexuality is constructed—biologically, developmentally, culturally, or whatever.

A DIMENSION FOR ORGANIZING
SOCIAL SCIENCE APPROACHES
TO SEXUALITY AND LOVE

One way to understand the variety of approaches to the relation between sexuality and love is to think of these approaches as lying along a dimension having two extremes—one arguing that love is a mere by-product of sexuality, of the physiological and behavioral reproductive systems dictated by human genes, and the other arguing that sexuality is a mere by-product of the cosmic yearning for love, for fusion, for union (see Fig. 2.1). In between, of course, lie the views that neither sexuality nor love is the cause of the other, but influence each other to varying degrees. (Or, at the midpoint, they are seen as two factors having relative importances that are either equal or undiscussed.)

Position A: Approaches to Sexuality that Ignore Love
or Consider Love a Result of Sexuality

Returning to the first extreme of the dimension, the view that "all love is really sex" probably began with Charles Darwin, but in psychology it is of course associated with Sigmund Freud. For most of his life, Freud (e.g., 1920/1952) held to the idea that libido, the psychic energy generated by the desire to obtain

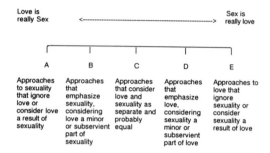

FIG. 2.1   A dimension for organizing theory, data, and attitudes on the relation between love and sexuality.

sexual gratification from objects, was the energy driving all of mental life. Thus, not only were all love relationships really sexual, according to Freud, but so were all human relationships of any sort—if their sexuality was not obvious, it was sublimated.

Today the reduction of love to reproduction is most often represented by sociobiology, which holds that, in the long run, evolution has selected for those individuals who behave in all human relationships so as to enhance the survival of their own genes. Obviously this is especially the case for dating or courtship, in which "reproduction is the central organizing theme" (Kenrick & Trost, 1987, p. 68). To be successful in passing on their genes, males and females must adopt conflicting strategies (Gallup, 1986). A female has no need to worry about identifying her genetic relationship to her offspring, but their numbers will be quite limited and her biological investment as she bears and raises them will be high. Because her every try at mating counts, her best strategy is to take her time and study a potential mate. Her ideal is someone "of high genetic quality who is willing to make a long-term commitment to provisioning the female and her offspring" (Gallup, 1986, p. 22). A male, on the other hand, cannot be certain if an offspring is his own, but he can potentially sire a great many in his lifetime while his biological investment in the raising of them could be nil. As a result, "males have been selected to attempt to copulate with many females on a high frequency basis" (p. 23), and a male's best strategy is to seek to mate as soon as possible in a relationship. His ideal is someone exhibiting health, youth, and other physical features suggesting her offspring will survive (Buss, 1988; Symons, 1987).

The conflicting strategies of males and females are resolved differently in different cultures, but males usually give up quantity for certainty of paternity. That is, the reproductive relationship tends toward monogamy and an emphasis on fidelity. Love—or "love acts" (Buss, 1988), such as giving gifts or demonstrating fidelity—serves the important purpose of (a) encouraging a display of resources prior to selecting a life-long mate and (b) maintaining exclusivity and commitment to raising offspring after mating. Love is entirely the product of reproduction, and for many sociobiologists, an epiphenomenon.

Position B: Approaches that Emphasize Sexuality, Considering Love a Minor or Subservient Part of Sexuality

Closer to the midpoint on the dimension are those views that still give sexuality the greater role but hold that love can also be an important or interesting motivation, even if it is nothing more than an elaboration of a biological system. "Classical" attachment theory (Bowlby, 1969) is the prime example. It holds that what appears as adult love is the result of the melding of three matured biological systems. One, of course, is the sexual system. But primate and human reproduction, with its long childhood, necessitates two others—(a) the infant's attachment system, organizing the close bonding of the infant to the parent, and (b) the adult's caregiving system, organizing the parent's or potential parent's continued nurturing of the infant, and also the mate and other members of the social group.

Here also lie the theorists who interpret love in terms of physiology—for example, the hormones associated with the euphoria typical of love (Liebowitz, 1983). Berscheid (1988), a noted researcher on love, wrote that, in the case of romantic love, if she were "forced against a brick wall to face a firing squad who would shoot if not given the correct answer [when asked to define love] . . . would whisper 'It's about 90 percent sexual desire as yet not sated' " (p. 373).

Position C: Approaches that Consider Love and Sexuality as Separate and Probably Equal

Of the at least six views that we have identified as lying at the midpoint of the dimension, those of Reiss (1986a, 1986b) remain closest still to giving sexuality greater importance. He saw only a loose connection between sexuality and reproduction—sexuality serves reproduction only when it holds together kin so that children are raised. To Reiss the essential elements of sexuality are pleasure and self-disclosure. While the physical–pleasure aspect is a typical description of sexuality (from the viewpoint of the mating individual), Reiss' self-disclosure aspect has a different quality. It is said to arise from a desire to share the private, altered state of consciousness of sex with another. This desire in turn arises because "almost all humans value . . . the psychic release and intimacy potential of self-disclosure" (p. 35). Sexual self-disclosure is not necessarily in itself affectionate—one can be affectionate and not disclose sexually, and one can disclose sexually and not feel affection. But the "elemental physical and emotional disclosures of sexuality can promote further and deeper psychic disclosures" (1986b, p. 35). In other words, according to Reiss a desire to disclose to another is inherent in human sexuality, and it at least promotes affection. The motive is as important as physical pleasure and, more importantly, does not seem to arise from either the reproduction motive (privacy might safeguard mating but need not be a source of pleasure) or the pleasure motive (for otherwise, in the latter case, another person would not be necessary at all). In other words, to us Reiss seems to be identifying and raising to equal status a fundamental motive to share and join with another, which seems very much like something at the root of love.

Love receives still more status in the second view of the six, provided by sociologists and social psychologists. The former often emphasize social patterning of sexuality (norms, scripts, roles) as including aspects of love as well (DeLamater, 1987; McKinney, 1986; Simon & Gagnon, 1987). And social psychologists have sometimes referred to social scenarios of love (Aron, Dutton, Aron, & Iverson, 1989; Averill & Boothroyd, 1977), which explicitly or implicitly entail sexuality. These various views are generally not very concerned with the ultimate source—sexuality or love—of the social patterning in sexuality or of the scenarios in love. Rather, the interest is in how social patterns and scenarios influence behavior, and sexuality and love share the same status.

The third view, exchange theory (e.g., Thibaut & Kelley, 1959), which has been particularly influential in the area of love and close relationships (e.g., Kelley et al., 1983; Sprecher, in press), sees love and sexuality as separate resources to be exchanged: They serve as potential rewards that a person can receive from another and that are taken into account in calculating the potential outcome of any given act. Foa and Foa (1974) listed love as one of six such interpersonal resources, along with status, services, information, goods, and money. Sex was also explicitly mentioned but was considered an amalgam of love and services (others, however, in using Foa & Foa's list, have simply added sexuality as a seventh resource—cf. Cate, Lloyd, Henton, & Larson, 1982). Similarly, Safilios-Rothschild (1976) prominently included both love and sex among the major resources potentially exchanged between spouses. Interestingly, Rettig and Bubolz (1983) used this approach and found that among married individuals there was a high correlation between the quality of love and of sex that they received from their spouse ($r = .65$ for wives, .69 for husbands), implying that, when one of these rewards is plentiful, so is the other.

Fourth, the historical/economic view (as described, e.g., in DeLamater, 1987) emphasizes that love arose as a result of the growth of capitalism, which made family life less important for production and more important as a source of interpersonal support. Love, in other words, arose quite independent of sexuality. According to this view, it was only because the family was also the locus of reproduction, and hence sexuality, that love and sexuality became associated at all in our culture.

Fifth, Reik (1949), arguing from a neo-Freudian clinical perspective, also held that sexuality and love have separate but roughly equal influence. For example, he noted that sex is blatantly selfish, whereas in the case of love "it is very difficult to name its selfish aims, other than that of being happy in the happiness of the beloved person" (p. 21). "Sex is a passionate interest in another's body; love a passionate interest in another's personality. . . . Sex does not feel pain if its object is injured, nor joy when it is happy" (p. 21). "Sex . . . is undiscriminating . . . love is highly discriminating . . . there is no such thing as impersonal love" (p. 20).

Love arises, according to Reik (and with some research support from Mathes & Moore, 1985), from the desire to realize one's ideal self vicariously (by forming a relationship with one who is perceived to possess your own ideal traits). As Reik (1949) put it, "tell me whom you love and I will tell you who you are and, more especially, who you want to be" (p. 96). Although this ego-oriented approach to love is said to arise entirely independently of the sex drive (which Reik thought Freud had described far too broadly), Reik believed that the most fulfilling romantic relationship arose when love and sex went together. Certain other psychodynamic writers have also argued that sex and love are independent but potentially complementary forces in romantic attraction (e.g., Berl, 1924).

Finally, Grant (1976), a psychologist with a more eclectic approach, also argued (based in part on the earlier writing of Moll, 1912), that the sex drive and what he called the "amorous emotion" are independent aspects of "sexual love." In support of this position he made a number of points. Among them were (a) people report being willing to die for the love of a particular other person, even when sexual gratification may be quite available from someone else; (b) it is quite common for young children to report intense romantic love; and (c) the person whom an individual most desires sexually and the person with whom an individual feels most in love may be different. Grant also argued that there may be a third emotion, a nonsexual tenderness-love, which has its roots in attachment to the mother.

We will only mention here yet another group of approaches, which considers love and sexuality to be relatively equal and independent factors arising from other, common motivational forces. These closely related views include (a) the reattribution of arousal (Dutton & Aron, 1974) or the two-factor theory of love (Berscheid & Walster, 1974), and associated theories (e.g., Allen, Kenrick, Linder, & McCall, 1989; Clark, 1982; G. L. White & Kight, 1984); (b) love and sexuality as special cases of a general desire for passionate experience (Aron, 1970; Bataille, 1962; Stendhal, 1927); and (c) love and sexuality as special cases of opportunities for self-expansion (Aron & Aron, 1986). However, because these positions have a there's-a-third-cause-of-both interpretation of the link between sex and love, we will postpone considering them until after reviewing the entire continuum of theories on sexuality and love.

Position D: Approaches that Emphasize Love, Considering Sexuality a Minor or Subservient Part of Love

The approaches found at the next point along the continuum all come from the social-psychological study of love. These approaches emphasize love, their topic, and make sexuality a minor although real component of their theories—perhaps a small subset of all the types of love. Although some even hold sexuality to be immensely important at times, it is simply not their emphasis.

Beginning with the theories least preoccupied with the measurement of love, we can describe Sternberg's (1986) triangular theory of love as having three components—decision/commitment, intimacy, and passion. Sexuality was considered an aspect of only the third component. Hatfield and Walster (1978) divided love into "passionate" and "companionate" categories, and sexuality played only a small role in the former category. Indeed, Hatfield and Rapson (1987) verified Grant's (1976) anecdotal evidence about strong romantic love in young children, showing that passionate love occurs as frequently in 5-year-olds as in 18-year-olds, and pointing out that it would be hard to explain the passion of the former in terms of physiological sexuality.

Lee (1977) proposed six styles of love: eros (romantic, passionate love), ludus (game-playing love), storge (friendship love), mania (possessive, dependent love), pragma (logical, "shopping-list" love), and agape (all-giving, selfless love). These styles were constructed from the reduction of data acquired through an extensive interview procedure using questions including "only a very small number . . . that referred to sexual events" (p. 176). Similarly, C. Hendrick and Hendrick (1986), in constructing their scales of Lee's six love styles, included only two sexually relevant items (two of the seven items in the eros category—"Our lovemaking is very intense and satisfying" and "My lover and I have the right physical 'chemistry' between us" (p. 395). However, they have suggested that the tendency for males to be more permissive in their sexual attitudes is somehow related to males being more likely to manifest the ludus love style (S. Hendrick, Hendrick, Slapion-Foote, & Foote, 1985). In a later study (S. Hendrick & Hendrick, 1987) they systematically related the love styles to sexual attitudes and practices and found few gender differences in love styles. They did find, however, a pattern of associations with love styles that was consistent with the structure of their model. For example, eros lovers are intense about sexuality, pragma lovers are practical about sexuality, and so forth. More generally, Hendrick and Hendrick concluded that "love and sexuality are strongly linked to each other and to both the physical and spiritual aspects of the human condition" (1987, p. 293).

Although, as already noted, Bowlby's (1969) attachment theory gives love a strong biological basis, the research of Hazan and Shaver (1987) on love as attachment focused more on adolescent and adult relationships and is considerably less dependent on either biology in general, or sexuality in particular. Nor have their results indicated much of a role for sexuality in the three attachment styles described by attachment theory: secure, anxious/ambivalent, and avoidant. For example, of the various measures Hazan and Shaver related to attachment style in their studies, one subscale of one measure consisted of four items about "sexual attraction" (e.g., "I (was/am) very physically attracted to ____" [p. 514]). These items did have an adequate level of internal consistency, and anxious/ambivalent-type adult respondents to a newspaper questionnaire were slightly more likely to endorse them than were avoidant or secure types (consistent with a general pattern of anxious/ambivalents to endorse items associated with more intense feelings). However, a replication of this study with a college-student sample, although quite consistent overall with the results of the newspaper-survey sample, did not replicate the particular finding on the sexual-attraction subscale.

Rubin's (1970) study of romantic love has resulted in a Romantic Love Scale, which was developed from a large pool of potentially relevant items, at least some of which emphasized "physical attraction" (p. 266). After some initial screening by a panel of judges, 70 items were selected to be administered to a large class, asked (among other things) to complete them with regard to a boyfriend or girlfriend. A single factor emerged, and the items with the highest loadings were included in the scale. Not one of these items made any reference to sexuality or physical attraction (perhaps more of a comment on the students' views of love and sexuality than of the actual relationship). Instead, the items were about needing, caring, and exclusiveness/absorption. However, Rubin commented that the need component "evokes . . . Freud's [(1921/1951)] view of love as sublimated sexuality" (p. 268).

Two other approaches to romantic love has resulted in scales, neither of which have given sexuality much explicit emphasis. Hatfield and Sprecher's (1986) Passionate Love Scale was designed to include "cognitive, emotional, and behavior indicants of 'longing for union' " (Hatfield, 1988, p. 193). Only 6 of the 30 items include content that could be interpreted as sexual—for example, "I want ____—physically, emotionally, mentally" and "I eagerly look for signs indicating ____ 's desire for me" (p. 195). And Mathes (1982) developed a Romantic Symptoms Checklist, on which the respondent is instructed to "check the feelings elicited by the thought of your beloved, *now.*" The checklist includes items such as "Carefree," "Oneness," "Sunny," and "Wow!" Of the 35 items on the checklist (short form), only 4 are explicitly physical— "Tingly," "An increased heart beat," "An increased metabolism," and "A big rush inside me." None are explicitly sexual.

Given all these scales, it is also of some interest to consider some studies that have factor-analyzed various subsets of these scales (C. Hendrick & Hendrick, 1989; Levy & Davis, 1988; Sternberg & Grajek, 1984). Of course, because these analyses were only encompassing the above sorts of measures, which have all minimized the role of sexuality in love, the role of sexuality in love is of course small in their results. Nevertheless, in the most recent of these studies (C.

Hendrick & Hendrick, 1989) "passion"—which had very high factor loadings for the eros love style, Hatfield and Sprecher's (1986) passionate love scale, and two other passion subscales from other tests—was the first of five factors and accounted for 32% of the variance in responses of college students. (The next factor, accounting for 14% of the variance, generally included measures of closeness; two subsequent factors represented the three Hazan & Shaver, 1987, attachment styles; and finally one included Lee's, 1977, practical and friendship love styles.) Hendrick and Hendrick also conducted separate factor analyses of the items within each scale. The passion scales and subscales were all homogeneous, having single-factor solutions. This suggests that, although passion may be an important part of love, the sexuality-related items in scales of passion are not differentially contributing to what these scales measure.

Finally, in a study quite different from the above, Swensen (1961) explored love as a behavior, having 100 college students rate five love relationships (mother, father, sibling, same- and opposite-sex friend). Respondents were instructed to rate only relationships in which they "genuinely loved" the other person. One relationship was rated per week over 5 weeks on 293 possible behaviors of love in seven categories, as to whether each behavior was true (received or given) in that particular relationship. An item was considered true of a type of relationship only when at least 75% of the respondents had marked it as "always true." For the rating for their "fiancee or closest friend of the opposite sex" (p. 168—a characterization that might have led to ratings of a platonic relationship for some respondents), two of the five behaviors in the physical expression category, hugging and kissing, were so rated. None of the other relationship types had any physical expressions as always true for 75% of the students. "Nonmaterial evidence" ("advice, encouragement, etc."), "shared activities (games, shows, etc.)," "self-disclosure," and "verbal expression of feelings" appeared to be most important in this fiance or opposite-sex-friend relationship type, the last behavior category being nearly unique to it.

Overall, much of this recent social-psychological work on love seems to differentiate a nonsexual aspect or type of love from what is usually called *passionate love,* a category generally conceptualized as including sexuality to various degrees, but much more than sexuality as well.

Position E: Approaches to Love that Completely Ignore Sexuality or Consider Sexuality a Result of Love

The extreme end of the dimension posits that love is what is relevant and sexuality is a mere epiphenomenon in some love relationships. One group falling here includes the social psychologists who have studied love while for the most part utterly ignoring sexuality. For example, Dion and Dion (1973, 1975) conducted a series of studies of the relation of personality variables, such as self-esteem and locus of control, to the number of love relationships their respondents have had. More recently, these same authors (Dion & Dion, 1988) have discussed the impact on love of cross-cultural differences in individualism and collectivism, all with very little reference to sexuality. Another example is the recent work of Rousar (1990), who examined the implications of the theory that the essence of love is the valuing of the other person for his or her fundamental being, rather than for any particular resources (presumably, although it was not explicitly mentioned, these irrelevant resources include sexuality).

An interesting addition to this end of the dimension is the work of object relations theory, which has its roots in Freud (1920/1952), but much of its source in various analysts' dissatisfaction with Freud's libido theory. Object relations theory (e.g., Kohut, 1977; Mahler, 1968) emphasizes early childhood development—a cognitive fusion with the mother at birth, then a separation from her, followed by rapprochement with selfhood at around 2 years—along with the effects of exigencies on this process for adult development. Person (1987) cited object relations theorist Lichtenstein (1977) as arguing that the purpose of infantile sexuality is not to promote reproduction but pair bonding, and Fairbairn (1952) as seeing the sex drive as object seeking rather than pleasure seeking. (After all, although humans must mate in order to survive as a species, they in fact mate for some other reason. A subtler reason, according to this theory, would be to achieve pair bonding, and perhaps to affirm one's personal existence as well.) In this sense, object relations theory resembles Bowlby's (1969) biologically based attachment theory—that love receives contributions not only from the sexual system but from the mother-child attachment and caregiving systems. But the emphasis here seems to be far more cognitive, and to give all the causal power in the sex-love equation to love or affection. According to Person (1987), "rather than viewing libido as controlling interpersonal relations, it [object relations theory] emphasizes the way in which early object relations shape the experience of desire" (p. 397). For example, Person's concept of sex print—the "particular erotic prerequisites to sexual arousal in any given individual" (p. 400)—includes the idea that sex prints vary in whether the person uses sex "for pleasure, for adaptation, for the resolution of unconscious conflict" (p. 401), and whether sexuality will be central or peripheral to life—all of which is determined by the nature of prior relationships. That is, sex-is-really-love, in that its motivation and expression arise from past experience in human bonds.

But there is a far stronger version of this extreme of the continuum, and it is that Love with a capital "L" is primary or even the cosmic source of life and therefore of sexuality. This very ancient tradition is first accessible in the West in Plato, although Socrates reportedly received his knowledge from the Pythagorians, who are thought to have been greatly influenced by both Eastern sources and the pre-Indo-European Old Europe culture (through various learned women in that tradition—Eisler, 1987). Looking ahead from Plato, we know that Platonic ideas—especially the dualism of mind and body and the idea of a personal, active striving for transcendence—were the major source of Christian theology (Bullough, 1987), and thus have deeply shaped our culture.

In the earliest clear expression of this tradition in the West, Plato (400 BC/ 1892) said that "the mortal nature is seeking as far as is possible to be everlasting and immortal . . . love is of the immortal" (p. 332). For some, love fulfills the need to be immortal through the children who result from love—the next generation. But for others, with "souls which are pregnant . . . [they] conceive that which is proper for the soul to conceive or contain" (p. 333): temperance, justice, beauty. Naturally such a person "embraces the beautiful rather than the deformed body; above all when he finds a fair and noble and well-nurtured soul, he embraces the two in one person [body and soul] . . . and they are married by a far nearer tie and have a closer friendship than those who beget mortal children" (p. 333). In other words, for a special few a higher form of love leads to a higher form of immortality, through immortal truths.

That, however, is only the beginning of the story of love's nature. Plato claimed to be recording Socrates' words, who in turn was quoting the words of Diotima of Mantineia, "a woman wise in this and in many other kinds of knowledge" (p. 327). According to Socrates, Diotima told him that all the above thoughts "are the lesser mysteries of love" (p. 334), and went on to describe the stages of achieving a "greater and more hidden" love, "the crown of these" (p. 334). First, the student appreciates lovely objects, until he or she "becomes a lover of all beautiful forms" (p. 334). Then the student turns inward and loves the beauty of the mind—at first, thoughts on various beautiful concepts, until he or she sees the underlying beauty of the unity of all. Still, this is only a step, for then the student experiences "under the influence of true love" that which is "not growing or decaying, or waxing or waning . . . not fair in one point of view and foul in another . . . [but] beauty absolute, separate, simple, and everlasting" (p. 335).

In short, it was Diotima's experience that love has no limits—certainly no physical or biological limits such as hormones and gametes—but is both transcendental, "of the immortal," and a means to a unified state containing both love and everything else. Far removed from scientific psychology as it seems, this view of love is extremely important to appreciate for its persistent influence, at least in Indo-European-based cultures (Western and the Vedic-influenced Eastern cultures, which are those with Hindu or Buddhist underpinnings). (We grasp this influence better in the next section.)

Turning to less ancient theories of love and sexuality that fall at this extreme of the continuum, we must mention Freud in passing, for his (largely discounted) later writings on the life and death instinct (e.g., 1920/1959), and we must also discuss Carl Jung. Actually, Jung (1925/1959) saw love as arising purely out of sexuality in the first half of a person's life. (Jung would have agreed heartily with the sociobiologists on the function of the reproductive years.) It was his opinion that youths are more or less slaves to the reproductive needs of their species. Mating decisions are made on the basis of the anima/animus archetypes of the ideal man or woman (a sort of cognitive sociobiology). The entire process is largely unconscious, and therefore any love involved is not a valuing of the other person but of one's projection of the archetype onto that person.

Jung (1928) argued, however, that matters change in the second half of life. Our species' longevity past the age of reproduction allows humans to make their larger contribution to the evolution of the species, not through their genes, but through the insights and cultural contributions that arise from their greater experience. When a person does not resist the maturing process, relationships in the second half of life can become less driven by biological/reproductive considerations, and therefore less driven by unconscious projections. Instead, relationships provide opportunities for conscious work on the personal and collective task of achieving wholeness or balance among parts of the personality, and love is what draws one on through the often-difficult process (Jung, 1965). Or as the Jungian Guggenbuhl-Craig (1981) wrote in the context of marriage, love relationships are for salvation. Sexuality can be present or not; it is largely irrelevant.

In a similar vein, Maslow (1962) compared D-love (for deficiency) and B-love (for being) in a way that idealized the latter, calling it "richer, 'higher,' more valuable" (p. 43). Further, he too implied that sexuality is irrelevant to this higher love, in that "the concept 'gratification' hardly applies" to it (while "D-love *can* be gratified"), and that B-love is "admiring rather than needing" and "can never be sated" (pp. 42–43). Also echoing Plato, he stated that B-love allows the "truest, most penetrating perception of the other"; in fact, it "creates the partner" (p. 43) by allowing the partner to grow.

Others in the therapeutic traditions, such as Gaylin (1988), have also asserted that love is emphatically more important to humans than sexuality. Retelling the Indo-European myth that long ago humans were divided by the gods and are seeking their other half when they seek a mate, Gaylin wrote that "while intercourse is one intense, passionate form of such fusion it is not the essential mechanism. Rather, that mechanism is the rediscovering of the self in another. Any sophisticated concept of love must ultimately embrace this ancient concept. . . . Love is a fusion, a blurring of identities, and it is a fixed part of our species needs" (p. 57).

Finally, Brehm (1988), admitting that her conclusions fall in the Platonic tradition, and building on the Platonic views of the Christian mystics and of Stendhal, concluded that the core of passionate love is "the capacity to construct in one's imagination an elaborated vision of a future state of perfect happiness" (p. 253). As for sexuality, she did not see it as a necessary component of passionate love, but rather as a channel for the more general process of attachment—a channel that can be encouraged by cultural context. "But it is a serious mistake to regard all forms of passionate love as essentially sexual in origin or purpose" (p. 257).

ANOTHER DIMENSION—WHAT PEOPLE THINK
ABOUT LOVE AND SEXUALITY

As we said at the outset, social scientists are not the only ones who have drawn conclusions about sexuality and love. People generally have strong ideas on these topics, and social scientists have accumulated a large body of information on the attitudes and behaviors in various populations. As we turn to this information, the above dimension with its "love-is-just-sex, sex-is-just-love" extremes seem to be a good way to organize this work. Indeed, although we will not review the cross-cultural anthropological work on the subject, this is exactly how an-thropologists categorize cultures—by whether affection and sexuality are seen as one thing, occurring in one relationship, or whether they are seen as quite separate (Davenport, 1977).

Our own culture seems to link sexuality and love rather closely. Questionnaire data have consistently found sexual behavior or attitudes strongly linked to whether the persons involved are in love (or engaged, going steady, strongly committed)—the more in love, the more sexuality is acceptable. That is, this attitude is saying that love is primary and sex must wait for it. (Presumably, this would also mean that at other times in a relationship when sexual relations are impossible—for example, during physical illness—the relationship should con-tinue, for its ultimate foundation is love and not sex.) In short, the prevailing view falls a little past the midpoint on our continuum, lying in the direction of sex-is-really-love.

For example, Kaats and Davis (1970) found that college students are more permissive about sexual activities according to whether couples are "not particu-larly affectionate, strongly affectionate, in love, and engaged" (p. 393). Chris-topher and Cate (1984) factor-analyzed responses of 430 college students to 43 items about what has or would influence the respondents' decision to engage in intercourse. The first factor was Positive Affect/Communication, with love for partner and partner's love for self producing the highest correlations, followed closely by commitment. McCabe and Collins (1984) made going steady, con-sistent dating, and first date the predictor in a study of couples' agreement on their desired level of sexual involvement and their actual involvement, finding going steady correlated with more agreement. Finally, Sprecher (1989) has re-fined the Premarital Sexual Permissiveness Scale after the work of Reiss (1964), using the categories of first date, casually dating (dating for less than one month), seriously dating (dating almost one year), and engaged. These yield significant differences in what men and women feel is acceptable sexual behavior in target persons of differing gender, age, and personal relationship to the respondent. (Men were more permissive; less sexual behavior was acceptable for younger and personally related targets.)

Looking at recent trends, Sherwin and Corbett (1985) found sexual norms at a midwestern university had liberalized between 1963 and 1978, but that most of this increased permissiveness applied only to couples who felt affection for and commitment to each other. Earle and Perricone (1986) found similar changes at a small southern university between 1970 and 1981, with engaged, dating regularly, and casual acquaintance being the variable associated with permissiveness. And Kon (1987) reported that in Soviet universities, too, a change has been observed, so that now "the most important moral criterion for evaluating the moral appropriateness of sexual intimacy is not wedlock, but rather the presence of love and emotional involvement" (p. 265).

A 2-year study of college-age dating couples by Peplau, Rubin, and Hill (1977) also arrived at the same sort of distinctions (different behaviors being acceptable when no affection is felt, some is felt, or there is full commitment). After gathering data from 231 college-age dating couples recruited from a random sample of 5,000 in the Boston area, and after interviewing a smaller subset, the researchers described three orientations toward the "links between sex and love" (p. 97). For *sexually traditional couples* love alone was an insufficient reason for intercourse before marriage, and abstaining from intercourse was a sign of love. As noted above, one would expect that such couples would also hold that even in marriage, if circumstances made sexual fulfillment impossible, love could exist and should suffice to maintain the relationship (Position E). *Sexually moderate couples* saw love as a prerequisite for sex, and sex as an expression of love. Presumably they, too, held that love can thrive independent of sex and that sex does not have much place without love. Thus, they move closer to the midpoint (Position D). Finally, *sexually liberal couples* said sex with love is desirable, but sex without love is also acceptable. Here it is not clear if love could exist without sex. Love enhances sex. And sex can certainly manage to get along without love. They are roughly independent, and thus fall at the midpoint of our continuum (Position C).

This tendency to view sex as properly a part of love (or perhaps independent of it, but never love as a part of an effect of sexuality) is also reflected in the work of Fehr (1988), who attempted to identify the contents of prototypes of love. Again using North American college students as subjects, Fehr found that the most frequently mentioned attributes, and those shown to be most central to the prototype of love using a variety of social cognition procedures, did not include any sexuality-relevant terms, but focused instead on themes of caring, closeness, devotion, and the like. A number of sexuality-relevant terms did appear among the more peripheral features; these included *touching, sexual passion,* and *physical attraction.* Luby and Aron (1990) repeated Fehr's study comparing attributes of the prototype of loving someone with being in love with someone, and the pattern for loving someone was similar to that obtained by Fehr. However, the in-love prototype included 6 sexually relevant terms among its 29 central attributes: *touching, desire, excitement, sexual arousal, physical attraction,* and *sex.*

In a study of emotions, Shaver, Schwartz, Kirson, and O'Connor (1987) had students sort 135 emotion words into groupings that represented what the subjects thought people in general would consider to go together. A hierarchical cluster analysis identified a group of words the authors identified as love—1 of 5 major groupings, along with joy, anger, sadness, and fear. There were 3 subclusters within the love cluster, which they identified as affection (consisting of words such as *fondness, liking,* and *caring*), longing (consisting of only the word *longing*), and lust (consisting of *arousal, desire, lust, passion,* and *infatuation*). Two of the 5 words in the lust subcluster (*arousal, lust*) included all of the love-related words in the list of 135 related to sexuality (*desire* may also fit in this category). However, this subcluster also included the only 2 other love-related words (*passion* and *infatuation*) that could be used to describe intense nonsexual love. Thus all in all, subjects did not appear to separate sexuality sharply from love.

Some of the social-psychological research on love described earlier, such as reports of behaviors of love (Swensen, 1961) and measures of love (e.g., C. Hendrick & Hendrick, 1989), can also be interpreted as being descriptive of the view of love held by our culture—or at least its college students—and these findings also consistently suggested that people do not report sexuality as playing much of a role in love except when love is passionate or romantic (or a case of being in love with someone). And even in these instances the role is minor.

Finally, Reiss (1981) has tried to summarize the fundamental philosophies about sexuality underlying our culture's public debates on topics such as abortion, gender differences, pornography, and homosexuality by reviewing the large body of research that has studied the relation between general attitudes toward love and sexuality and views on these specific issues. Reiss concluded that there are two major ideologies in our own culture. One is the Modern-Naturalistic view, which emphasizes similar gender roles and equal gender rights. This position holds that the goal of sexuality is both pleasure and intimacy, that sex without love ("body-centered sexuality") "is of less worth than person-centered sexuality" (p. 280) but still has positive value, and that a wide range of sexual behaviors are acceptable if no force or fraud is involved. In short, love and sex are independent—Position C on the continuum we have described. The Traditional-Romantic view holds that gender roles do and should differ, and that males are and should be dominant—and frequently sees these two points as biological givens. Also, Reiss described this position as contending that "the major goal of sexuality is heterosexual coitus and that is where the man's focus should be placed" (p. 279). As for sexuality and love, "body-centered" sexuality should be avoided by women (the double standard) and "love redeems sexuality from its guilt, particularly for females" (p. 280). Also, sexuality is a powerful emotion (again, to be feared more by women). In sum, it would seem that the Traditional-Romantic view holds a double standard: The love-is-really-sex end of the continuum (Position A) applies to men; the sex-is-really-love end (Position E) applies to women.

Reiss did not hide his bias in favor of the Modern-Naturalistic view, and so places himself squarely with the views of college students reviewed above. He wrote: "Many people in the Western world lack awareness of what adherence of these [Traditional-Romantic] beliefs force them to include and exclude from their life styles. One purpose of this paper is to increase such awareness" (p. 280). All of this serves to remind us that social scientists and college students have probably influenced each other a great deal! Indeed, culture generally influences what science finds interesting to study, and it should be no surprise that if the whole range of views, from love-is-really-sex to sex-is-really-love, is easily identified in social science theory, it is also apparent in the people it studies and from which it sprang.

SEXUALITY AND LOVE AS TWO EXPRESSIONS OF A THIRD, UNDERLYING MOTIVE, AS DESCRIBED BY THE SELF-EXPANSION MODEL

We have seen that scientific approaches and the general public's approach to sexuality and love both can be understood as falling along a continuum from emphasizing sexuality to emphasizing love. It is, we hope, not too much of a simplification of the extremes of this continuum to say that at one end (Position A) we find views that sexuality (or natural selection in favor of good reproductive strategies) "causes" love, and at the other end (Position E) views that love (as some essence of the universe or of being human) "causes" sexuality. In the middle lie views arguing that either the two are mostly independent or that they cause each other. But still another view is also possible—a spurious relationship, that some third factor causes both love and sexuality. In this section we review approaches suggesting this possibility. As such, they do not quite fit on this continuum (although for completeness, we provisionally stationed them at midpoint, Position C). Rather, it seems that these views more or less transcend the continuum.

One such approach focuses on physiological arousal. A number of researchers (e.g., Allen et al., 1989; Aron, 1970; Dutton & Aron, 1974, 1989; White, Fishbein, & Rutstein, 1981; G. L. White & Kight, 1984) have demonstrated that romantic attraction is more likely to occur under conditions of physiological arousal, created by means as various as fear of electric shock, mirth over a Steve Martin comedy routine, or just running in place for 4 minutes. Sexual arousal has also been found to lead directly to greater general romantic attraction (e.g., Stephan, Berscheid, & Walster, 1971). One interpretation of this work (e.g., Berscheid & Walster, 1974; Dutton & Aron, 1974) has been that generalized physiological arousal, in the presence of an appropriate object of attraction, is misattributed to feeling attraction to the object. This interpretation follows the line of reasoning about emotions advanced by Schachter and Singer (1962). Other interpretations have also been advanced (e.g., Allen et al., 1989; Aron,

1970; Clark, 1982; Kenrick & Cialdini, 1977; G. L. White & Kight, 1984). But all of these various interpretations are consistent with the idea that love or sexuality could arise as a special case of some more general arousal.

Lately we have preferred to focus on the motivational aspect of love and sexuality, love being a motivation to enter and maintain a close relationship, and the experience of sexuality (or sexual desire) being a motivationally desirable goal state. The question we would then pose is, Do the two motivational goals, close relationships and sexual experiences, have any common elements?

Bataille (1962), Stendhal (1927), and one of us in earlier writings (Aron, 1970), all argued that the goal of both sex and love is passion, or boundary breaking—a desire to escape the ordinary. Bataille, in particular, argued that life is lived in two phases, the mundane and the passionate. The former includes the world of work and everyday life; the latter, such extremes as love and sex. Society seeks to reduce all passionate experience to the mundane—for example, by reducing spiritual passion to religion or sexual and romantic passion to conventional marriage.

But it seemed to us that the longing for passion found in some people might only be a glimpse of a much larger motivation found in all—to expand the self in whatever ways one perceives is serving the purpose. The self-expansion model (Aron & Aron, 1986) hypothesizes that all behavior is motivated by a desire to increase the self's potential efficacy (an idea similar to the motivational work of Bandura, 1982; Deci, 1975; and R. W. White, 1959). Thus, passion is desired because it is perceived as a moment of limitless potential efficacy, or connection with a source of such limitless power. But the self-expansion model also holds that more mundane rewards such as wealth, information, and status all derive their rewarding effect from their perceived potential for expansion. (Even the relief of pain and other outcomes associated with survival, we would argue, have arisen in order to support this goal of self-expansion. But the latter arguments are not essential to the points we are making here. We might add, however, that our reading of sociobiology causes us to wonder if this very general, flexible motivation of self-expansion might be what has been selected for, instead of a more rigid reproductive strategy. That is, on the average, what one perceives to be good for the self under some particular living conditions or in a specific culture is also good for one's offspring.)

The model also holds that the process of expansion itself is both highly pleasurable and a motivational goal. Thus, especially sought out is anything experienced as rapidly expanding the self, such as bursts of creative insights, religious conversions, discoveries, winning lotteries, and the like—and, notably, falling in love and intense sexual experiences. (However, all expansion experiences must also be integrated into the self, so that the expansion process proceeds as an expansion-integration cycle. And circumstances, past experience, and dispositional differences predispose individuals to pursue some means of self-expansion and expect others to lead to no expansion or even to cause de-expansion—that is, a loss of some expansion already gained.)

Why are love and/or sexuality such favored means of self-expansion? First, they have the advantage of being seen as available to almost everyone, as evidenced by stories in the popular media of success in these areas being independent of wealth, social status, education, and so forth. Second, in our culture they are often combined, so that they are perceived to provide added (if not multiplied) expansion opportunities from the single pursuit of forming an intimate relationship with an appropriate other. Finally, Jungian psychology suggests that in each culture there are symbols helping its members gain psychological wholeness (which is, in our model, another, prime expression of the self-expansion motive). Yet as Guggenbuhl-Craig (1981) has asked, "But where do we find living, working symbols? Symbols that are as living and effective as the gods of the ancient Greeks or the alchemical process?" (p. 82). His answer is that in our culture today symbols of sexuality and romance have replaced the gods themselves. (Whitmont, 1982, another Jungian, has added symbols of "relatedness"—that is, of a conscious relationship to interpersonal reality and social collectivity" [p. 340].) These symbols are preoccupying, "numinous." They are our current means for a woman to come to terms with her masculine side, a man with his feminine side, and both with the wilder, more bizarre sides—to submit, to dominate, or whatever. That is, sexuality and love are our current means of gaining wholeness through glimpsing and then integrating the otherwise neglected or rejected sides of ourselves.

A FINAL NOTE

One more thought about love and sexuality. We would suggest that the self-expansion motive prods humans to elaborate and expand every element of themselves. Like the bit of sand inside the oyster, secretions are added to that original something—the older the culture, the larger the pearl. The relatively simple communications of other animals become, in humans, language, education, culture, politics, screenplays, poetry, the evening news, and on and on. Eating becomes preparation rituals, the food industry, gourmet cooking, table manners, tea ceremonies, and on and on. Perception becomes art, aesthetics, concepts of beauty, museums, astronomy, photography, symphonies, and on and on. Mating becomes freighted with fantasies, rites, institutions, medical specialties, Jung's concept of individuation, and on and on. Social bonding becomes kinship rituals, fraternities, pen pals, family reunions, team sports, and on and on.

The point has been made in other ways before—functional autonomy, secondary reinforcers. That is, food may be a reinforcer built in by biology, and money may be something we must learn to accumulate in order to buy food, but in time money can become an end in itself. In such cases the elaborations surrounding the primary reinforcer have become such independent preoccupations that it sometimes seems that the original function of the core as fallen away. Likewise, we may be biologically programed to find sexuality, attachment, and caregiving rewarding, but these bits of sand also seem to have grown into much, much more—not only for the Platos and the Stendhals, but for the majority in Western culture since them, who have found a fresh ring of truth in this linking of love with the search for the infinite and immortal. To say a pearl is only a bit of sand plus some stuff around it seems to greatly miss the essence of the pearl. If we want to say something in general about both the bit of sand, which may be biological, and its outer accretions, called culture, perhaps the most interesting commonality is found in the purpose of each—the expansion of human life.

ACKNOWLEDGMENTS

We are grateful to Bryan Strong and to the editors of this volume, Kathleen McKinney and Susan Sprecher, for their helpful comments on an earlier draft of this chapter.

REFERENCES

Allen, J. B., Kenrick, D. T. Linder, D. E., & McCall, M. A. (1989). Arousal and attraction: A response-facilitation alternative to misattribution and negative-reinforcement models. *Journal of Personality and Social Psychology, 57,* 261–270.

Aron, A. (1970). *Relationship variables in human heterosexual attraction.* Unpublished doctoral dissertation, University of Toronto, Toronto.

Aron, A., & Aron, E. N. (1986). *Love and the expansion of self: Understanding attraction and satisfaction.* New York: Hemisphere.

Aron, A., Aron, E. N., Tudor, M., & Nelson, G. (1991). Close relationships as including other in the self. *Journal of Personality and Social Psychology, 60,* 241–253.

Aron, A., & Dutton, D. G., Aron, E. N., & Iverson, A. (1989). Experiences of falling in love. *Journal of Social and Personal Relationships, 6,* 243–257.

Averill, J. R., & Boothroyd, P. (1977). On falling in love in conformance with the romantic ideal. *Motivation and Emotion, 1,* 235–247.

Bandura, A. (1982). Self-efficacy mechanism in human agency. *American Psychologist, 37,* 122–147.

Bataille, G. (1962). *Eroticism* (M. Dalwood, Trans.). London: Calder.

Beach, F. A. (1977). Human sexuality in four perspectives. In F. A. Beach (Ed.), *Human sexuality in four perspectives* (pp. 1–21). Baltimore: Johns Hopkins University Press.

Berl, E. (1924). *The nature of love* (F. Rothwell, Trans.). London: Chapman & Hall.

Berscheid (1988). Some comments on love's anatomy: Or, whatever happened to old-fashioned lust? In J. Sternberg & M. Barnes (Eds.), *The psychology of love* (pp. 359–374). New Haven, CT: Yale University Press.

Berscheid, E., & Walster, E. H. (1974). A little bit about love. In T. L. Huston (Ed.), *Foundations of interpersonal attraction* (pp. 355–381). New York: Academic Press.

Berscheid, E., & Walster, E. H. (1978). *Interpersonal attraction* (2nd ed.). Reading, MA: Addison-Wesley.

Bowlby, J. (1969). *Attachment and loss: Vol. 1. Attachment.* New York: Basic Books.

Brehm, S. (1988). Passionate love. In R. J. Sternberg & M. Barnes (Eds.), *The psychology of love* (pp. 232–263). New Haven, CT: Yale University Press.

Bullough, B. L. (1987). A historical approach. In J. H. Geer & W. T. O'Donohue (Eds.), *Theories of human sexuality* (pp. 49–63). New York: Plenum Press.

Buss, D. M. (1988). Love acts: The evolutionary biology of love. In R. J. Sternberg & M. Barnes (Eds.), *The psychology of love* (pp. 100–118). New Haven, CT: Yale University Press.

Cate, R. M., Lloyd, S. A., Henton, J. M., & Larson, J. H. (1982). Fairness and reward level as predictors of relationship satisfaction. *Social Psychology Quarterly, 45,* 177–181.

Christopher, F. S., & Cate, R. M. (1984). Factors involved in premarital sexual decision-making. *Journal of Sex Research, 20,* 363–376.

Clark, M. S. (1982). A role for arousal in the link between feeling states, judgments, and behavior. In M. S. Clark & S. T. Fiske (Eds.), *Affect and cognition: The seventeenth annual Carnegie Symposium on cognition* (pp. 263–289). Hillsdale, NJ: Erlbaum.

Clark, M. S., & Mills, J. (1979). Interpersonal attraction in exchange and communal relationships. *Journal of Personality and Social Psychology, 37,* 12–24.

Davenport, W. H. (1977). Sex in cross-cultural perspective. In F. A. Beach (Ed.), *Human sexuality in four perspectives* (pp. 115–164). Baltimore: John Hopkins University Press.

Davis, K. E., & Todd, M. J. (1982). Friendship and love relationships. In K. E. Davis & T. O. Mitchell (Eds.), *Advances in descriptive psychology* (Vol. 2, pp. 79–122). Greenwich, CT: JAI Press.

Deci, E. L. (1975). *Intrinsic motivation.* New York: Plenum Press.

DeLamater, J. (1987). A sociological approach. In J. H. Geer & W. T. O'Donohue (Eds.), *Theories of human sexuality* (pp. 237–355). New York: Plenum Press.

Dion, K. K., & Dion, K. L. (1975). Self-esteem and romantic love. *Journal of Personality, 43,* 39–57.

Dion, K. L., & Dion, K. K. (1973). Correlates of romantic love. *Journal of Consulting and Clinical Psychology, 41,* 51–56.

Dion K. L., & Dion, K. K. (1988). Individual and cultural perspectives. In R. J. Sternberg & M. Barnes (Eds.), *The psychology of love* (pp. 264–289). New Haven, CT: Yale University Press.

Dutton, D. G., & Aron, A. P. (1974). Some evidence for heightened sexual attraction under conditions of high anxiety. *Journal of Personality and Social Psychology, 30,* 510–517.

Dutton, D. G., & Aron, A. (1989). Romantic attraction and liking for sources of conflict-based arousal. *Canadian Journal of Behavioral Science, 21,* 246–257.

Earle, J. R., & Perricone, P. J. (1986). Premarital sexuality: A ten-year study of attitudes and behavior on a small university campus. *Journal of Sex Research, 22,* 304–310.

Eisler, R. (1987). *The chalice and the blade.* San Francisco: Harper & Row.

Fairbairn, W. R. D. (1952). *An object relations theory of personality.* New York: Basic Books.

Fehr, B. (1988). Prototype analysis of the concepts of love and commitment. *Journal of Personality and Social Psychology, 55,* 557–579.

Foa, U. G., & Foa, E. B. (1974). *Societal structures of the mind.* Springfield, IL: Charles C. Thomas.

Freud, S. (1921/1951). *Group psychology and the analysis of the ego* (J. Strachey, Trans.). New York: Liveright.

Freud, S. (1920/1952). *A general introduction to psycho-analysis* (J. Riviere, Trans.). New York: Washington Square Press.

Freud, S. (1920/1959). *Beyond the pleasure principle* (J. Strachey, Trans.). New York: Bantam.

Gaylin, W. (1988). Love and the limits of individualism. In W. Gaylin & E. Person (Eds.), *Passionate attachments: Thinking about love* (pp. 41–62). New York: Free Press.

Gallup, G. G. J. (1986). Unique features of human sexuality in the context of evolution. In D. Byrne & K. Kelley (Eds.), *Alternative approaches to the study of sexual behavior* (pp. 13–42). Hillsdale, NJ: Erlbaum.

Grant, V. W. (1976). *Falling in love: The psychology of romantic emotion.* New York: Springer.

Guggenbuhl-Craig, A. (1981). *Marriage: Dead or alive* (M. Stein, Trans.). Dallas, Spring. (Original work published 1977).

Hatfield, E. (1988). Passionate and companionate love. In R. J. Sternberg & M. Barnes (Eds.), *The psychology of love* (pp. 191–217). New Haven, CT: Yale University Press.

Hatfield, E., & Rapson, R. (1987). Passionate love: New directions in research. In W. H. Jones & D. Perlman (Eds.), *Advances in personal relationships, Vol. 1* (pp. 109–139). Greenwich, CT: JAI Press.

Hatfield, E., & Sprecher, S. (1986). Measuring passionate love in intimate relations. *Journal of Adolescence, 9,* 383–410.

Hatfield, E., & Walster, G. W. (1978). *A new look at love.* Reading, MA: Addison-Wesley.

Hazan, C., & Shaver, P. (1987). Romantic love conceptualized as an attachment process. *Journal of Personality and Social Psychology, 52,* 511–524.

Hendrick, C., & Hendrick, S. (1986). A theory and method of love. *Journal of Personality and Social Psychology, 50,* 392–402.

Hendrick, C., & Hendrick, S. S. (1989). Research on love: Does it measure up? *Journal of Personality and Social Psychology, 56,* 784–794.

Hendrick, S., & Hendrick, C. (1987). Love and sexual attitudes, self-disclosure and sensation seeking. *Journal of Social and Personal Relationships, 4,* 281–297.

Hendrick, S., Hendrick, C., Slapion-Foote, M. J., & Foote, F. H. (1985). Gender differences in sexual attitudes. *Journal of Personality and Social Psychology, 48,* 1630–1642.

Jung, C. G. (1928). *Two essays in analytical psychology* (H. G. & C. F. Baynes, Trans.). London: Bailliere, Tindall & Cox.

Jung, C. G. (1925/1959). Marriage as a psychological relationship. In V. S. DeLaszlo (Ed.), *The basic writings of C. G. Jung* (R. F. C. Hull, Trans.) (pp. 531–544). New York: Modern Library.

Jung, C. G. (1965). *Memories, dreams and reflections* (A. Jaffe, Ed.). New York: Vintage.

Kaats, G. R., & Davis, K. E. (1970). The dynamics of sexual behavior of college students. *Journal of Marriage and the Family, 32,* 390–399.

Kelley, H. H., Berscheid, E., Christensen, A., Harvey, J. H., Huston, T. L., Levinger, G., McClintock, E., Peplau, L. A., & Peterson, D. R. (1983). *Close relationships.* New York: Freeman.

Kenrick, D. T., & Cialdini, R. B. (1977). Romantic attraction: Misattribution versus reinforcement explanations. *Journal of Personality and Social Psychology, 35,* 381–391.

Kenrick, D. T., & Trost, M. R. (1987). A biosocial theory of hetersexual relationships. In K. Kelley (Ed.), *Females, males, and sexuality: Theories and research* (pp. 59–100). Albany: State University of New York Press.

Kohut, H. (1977). *The restoration of self.* New York: International Universities Press.

Kon, I. S. (1987). A sociocultural approach. In J. H. Geer & W. T. O'Donohue (Eds.), *Theories of human sexuality* (pp. 257–286). New York: Plenum Press.

Lee, J. A. (1977). A typology of styles of loving. *Personality and Social Psychology Bulletin, 3,* 173–182.

Levy, M. B., & Davis, K. E. (1988). Lovestyles and attachment styles compared: Their relations to each other and to various relationship characteristics. *Journal of Social and Personal Relationships, 5,* 439–472.

Lichtenstein, H. (1977). *The dilemma of human identity.* New York: Jason Aronson.

Liebowitz, M. R. (1983). *The chemistry of love.* Boston: Little, Brown.

Luby, V., & Aron, A. (1990, July). *A Prototype structuring of love, like, and being in love.* Paper presented at the International Conference on Personal Relationships, Oxford.

Mahler, M. (1968). *On human symbiosis and the vicissitudes of individuation: Infantile psychosis* (Vol. 1). New York: International Universities Press.

Maslow, A. H. (1962). *Toward a psychology of being.* Princeton, NJ: Van Nostrand Reinhold.

Mathes, E. W. (1982). Mystical experiences, romantic love, and hypnotic susceptibility. *Psychological Reports, 50,* 701–702.

Mathes, E. W., & Moore, C. (1985). Reik's complementarity theory of romantic love. *Journal of Social Psychology, 125,* 321–327.

McCabe, M. P., & Collins, J. K. (1984). Measurement of depth of desired and experienced sexual involvement at different stages of dating. *Journal of Sex Research, 20,* 377–390.

McKinney, K. (1986). The sociological approach to human sexuality. In D. Byrne & K. Kelley (Eds.), *Alternative approaches to the study of sexual behavior* (pp. 103–129). Hillsdale, NJ: Erlbaum.

Moll, A. (1912). *The sexual life of the child* (E. Paul, Trans.). New York: Macmillan.

Peplau, L. A., Rubin, Z., & Hill, C. T. (1977). Sexual intimacy in dating relationships. *Journal of Social Issues, 33,* 86–109.

Person, E. S. (1987). A psychoanalytic approach. In J. H. Geer & W. T. O'Donohue (Eds.), *Theories of human sexuality* (pp. 385–410). New York: Plenum Press.

Plato (1892). Symposium. In B. Jowett (Ed. & Trans.), *The dialogues of Plato* (pp. 301–345). New York: Random House.

Reik, T. (1949). *Of love and lust: On the psychoanalysis of romantic and sexual emotions.* New York: Farrar, Straus & Giroux.

Reiss, I. L. (1964). The scaling of premarital sexual permissiveness. *Journal of Marriage and the Family, 26,* 188–198.

Reiss, I. L. (1981). Some observations on ideology and sexuality in America. *Journal of Marriage and the Family, 43,* 271–283.

Reiss, I. L. (1986a). *Journey into sexuality: An exploratory voyage.* Englewood Cliffs, NJ: Prentice Hall.

Reiss, I. L. (1986b). A sociological journey into sexuality. *Journal of Marriage and the Family, 48,* 233–242.

Rettig, K. D., & Bubolz, M. M. (1983). Interpersonal resource exchanges as indicators of quality of marriage. *Journal of Marriage and the Family, 45,* 497–509.

Rousar, E. E. (1990). *Valuing's role in romantic love.* Doctoral dissertation, Pacific Graduate School of Psychology, Palo Alto, CA.

Rubin, Z. (1970). Measurement of romantic love. *Journal of Personality and Social Psychology, 16,* 265–273.

Safilios-Rothschild, C. (1976). A macro- and micro-examination of family power and love: An exchange model. *Journal of Marriage and the Family, 38,* 355–362.

Schachter, S., & Singer, J. (1962). Cognitive, social and physiological determinants of emotional state. *Psychological Review, 68,* 379–399.

Shaver, P. R., & Hazan, C. (1988). A biased overview of the study of love. *Journal of Social and Personal Relationships, 5,* 473–501.

Shaver, P., Schwartz, J., Kirson, D., & O'Connor, C. (1987). Emotion knowledge: Further exploration of a prototype approach. *Journal of Personality and Social Psychology, 52,* 1061–1086.

Sherwin, R., & Corbett, S. (1985). Campus sexual norms and dating relationships: A trend analysis. *Journal of Sex Research, 21,* 258–274.

Simon, W., & Gagnon, J. H. (1987). A sexual scripts approach. In J. H. Geer & W. T. O'Donohue (Eds.), *Theories of human sexuality* (pp. 363–383). New York: Plenum Press.

Sprecher, S. (1989). Premarital sexual standards for different categories of individuals. *Journal of Sex Research, 26,* 232–248.

Sprecher, S. (in press). Social exchange perspectives to the dissolution of close relationships. In T. L. Orbuch (Ed.), *Close relationship loss: Theoretical approaches.* New York: Springer-Verlag.

Sprecher, S., & Metts, S. (1989). Development of the 'Romantic Beliefs scale' and examination of the effects of gender and gender-role orientation. *Journal of Personal and Social Relationships, 6,* 387–411.

Stendahl (Marie-Henri Beyle) (1927). *On Love* (H. B. V., Trans.). New York: Boni & Liveright.

Stephan, W., Berscheid, E., & Walster, E. (1971). Sexual arousal and heterosexual perception. *Journal of Personality and Social Psychology, 20*, 93–101.

Sternberg, R. J. (1986). A triangular theory of love. *Psychological Review, 93*, 119–135.

Sternberg, R. J., & Grajek, S. (1984). The nature of love. *Journal of Personality and Social Psychology, 47*, 312–329.

Strong, B., & DeVault, C. (1988). *Understanding our sexuality* (2nd ed.). St. Paul: West.

Swensen, C. H., Jr. (1961). Love: A self-report analysis with college students. *Journal of Individual Psychology, 17*, 161–171.

Symons, D. (1987). An evolutionary approach: Can Darwin's view of life shed light on human sexuality. In J. H. Geer & W. T. O'Donohue (Eds.), *Theories of human sexuality* (pp. 91–125). New York: Plenum Press.

Thibaut, J. W., & Kelley, H. H. (1959). *The social psychology of groups.* New York: Wiley.

White, G. L., Fishbein, S., & Rutstein, J. (1981). Passionate love and misattribution of arousal. *Journal of Personality and Social Psychology, 41*, 56–62.

White, G. L., & Kight, T. D. (1984). Misattribution of arousal and attraction: Effects of salience of explanations for arousal. *Journal of Experimental Social Psychology, 20*, 55–64.

White, R. W. (1959). Motivation reconsidered: The concept of competence. *Psychological Review, 66*, 297–333.

Whitmont, E. C. (1982). Recent influences on the practice of Jungian analysis. In M. Stein (Ed.), *Jungian analysis* (pp. 335–364). La Salle, IL: Open Court Publishing.

3 Emotions and Sexuality[1]

John DeLamater
University of Wisconsin–Madison

This chapter analyzes the interrelations of emotions and sexuality within close relationships and reviews the recent relevant literature within psychology, sociology, and sexology.

Psychologists and sociologists concerned with emotion rarely mention sexuality, and those who study human sexual expression mention emotion only slightly more often (Everaerd, 1988). Among them, there is considerable disagreement about the definition of emotion. For the present, emotion is defined as a combination of physiological response and subjective experience whose meaning is influenced by cognitive appraisal (Victor, 1980). A definition of sexuality is offered by Aron and Aron (this volume): "the constellation of sensations, emotions, and cognitions that an individual associates with physiological sexual arousal and that generally gives rise to sexual desire and/or behavior." The concept of sexuality is much broader than overt sexual behavior; in addition, it includes internal or subjective responses to stimulation.

In the first section I review the literature on emotion and consider the two prominent psychological perspectives on emotion, the "two-factor" and "three-factor" theories. The debate between them concerns the components of the experience of emotion by the person. I then turn to the literature on overt expression of emotion and two current arguments: (a) whether the behavioral expression of emotion reflects inner experience and (b) whether "emotional" behavior is more heavily influenced by social norms than by internal state.

The ensuing analysis of the relationship between emotions and sexuality in close relationships is divided into three discussions: emotion as an antecedent of

[1] I thank Corey Keyes, Kathy McKinney, and Susan Sprecher for their detailed and very helpful comments on drafts of this paper.

sexuality, emotion as a component of sexual behavior, and emotion as a consequence of sexual desire and behavior. The final section of the chapter briefly discusses sexual jealousy, which combines sexuality and emotion.

EMOTION

This section considers two topics, the nature of the subjective experience, which constitutes emotion, and the factors that influence the expression of emotion.

The Nature of Emotion

One prominent view of the nature of emotional experience is the two-factor theory, frequently associated with the work of Schachter (1964). According to this view emotional experience involves (a) perceptible autonomic arousal and (b) cognitive processing that results in the attachment by the person of an emotion label to that arousal. The alternative view is the three-factor theory, which holds that emotion consists of (a) physiological arousal, (b) subjective feeling, and (c) behavioral expression.

Two-factor theory.   This theory describes an emotional experience as involving arousal and cognition. Arousal is portrayed as a generalized, undifferentiated state involving increased heart rate, blood pressure, muscular tension, and other internal physiological changes (Berscheid, 1983). These changes can occur in response to a wide variety of internal or external stimuli. Thus, when the individual experiences (recognizes) arousal, he or she must interpret it. This involves cognitive processing of available information, which results in the person attributing the arousal to a particular stimulus. It is the attribution that defines the emotion for the person.

Imagine a man and a woman having dinner by candlelight. The woman notices that she feels warm; in turn, she becomes aware that her heart is beating rapidly, her mouth is dry, and her body is tense. These sensations are the subjective or experiential component of emotion. However, because they can result from a wide range of stimuli, the woman must determine their cause by processing available information. Given the setting, she may attribute the arousal to love for her companion. Alternatively, if she has been thinking about making love, she may conclude that she is sexually aroused. Finally, if the two fought on their way to the restaurant, she may interpret the arousal as anger.

In the two-factor theory, the type (or nature) of emotion being experienced is determined by the cognitive process, by the attribution that the person makes. Thus, Lazarus (1982) argued that the experience of emotion is inseparable from cognitive processes. "Stimulus events are assessed, interpreted or appraised, consciously or unconsciously, before these events result in emotions" (Everaerd,

1988, p. 4). This view emphasizes the importance of cognitive appraisal, and thus renders emotion as fundamentally cognitive.

It also suggests that emotion is responsive to external cues, to what sociologists term the definition of the situation. Thus, the two-factor theory is congruent with a major sociological theory, symbolic interactionism. Writers in this theoretical tradition assert that meaning is a social product. As people interact, they collectively define what is going on; once created, the definition influences both cognitive processes and behavior. Based on the definition of the situation, people engage in both selective attention and selective interpretation. A man alone with an attractive woman in her apartment will be more alert for cues suggesting sexual arousal; the same man alone in a house with his mother will be more alert for cues suggesting other sources of arousal. Similarly, arousal that occurs during a lecture on human sexuality is more likely to be interpreted as sexual, whereas arousal in the context of a church service is more likely to be interpreted as guilt for one's past violations of religious norms.

Several experimental studies provide evidence that supports the two-factor theory. These studies show that the attributions subjects make about the sources of their arousal can be influenced by manipulating the cues available in the setting in which the arousal occurs. Thus, if a man is aroused by fear (Dutton & Aron, 1974) or strenuous exercise (White, Fishbein, & Rutstein, 1981) when an attractive woman is present, he will attribute the arousal to sexual or romantic attraction.

Three-factor theories.   These theories suggest that an emotion has three components: physiological, experiential, and behavioral expression. For example, emotion is defined as a subjective experience accompanied by certain somatic events and revealed by facial and other expressions (Oatley & Johnson-Laird, 1987). Similarly, Everaerd (1988), in a discussion of the emotional aspects of sexuality, identified neurophysiological-biochemical, behavioral expressive, and feeling-experiential components of emotion.

Theories of this type reject the view that a single, generalized state of arousal underlies all emotions. Instead, proponents argue that each emotion is accompanied by (somewhat) distinctive physiological events. Appraisal is therefore not essential to the definition of an emotion. The feeling or subjective experience is a result of the distinctive internal sensations. Thus, a person who becomes aware of increased heart rate, blood pressure, and bodily tension experiences anger. An individual who becomes aware of increased heart rate, blood pressure, and vasocongestion in the genitals experiences sexual arousal.

These theories assume, implicitly if not explicitly, that emotions exist (Strongman, 1987), in contrast to the two-factor view, which reduces emotional experience to the application of a cognitive label. Further, they assume that emotions vary along two dimensions, hedonic sign (positive or negative) and intensity. It is the combination of sign and intensity that results in the distinctive feeling associated with each emotion. Often these theories assume that there are a small number (five, eight, and nine have been suggested) of primary emotions, with distinctive characteristics, and a larger number of secondary emotions that are combinations of two or more of the primary ones.

One of the most sophisticated theories of emotion was developed by Leventhal (1980, 1984). In his perceptual-motor theory, he described an adult emotion as a complex behavioral reaction that reflects the constructive activity of a hierarchical processing system (Leventhal & Scherer, 1987). A stimulus triggers not only autonomic arousal but also a cognitive processing system that contains prototypes or templates of emotional experiences based on past experience. The linking of the current stimulus setting with prior emotional episodes organizes the experience of emotion and emotional behavior.

A research program carried out by Shaver and his colleagues provides evidence that supports the view that prototypes of emotional experience influence our interpretation of present feelings. Undergraduate students sorted 135 names of emotions into categories based on similarity. A hierarchical cluster analysis of the sorts suggests that there are five basic emotion prototypes: love, joy, anger, sadness, and fear (Schwartz & Shaver, 1987). In another study (Shaver, Schwartz, Kirson, & O'Connor, 1987), subjects described personal emotional experiences. Analyses of these descriptions indicate that prototypes guide people's memories and reporting of such experiences.

Evaluation of three-factor models.   Strongman (1987) reviewed and assessed the evidence for the importance of each of the three components of emotion.

1. *Psychophysiological component.* There is no convincing evidence of distinct central or peripheral processes associated with each emotion, nor of direct links between physiological and behavioral responses.

2. *Cognitive component.* Recent research has clearly shown that emotion and cognition are intertwined. "Cognitive functions must be taken into account to give a reasonable picture of emotion" (Strongman, 1987, p. 110). Strongman suggested that emotion and cognition are both independent and interacting. Both may operate preconsciously, without awareness. Only emotion, he asserted, is capable of producing subjective feeling.

3. *Expressive component.* Work to date suggests that the link between internal state and behavior/expression of the state is quite complex. There is no direct relationship between internal state and a variety of behaviors (Strongman, 1987). The exception is facial expressions. Adelmann and Zajonc (1989) suggested a close relationship between "facial efference" and internal state. Research has shown that increased physiological arousal is correlated with increased facial expressiveness. Further, "exaggeration of facial efference congruent with an emotional stimulus increases corresponding subjective experience of an emotion while inhibition reduces it" (p. 267). Finally, Adelmann and Zajonc concluded

that the literature confirms the facial feedback hypothesis: Spontaneous facial efference can initiate the subjective experience of the corresponding emotion. Adelmann and Zajonc (and others) suggested that distinctive patterns of facial feedback determine which emotion one experiences.

The Expression of Emotion

In the past decade, several sociologically oriented writers have suggested that, in addition to internal state, there are important social influences on the expression of emotion.

Feeling rules. Emotional expression, like all other behavior, is subject to social control. Every society has social norms that specify as appropriate particular emotions in particular situations (Shott, 1979). In American society, norms prescribe love and happiness as appropriate emotions for the bride and groom to experience on their wedding day. Anger is inappropriate at a wedding. Such norms, or feeling rules, are an important influence on the expression of emotions. Generally, competent actors will express acceptable emotions in behavior (e.g., by smiling and gazing tenderly at one's bride) and suppress unacceptable ones (e.g., slapping one's betrothed). Thus, an important reason why subjective experience may not be expressed in overt behavior is that the feeling is inconsistent with feeling rules.

An emphasis on the importance of feeling rules (i.e, the influence of social definitions) is compatible with a two-factor theory of emotion. If arousal is a generalized state, and the substance of an emotion is determined by the label that is applied, then the culture's feeling rules can essentially determine the subjective feelings one experiences. Thus, "affective labeling of physiological states can be manipulated to a great extent, . . . within a range bounded by recognition of cues indicating minimal arousal and intense arousal" (Shott, 1979, p. 1330).

An emphasis on the importance of social definitions is also compatible with a three-factor view of emotion. Hochschild (1983) also emphasized the impact of social definitions on our expression of emotions. But she assumed that people experience spontaneous feelings; whether individuals express them in behavior depends on the feeling rules governing the interaction or situation. Feelings that are inconsistent with the rules produce emotion work; people attempt to change the emotion they are experiencing, to bring feelings into line with the social norms. They may have to suppress an inappropriate feeling, evoke a feeling that is not initially felt, or exaggerate a feeling that is not intense enough. This perspective is very similar to Leventhal's (1984) perceptual-motor theory; both recognize that people's expressive behavior reflects not only the subjective feeling but also their conscious control over behavior.

Within the two-factor theory, then, feeling rules influence the emotion label, and thus the experience of emotion. Within the three-factor models, feeling rules affect the expression of emotion but not the subjective experience.

The members of a culture or subculture learn the prevailing norms, beliefs, and vocabularies of emotion (Gordon, 1990). Research on the process of emotional socialization is beginning to appear. Simon (1989) reported a study of teenage girls' learning of the feeling rules for romantic love. Observation of the interactions of 12- and 13-year-old girls identified several rules that were being taught: (a) Romantic love is heterosexual; (b) romantic relationships should be important, but not everything in life; (c) one should not have romantic feelings for more than one boy at a time (serial monogamy); (d) one should not have romantic feelings for a boy who is already attached (exclusivity). These rules were inferred from explicit statements, gossip about girls who may have violated these rules, and teasing and other negative sanctions directed at group members thought to have violated them.

Thorne and Luria (1986) also observed emotional socialization among school-children. They focused on the development of gender differences in attitudes toward sexuality. Girls and boys learn to define sexual behavior in different contexts. Boys' interactions are oriented toward producing excitement by violating rules and girls' interactions are oriented toward constructing intimacy by mutual self-disclosure. Once established, patterns of teasing maintain these differences. Thorne and Luria also noted the emphasis on heterosexual attachments and the hostility expressed toward homosexual ones.

Rules governing sexual feelings and behavior are also taught by the mass media (Metts & Cupach, 1989). Models of sexual scripts, how men and women meet and achieve sexual intimacy, are regularly portrayed in films, television programs, and rock music videos. Visual presentations of sexual behavior include provocative dress, touching and hugging, and passionate embraces and kisses. Opening lines, verbal statements that can be used to initiate interaction, are a staple of movies and prime-time television programs directed at teenagers, and most references to sexual intercourse involve partners who are not married, or not married to each other.

The social construction of emotion.   A recent extension of this sociological perspective, the social constructionist viewpoint (Harre, 1986; McCarthy, 1990), places even greater emphasis on the social influences on emotional behavior. According to this view, people's experience of emotions is determined by the cultural vocabulary of emotion words to which they have been socialized. It is "by way of its linguistic practices and the moral judgements in the course of which the emotional quality of encounters is defined" (Harre, 1986, p. 5). In this view, emotions are attitudes or beliefs that are learned via socialization. Emotional behavior is prescribed by social norms as appropriate in a given situation. People behave angrily because they have learned that angry behavior is appropriate in the situation; others observe normatively required angry behavior and conclude a person is angry. This perspective might be termed a *one-factor theory* because physiological sensation or feeling is not a necessary condition for the occurrence of emotion.

Blumstein and Schwartz (1990) presented a constructionist view of sexual desire: "Fundamental categorical desire may not even exist. Rather, it is culture that creates understandings about how people are sexual" and determines what types of persons one will desire. They recognized the importance of language, arguing that it provides people with the meanings they apply to situations and other people.

EMOTION IN CLOSE RELATIONSHIPS

Most emotional experiences arise in the context of social, and especially intimate, relationships (Clark & Reis, 1988).

Schwartz and Shaver (1987) asked subjects to describe an emotional experience, including its antecedents, behavioral expression, and coping techniques. Analyses of the descriptions indicated that most experiences had their antecedents in relationships. Fear is often a consequence of the threat of rejection, or of the loss of a relationship. Sadness is frequently caused by illness or death of a loved one, rejection by another person, or the end of a relationship. Anger may be due to loss of respect or an insult. Joy is caused by receiving esteem or praise, or being the object of affection or love. Last but not least, love is uniquely interpersonal. Analyses of the experiences of each type found that all of the reported episodes of love involved relationships, as did 91% of the anger experiences, 90% of the sadness episodes, and 47% of the fear and 40% of the joy episodes. In addition, the behaviors that subjects reported engaging in were typically social as well.

Denzin (1984) argued that all emotions are interpersonal, that every emotion has the self or the self of another as a referent. Furthermore, emotions arise from social acts engaged in by the person, or directed at the person by others. Like other sociologically oriented writers, he argued that emotions are interpreted in terms of one's relationships to others.

EMOTION AS AN ANTECEDENT
OF SEXUAL EXPRESSION

Most sexual expression involves two (sometimes more) people. Inevitably, it will be influenced by their relationship and emotions. Emotion can play an important role in determining whether sexual behavior occurs, and may influence which activities the persons engage in. Three emotions that may be antecedents are love, anxiety, and depression.

Love

In American society, an emotional bond is often a prerequisite for sexual behavior (DeLamater, 1981). This bond is typically called love. American culture is unique in the degree to which love and sexuality are linked (see Aron & Aron, this volume). Surveys of sexual attitudes or standards consistently find that the more emotionally intimate a relationship is, the more acceptable sexual behavior is. Similarly, studies of behavior indicate that the more intimate the relationship, or the longer its duration, the more likely the people are to engage in sexual intimacy (Sprecher, 1989).

Love is a particular type of emotion, a *sentiment,* that Gordon (1981) defined as "a socially constructed pattern of sensations, expressive gestures and cultural meanings organized around a relationship to an object, usually another person" (p. 566). Gordon differentiated between emotions and sentiments by stressing that the latter are culturally defined. Gordon argued that, although arousal is the stimulus for a sentiment, the emotional quality experienced is determined by the cultural meanings the person has learned. Sentiments are socially important because they persist over time and sustain the relationship with the object of the sentiment.

Love is defined by Aron and Aron (this volume) as "the constellation of behaviors, cognitions, and emotions associated with a desire to enter or maintain a close relationship with a specific other person." To the extent that love is a prerequisite for sexual intimacy, it is likely that voluntary sexual intimacy will occur primarily in on-going, rather than casual, relationships. Our understanding of love is heavily influenced by the mass media (Gordon, 1981). Advice columns in newspapers and magazines, popular books, and television shape both our definition and our expression of love. Many popular songs are about love or about sexual attraction; they often explicitly describe the feelings or other cues people can use to recognize love or desire. Media portrayals reinforce the feeling rules about love learned in childhood and adolescence.

In the social-psychological literature on love, it is common to distinguish between passionate love and companionate love. *Passionate love* is "a state of intense absorption in another. A state of intense physiological arousal" (Berscheid & Walster, 1978, p. 160). *Companionate love* is "the affection we feel for those with whom our lives are deeply intertwined" (Berscheid & Walster, 1978, p. 177). It involves strong attachment to and caring for another person. The elements of passion, on the other hand, include intense arousal, wishfulness or fantasy (as opposed to logic), mystery or elusiveness, and an element of danger (as opposed to acceptability) (Viederman, 1988). Passionate love is not the same as intense desire for sexual intercourse with a particular person, or lust (Stone, 1988). However, passionate love and sexual desire are closely linked (Hatfield & Rapson, 1987). Passionate love will often lead to intense and frequent sexual interaction, whereas companionate love may lead to enjoyable but less intense and less frequent sexual behavior (Brehm, 1985; Sprecher, 1989). Alternatively, companionate love may be associated with a nonsexual relationship, such as between parent and child or close friends.

Empirical research yields mixed results with regard to the existence of the two kinds of love. Fehr (1988) analyzed love from a prototype perspective and asked subjects to list as many features of love as came to their minds. Analyses revealed one large cluster, comprised of features reflecting positive feelings. Subsequent studies found that the central features of love are caring, attachment, and intimacy. None of the features of passionate love was central to these subjects' conception of love. On the other hand, Hendrick and Hendrick (1989) asked subjects to complete five questionnaire measures of love, including those used by Davis and Todd (1985), Hazan and Shaver (1987), Hatfield and Sprecher (1986), and Sternberg (1986), as well as their own. A factor analysis of the items from all five scales yielded five factors. The first and largest factor tapped passionate love. The second factor involved measures of closeness, or companionate love.

Stone (1988) suggested that the capacity for passionate love is not innate. Case histories of relationships involving passion are widespread across societies and throughout history, but are not universal. Thus, he concluded that the disposition to fall in passionate love with another person is the result of socialization. The romantic love complex, the prescription that love is highly desirable as a basis for marriage, is found in only a few societies, including contemporary American society (Goode, 1959). Clearly, the experience of romantic love and its relationship to sexual expression are heavily influenced by the culture.

Several analysts have suggested typologies or taxonomies comprised of more specific types of love. Clark and Reis (1988) presented a good review of these models.

Anxiety

In a close relationship, anxiety may be associated with actual or potential sexual behavior, or with the relationship.

Anxiety may be aroused by thoughts about sexual activity or by interpersonal interactions in which sexual overtures may be made. Many adolescents and young adults are anxious about sexual activity, in part because of its novelty (Hardy, 1964) and in part because of the lack of adequate sex education, either at home or in the schools (Orbuch, 1989). Anxiety in particular relationships may reflect concerns about the relationship rather than about sexual intimacy. A person may be anxious because of fear of intimacy, concern about the partner's commitment to the relationship, or fear of rejection. These considerations suggest that anxiety is likely in the early stages of most relationships. Uncertainty about the partner's intentions, about how much sexual intimacy the partner expects, and about how to initiate physical intimacy may all contribute to anxiety. As the relationship develops and partners establish interpersonal and sexual scripts, anxiety should lessen. It may increase when events (such as the birth of a baby) disrupt established scripts.

Anxiety can either facilitate or inhibit sexual arousal (Barlow, 1986). The two-factor theory suggests that arousal is generalized, that the difference between anxiety and sexual arousal is the label applied. Barlow reviewed literature indicating that anxiety increases arousal in sexually functioning persons. Perceived demands for performance and sexually aroused partners facilitate sexual behavior in such persons. Beggs, Calhoun, and Wolchik (1987) reported that both sexually pleasurable and anxiety-arousing narratives produced increased arousal in women, but the increases associated with pleasurable narratives were greater.

Kaplan (1979) wrote of the significance of anxiety in inhibiting sexual expression. She stated that anxiety is the basic cause of sexual dysfunctions, and that the more intense the anxiety, the more serious the disorder. Kaplan also discussed the many sources of anxiety that can lead to dysfunctions. Mild anxieties include concern about one's sexual performance, fears of rejection, unrealistic expectations, and residues of childhood guilt about sexual thoughts, feelings, and behavior. Moderate anxieties include concern about pleasure, fear of intimacy and commitment, and deep fears of rejection. Profound anxiety has its roots in hostility toward the partner, intimacy phobias, and high levels of guilt about sexuality.

A review of empirical studies that compare persons experiencing sexual dysfunctions with normal persons found that anxiety is common among those with dysfunctions (Norton & Jehn, 1984). At the same time, the authors pointed out that the level and nature of the anxiety vary greatly from one person to another. Beck and Barlow (1986) suggested that, in the dysfunctional male, anxiety distracts his attention from the erotic sensations and fantasies that contribute to arousal. In these men, increased arousal did not produce increased genital response.

Depression

Clinicians have long recognized that depression leads to loss of interest in sexual activity. In contemporary terms, depression is identified as a major cause of both inhibited sexual desire and absence of sexual desire (Rosen & Leiblum, 1987).

Reynolds et al. (1988) compared the sexual functioning of three samples of men: outpatients with major depressive disorders (n = 42), men with erectile disorders (n = 13), and healthy controls (n = 37). All three groups were composed of white, well-educated, middle-class heterosexuals; about one half of the men in each group were married or had a steady partner. Each man completed two sexual functioning inventories, and kept a log of sexual interest and activity for 14 days. Compared to healthy men, depressed men reported less frequent sexual thoughts and fantasies, less frequent sexual activity (about 50% less), less pleasure from their sexual activity, and less satisfaction with their sex lives. The researchers were also able to collect data from the partners of 12 depressed men and 14 controls. Partners of depressed men reported less frequent intercourse, and greater frequency of erectile dysfunctions. Partners of depressed men reported that, prior to the onset of depression, the men's sexual interest and activity had been greater and they had fewer erectile problems.

In summary, love, particularly passionate love, is associated with more intense and frequent sexual activity. Anxiety may either facilitate or inhibit sexual expression. Depression is associated with reduced sexual activity.

EMOTION AS A COMPONENT
OF SEXUAL EXPRESSION

Sexual Desire

Much of the recent work in the study of sexuality has focused on sexual desire. It is assumed that most sexual behavior is motivated by desire. Further, it is possible that desire is differentiated so that it predisposes the person to engage in some behaviors and not others. Thus, patterns in sexual behavior (e.g., high frequencies of oral sex) may reflect preferences associated with desire. Similarly, a preference for male or female partners may be tied to desire.

The nature of arousal.   Fundamental to sexual desire is physiological arousal. Like other emotions, sexual desire involves sympathetic arousal, visceral and muscular sensations associated with the flow of adrenalin. In addition, it involves vasocongestion, the flow of blood to certain tissues, especially the genitals; this process is controlled by the parasympathetic system and may be unique to sexual arousal (Mandler, 1984). Other symptoms of arousal include an increase in heart rate and/or blood pressure, feeling hot or flushed, and tremors. Cognitive appraisal is an essential component of sexual arousal. The internal or external stimulus must be interpreted as sexual; although some other emotions may occur in direct response to a stimulus, there is no evidence that this is true of sexual arousal (Everaerd, 1988). The cognitive schema associated with sexual arousal contain learned response tendencies or propositions. They reflect the person's past experiences in sexual situations. Sexual arousal activates cognitive schema. If the situation allows, the associated behaviors will occur.

Several writers have suggested that there is a circular or feedback process involved in arousal. As previously noted, a stimulus is followed by cognitive processing, which leads to an interpretation of the physiological arousal. This may in turn make the person more aroused and produce new interpretations (Gordon, 1981). With regard to sexual arousal, such a feedback loop between the physiological and the cognitive processes is quite plausible.

Mosher, Barton-Henry, and Green (1988) suggested that sexual arousal is an affect-cognition blend, consisting of awareness of physiological sexual arousal and one or more sexual affects: sexual interest, anticipatory excitement, sexual enjoyment, or sexual pleasure. Arousal "deepens [the person's] involvement by amplifying the perception of sexual stimulation, sexual cognitions, sexual behavior, physiological sexual response, and of itself" (p. 412). Members of a sample of college students were asked to recall and rate four sexual experiences. Sexual arousal was assessed by 11 questions that asked about genital, muscular, and physiological responses during the experience. The men and women also rated the maximum level of genital sensation during the experience. A third measure assessed affective arousal, ratings of the extent to which the person was lustful, sexually aroused, sensuous, hot, horny, passionate, and sexually excited. The median correlation among the three measures across the four experiences was .51. Thus, the greater the rated physiological arousal, the greater the rated emotional arousal, suggesting a feedback loop between the two.

Gender differences.   Recent research suggests that sexual desire in women is associated with hormonal factors. Stanislaw and Rice (1988) reported prospective data on the timing of reported sexual desire and various characteristics of the menstrual cycle. Sexual desire occurred and/or increased around the expected day of ovulation. These and other results suggest that sexual desire is influenced by the same hormonal process that regulates the menstrual cycle. Other research suggests that the level or intensity of sexual desire reported by women is correlated with their general arousability (Jupp & McCabe, 1989). Two judges assessed sexual desire by independently rating parts of a recorded interview for the woman's attitude toward sex and comfort with sexual activity. A 40-item self-report scale measured general arousability and included items such as "I get excited easily." In a sample of college students, there was a substantial (.43) correlation between arousability and rated sexual desire. One implication of these results is that, for some women, the frequency and timing during their cycle of desire for sexual activity are predictable. This should make it easier to develop a script with the partner that satisfies the woman's desires.

There is evidence of gender differences in the experience of sexual arousal. Males have a more obvious cue (erection) that sexual arousal is occurring. For females, the cues are more ambiguous: vaginal lubrication, erect nipples, and increased heart rate and blood pressure. Thus, males should be more likely to recognize sexual arousal when it is occurring (Rook & Hammen, 1977). Research in which physiological indicators of arousal are compared with self-reports indicates that men are more likely to report arousal when it is occurring (Heiman, 1975). There are also gender differences in the nature of the stimulus that produces arousal. Males are more likely than females to report that arousal is triggered by a visual stimulus—an attractive woman, pictorial or written representations of sexual activity—whereas females are more likely to report arousal triggered by a social or romantic context (Knoth, Boyd, & Singer, 1988). Further, males reported that their arousal is of greater intensity and more distracting than females'. These differences in the nature of sexual arousal are consistent with other evidence indicating that men have a more body-centered orientation toward sexuality and that women have a more person-centered orientation (DeLamater, 1987).

Research also suggests differences in motives for engaging in sexual behavior (Sprague & Quadagno, 1989). Young males reported that their motives are for physical pleasure and fun, whereas young females' motives include emotions and commitment. A sample of white, middle-class adults rated the importance of physical release and love as motives for intercourse. Men aged 22 to 45 rated physical release as more important than women of those ages, but men over 45 rated it as less important than did women over 45. Women 22 to 35 rated love as more important than did men, while women and men over 35 gave love similar ratings. Thus, the differences noted among younger men and women may lessen as they get older. These differences in motives clearly reflect differences in the socialization of men and women, and in the sexual scripts they are taught (Mac-Corquodale, 1989).

Sexual Behavior

Strongman (1987) suggested that sexual behavior involves complex emotions— "arousal through neural processes, hormones, external stimuli, imagery and thought in massive interaction, all tempered by learning and experience" (pp. 221–222).

Once the person begins to engage in sexual activity, his or her behavior is likely to lead to increased stimulation, producing increased arousal. Such a process is clearly involved in sexual foreplay, with increasingly intimate sexual behavior closely associated with increasing sexual arousal. The partner's tactile stimulation of various parts of the body, particularly the lips, breasts, inner thighs, and genitals, typically produces further sexual excitement.

EMOTION AS A CONSEQUENCE OF SEXUAL ACTIVITY

The occurrence of sexual activity is likely to cause emotions. If the activity produces sexual pleasure or orgasm, satisfaction may result; if the activity does not produce pleasure, dissatisfaction may result. Emotions may also result from more specific aspects of the sexual activity, such as types of foreplay, coital positions, settings in which the activity occurs, and partner's response. In this section, four emotions are discussed: sexual satisfaction/dissatisfaction, embarrassment, anxiety/fear, and frustration.

Sexual Satisfaction/Dissatisfaction

Contemporary research and writing about sexuality, particularly sexual expression within marriage, frequently include a discussion of sexual satisfaction. A substantial literature relates sexual satisfaction to a variety of other variables. This literature is reviewed in this section.

Concern about satisfaction or adjustment is a recent phenomenon. Prior to 1960, sexual partners were rarely concerned about the quality of their sexual relationship (Adams, 1986). The prevalence of this interest today and the fact that satisfaction is related to other individual and couple characteristics reflect cultural definitions. "In no past society known to me has . . . sexual fulfillment been elevated to such preeminence in the list of human aspirations" (Stone, 1988, p. 19). Stone went on to suggest that, if the Declaration of Independence were revised today, total sexual fulfillment would have to be added to the list of inalienable human rights. Adams (1986) suggested that sexual adjustment may be particularly problematic for middle-class couples, who are likely to feel guilty about sexual feelings and pleasure yet believe that sexual fulfillment is important.

Sexual satisfaction refers to the degree to which a person's sexual activity meets his or her expectations. A study of young women by Pinney, Gerrard, and Denney (1987) identified two dimensions: general sexual satisfaction, comprised of the woman's satisfaction with the types and frequency of her sexual behavior, and satisfaction with her partner. Satisfaction, then, has both a personal and an interpersonal component. Satisfaction in either case is clearly relative; it depends on the person's desires for type and frequency of sexual activity and type and behavior of partners. For example, one cannot help but be struck by the irony when one woman writes to Ann Landers, dissatisfied that her husband makes love to her as infrequently as once a month, and another woman complains that her husband makes love to her too often (at least once a week), and offers him to the first letter writer.

Within a relationship, a couple develops a sexual script, a sequence of specific behaviors that usually leads to intercourse. Once created, the script tends to be followed each time the couple engages in sexual activity. For these couples, satisfaction depends on whether the script allows for the desired amount of sexual pleasure. One's desire to engage in particular behaviors and to experience certain types of pleasure depends on past experience. The person who has had other sexual relationships will have a standard for comparison. Another important influence on people's standards today is the mass media. Newspaper and magazine articles often suggest that (almost) everyone ought to be experiencing satisfaction. In particular, one ought to be orgasmic; although men can generally take this outcome for granted, women cannot. A woman who adopts this standard may, as a result, become dissatisfied with what had in the past been a satisfying sexual script.

Because satisfaction reflects in part the sexual activities in which the couple engages, it is not surprising that sexual satisfaction is related to the extent of communication about sex. Both frequency and quality of a couple's talk about sex are related to sexual satisfaction (Metts & Cupach, 1989). In their report of the results of a survey conducted by *Redbook* magazine, Tavris and Sadd (1978) reported that more than 50% of the women who always discussed their sexual feelings with their husband were very satisfied, and that only 9% of those who never discussed their feelings were very satisfied. (See Cupach & Metts, this volume).

In general, sexual satisfaction is positively related to marital satisfaction. Those men and women who reported being satisfied with their sexual relationships also reported being satisfied with their marital relationships (Reiss & Lee, 1988).

There are gender differences in the immediate causes of sexual dissatisfaction (Hatfield, Sprecher, Pillemer, Greenberger, & Wexler, 1989). For women, the emotional quality of sexual interactions seems to be a more important influence on their evaluations of the sexual relationship. Therefore, women who are dissatisfied want more love, affection, and caring in their sexual relationships (Hatfield, 1982; Hite, 1976). For men, the quantity of sexual activity is more important. Men who are dissatisfied want more frequent, varied, and impulsive sexual behavior (Hite, 1981). As noted earlier, research suggests that this difference lessens with age (Sprague & Quadagno, 1989).

Dissatisfaction with sexuality is related to several important outcomes. First, dissatisfaction is associated with low marital satisfaction or happiness. This association is undoubtedly bidirectional. Dissatisfaction with sex can lead to dissatisfaction with the relationship and vice versa. In turn, dissatisfaction with the marital relationship is associated with involvement in extramarital sexual activity. This is another indicator of the importance of sexual fulfillment to many men and women.

Second, sexual dissatisfaction is associated with an increased incidence of sexual dysfunctions. A recent study found that couples experiencing dysfunctions were more likely than normal couples to report dissatisfaction with their sexual interaction (Kilmann et al., 1984).

The most prevalent sexual dysfunction seems to be inhibited sexual desire (ISD). According to media accounts, sex therapists report that one half or more of their clients are experiencing this disorder. (*Newsweek, 1987*). Although the causes of ISD are numerous, the underlying factor in many instances may be dissatisfaction with the current sexual relationship or partner (Everaerd, 1988). A study comparing married women who reported inhibited sexual desire and married women who reported normal desire found that those with ISD also reported lower levels of affection in and satisfaction with the marital relationship (Stuart, Hammond, & Pett, 1987).

Embarrassment

A second emotion that may result from sexual activity or attempts to engage in sexual activity is embarrassment. I discussed above the expectations that have developed in American culture about sexual fulfillment. Many people believe that their sexual interactions should be fulfilling. Often people believe that both participants in sexual activity should experience orgasms, and they may believe that the orgasms should be simultaneous.

Other related beliefs may be differentiated by gender. Women may believe they should be uninhibited, be able to participate in a variety of behaviors, or be able to experience multiple orgasms. Men may believe that they are solely responsible for their partner's pleasure, or that they should be able to delay ejaculation indefinitely. All of these expectations become performance standards, and the person judges the self and the sexual relationship in terms of these criteria. When actual experience falls below an individual's expectation, he or she is likely to feel embarrassed.

Embarrassment about one's past sexual performance can have a variety of effects on the person. He or she may be more inhibited in future encounters, or avoid completely the situation or person involved in the embarrassing episode. Such episodes can have an impact on the individual's self-image, causing the person to redefine the self as sexually inhibited or incompetent. Obviously, embarrassment may cause a sexual dysfunction. On the other hand, embarrassment may lead to more constructive outcomes, such as seeking out information about sexuality in books or from professionals.

Anxiety/Fear

Sexual interactions that result in physical or psychological trauma may create lasting anxiety or fear as the dominant emotion associated with sexuality. In the past decade, we have become more aware of the frequency and emotional impact of sexual abuse or sexual assault on the victim. A study of the prevalence of sexually stressful events among women (DiVasto et al., 1984) found that 21% had experienced harassment, 31% reported indecent exposure, 12% had experienced invasive fondling, 14% reported attempted assault, and 10% had been sexually assaulted. The cases of harassment and indecent exposure involved perpetrators who were strangers, whereas the cases of fondling and attempted and completed assault involved friends, relatives, or acquaintances. (See Muehlenhard, Goggins, Jones, & Satterfield, this volume.) The victims reported that the vast majority of these incidents were stressful.

Fear of sexual activity may lead to sexual aversion disorder (SAD), defined as persistent and extreme aversion to sexual intercourse (Katz, Gipson, Kearl, & Kriskovich, 1989). In addition to sexual trauma, severe conflicts about intimacy and serious relationship problems can cause SAD. Katz et al. developed a questionnaire measure of sexual aversion. The measure included items such as: The thought of sex makes me nervous; I'm not afraid of kissing or petting, but intercourse really scares me; I would like to feel more relaxed in sexual situations; and I would like to feel less anxious about my sexual behavior. The measure was completed by 382 college students. Women reported more fear of sexual intercourse than did men. Women were more concerned about criticism of their sexual behavior and were more inclined to avoid sexual situations.

Aversion to sexual behavior is likely to inhibit a person from initiating relationships in which sexual intimacy is possible. Within a close relationship, aversion in either partner undoubtedly reduces the frequency of sexual intimacy and may lead the unaffected partner to be dissatisfied with the sexual activity that does occur.

As already noted, anxiety is frequently a factor in causing sexual dysfunctions. It follows that therapeutic techniques that reduce anxiety should be effective in treating sexual dysfunctions. A recent review (Norton & Jehn, 1984) assessed the empirical support for that hypothesis. Anxiety-reduction procedures do reduce some, but not all, dysfunctions.

Frustration

A fourth emotional outcome of sexual activity is frustration. It may result from lack of sexual activity or from the absence of opportunities to experience sexual gratification. In the study of aversion by Katz et al. (1989), males reported greater frustration with their sexual activity than did females. Men indicated they would like to be more sexually active, but were afraid of contracting a sexually transmitted disease (STD). Lack of opportunity can be frustrating in part because American society emphasizes sexual fulfillment. Sexual motivation increases with abstinence, but there are no aversive internal sensations associated with deprivation (Singer & Toates, 1987). In this regard, sex is different from hunger and thirst.

SEXUAL JEALOUSY

Jealousy is clearly an emotion; it involves arousal, cognition, and behavioral expression. It is "a protective reaction to a perceived threat to a valued relationship or to its quality" (Clanton, 1990, p. 180). In adults, jealousy is usually associated with a threat to a romantic or sexual relationship.

Jealousy is a response to one's perceptions of the motives or behavior of another. Although jealousy may often be aroused by some external event (Berscheid, 1983), there need not be an external stimulus. Several writers noted that jealousy involves particularly intense arousal (e.g., Gordon, 1981). At the same time, the cognitive element seems to be especially important in determining the circumstances under which and toward whom jealousy is expressed.

Berscheid (1983) discussed influences on the severity of the jealousy one feels. Jealousy involves a threat to the relationship with the partner, to the continuation of the exchanges with the partner. Therefore, the more interdependent the relationship, the more vulnerable the parties are to jealousy. Further, the cause of the threat must be perceived as a third person or activity outside the relationship. Finally, the partner must be perceived as able to change the condition producing the threat. Again we see the importance of cognitive processes, of individual interpretations, in the occurrence of specific emotions.

According to Reiss (1986), jealousy is a boundary-setting mechanism; social norms define jealousy as appropriate when important social relationships are threatened. He argued that all societies allow a person to be jealous of his or her spouse's sexual activity with a third party. Yet there are situations, such as mate swapping, in which sexual behavior apparently does not always lead to jealousy. Finally, jealousy may be expressed in a variety of ways. Media reports call attention to cases in which sexual jealousy leads to aggression toward another person; at times it may lead to sexual aggression. At other times, jealousy may lead to more passionate consensual sexual activity (Hatfield & Rapson, 1987). Or jealousy may lead the offended party to seek a new sexual partner. In each of these cases, jealousy is an antecedent to sexual behavior.

For a more detailed discussion of jealousy, see Bringle and Buunk (this volume).

SUMMARY AND CONCLUSIONS

There is a continuing debate over the relative impact of physiological arousal and social learning on the experience of various emotions. However, there is agreement that sexual arousal involves the internal processes of vasocongestion and myotonia. There is also continuing discussion of the relative influence of social norms on the expression of emotion. Some believe emotional behavior reflects the person's internal state, and others believe that such behavior reflects the impact of norms requiring emotional behavior in the situation. Further research is needed in order to specify more precisely the interrelations of arousal, norms, and emotional behavior.

Several emotions are important antecedents to sexual expression. In American society, norms specify the sentiment of love as a prerequisite for sexual activity. The early stage of a romantic relationship often involves passionate love; the high degree of arousal that characterizes passionate love can enhance sexual arousal and lead to frequent and intense sexual activity. Companionate love may lead to less intense but enjoyable sexual expression.

Anxiety can either facilitate or interfere with sexual arousal. Research is needed to specify the conditions under which each effect occurs. Anxiety may be the underlying cause of most sexual dysfunctions. Depression seems to inhibit sexual arousal or desire.

A fourth emotion, sexual jealousy, may lead to either intense consensual sexual behavior or coercive sexual acts. Contemporary treatments of emotion in relationships overlook the possibility that the person may experience two or more emotions toward the same person (Berscheid, 1985). Thus, one might feel passionate love toward another person, yet experience high levels of anxiety about sexual activity with that person.

Cognitive appraisal is essential to sexual desire; it defines the arousal and activates response tendencies. If the situation allows, these tendencies will be enacted. Evidence suggests that arousal is more bodily centered for men and more person centered for women. It was suggested that arousal is an affect-cognition blend, and that there is a feedback loop between these two components.

Four emotional consequences of sexual (in)activity were discussed. Individuals evaluate their own frequency and type of sexual activity based on expectations about sexual expression. This evaluation may result in sexual satisfaction or dissatisfaction. Among married persons, satisfaction is associated with greater communication with the partner about sex, and with greater satisfaction with the marital relationship. Dissatisfaction is associated with reduced marital satisfaction, involvement in extramarital sexual activity, and an increased incidence of sexual dysfunctions, including inhibited sexual desire. Embarrassment may occur if the person fails to meet his or her own standards for sexual performance, and may inhibit future sexual expression. Anxiety or fear may result from traumatic experiences and lead to sexual aversion or other dysfunctions. Frustration may result from the absence of sexual activity.

REFERENCES

Adams, B. N. (1986). *The family: A sociological interpretation* (4th ed.). San Diego, CA: Harcourt Brace Jovanovich.

Adelmann, P. K., & Zajonc, R. B. (1989). Facial efference and the experience of emotion. *Annual Review of Psychology, 40,* 249–280.

Armon-Jones, C. (1986). The thesis of constructionism. In R. Harre (Ed.), *The social construction of emotions* (pp. 32–56). Oxford, England: Basil Blackwell.

Barlow, D. H. (1986). Causes of sexual dysfunction: The role of anxiety and cognitive interference. *Journal of Consulting and Clinical Psychology, 54,* 140–148.

Beck, J. G., & Barlow, D. H. (1986). The effects of anxiety and attentional focus on sexual responding. II: Cognitive and affective patterns in erectile dysfunction. *Behavior Research and Therapy, 24,* 19–26.

Beggs, V. E., Calhoun, K. S., & Wolchik, S. A. (1987). Sexual anxiety and female sexual arousal: A comparison of arousal during sexual anxiety stimuli and sexual pleasure stimuli. *Archives of Sexual Behavior, 16,* 311–319.

Berscheid, E. (1983). Emotion. In H. H. Kelley et al. (Eds.), *Close relationships* (pp. 110–168). New York: Freeman.

Berscheid, E. (1985). Interpersonal attraction. In G. Lindzey & E. Aronson (Eds.), *The handbook of social psychology* (Vol. 2, 3rd ed., pp. 413–484). New York: Random House.

Berscheid, E., & Walster (Hatfield), E. (1978). *Interpersonal attraction* (2nd ed.). Reading, MA: Addison-Wesley.

Blumstein, P., & Schwartz, P. (1990). Intimate relationships and the creation of sexuality. In D. P. McWhirter, S. A. Sanders, and J. M. Reinisch (Eds.), *Homosexuality/heterosexuality: Concepts of sexual orientation.* New York: Oxford University Press.

Brehm, S. S. (1985). *Intimate relationships.* New York: Random House.

Clanton, G. (1990). Jealousy in American culture, 1945–1985: Reflections from popular culture. In D. D. Franks & E. D. McCarthy (Eds.), *The sociology of emotions: Original essays and research papers* (pp. 179–193). Greenwich, CT: JAI Press.

Clark, M. S., & Reis, H. T. (1988). Interpersonal processes in close relationships. *Annual Review of Psychology, 39,* 609–672.

Davis, K. E., & Todd, M. J. (1985). Assessing friendship: Prototypes, paradigm cases, and relationship description. In S. Duck & D. Perlman (Eds.), *Understanding Personal Relationships: An interdisciplinary approach* (pp. 17–38). London: Sage.

DeLamater, J. D. (1981). The social control of sexuality. *Annual Review of Sociology, 7,* 263–290.

DeLamater, J. D. (1987). Gender differences in sexual scenarios. In K. Kelley (Ed.), *Females, males, and sexuality: Theories and Research* (pp. 127–140). Albany, NY: SUNY Press.

Denzin, N. K. (1984). *On understanding emotion.* San Francisco: Jossey-Bass.

DiVasto, P. V., et al. (1984). The prevalence of sexually stressful events among females in the general population. *Archives of Sexual Behavior, 13,* 59–67.

Dutton, D., & Aron, A. (1974). Some evidence for heightened sexual attraction under conditions of high anxiety. *Journal of Personality and Social Psychology, 30,* 510–517.

Everaerd, W. (1988). Commentary on sex research: Sex as an emotion. *Journal of Psychology and Human Sexuality, 1,* 3–15.

Fehr, B. (1988). Prototype analysis of the concepts of love and commitment. *Journal of Personality and Social Psychology, 55,* 557–579.

Goode, W. J. (1959). The theoretical importance of love. *American Sociological Review, 24,* 38–47.

Gordon, S. L. (1981). The sociology of sentiments and emotion. In M. Rosenberg & R. H. Turner (Eds.), *Social psychology: Sociological perspectives* (pp. 562–592). New York: Basic Books.

Gordon, S. L. (1990). Institutional and impulsive orientations in selectively appropriating emotions to self. In D. D. Franks & E. D. McCarthy (Eds.), *The sociology of emotions: Original essays and research papers* (pp. 115–135). Greenwich, CT: JAI Press.

Hardy, K. R. (1964). An appetitional theory of sexual motivation. *Psychological Review, 71,* 1–18.

Harre, R. (1986). An outline of the social constructionist viewpoint. In R. Harre (Ed.), *The social construction of emotions* (pp. 2–14). Oxford, England: Basil Blackwell.

Hatfield, E. (1982). What do men and women want from love and sex? In E. R. Allgeier & N. B. McCormick (Eds.), *Changing boundaries: Gender roles and sexual behavior* (pp. 106–134). Palo Alto, CA: Mayfield.

Hatfield, E., & Rapson, R. L. (1987). Passionate love/sexual desire: Can the same paradigm explain both? *Archives of Sexual Behavior, 16,* 259–278.

Hatfield, E., & Sprecher, S. (1986). Measuring passionate love in intimate relations. *Journal of Adolescence, 9,* 383–410.

Hatfield, E., Sprecher, S., Pillemer, J. T., Greenberger, D., & Wexler, P. (1989). Gender differences in what is desired in the sexual relationship. *Journal of Psychology and Human Sexuality, 1,* 39–52.

Hazan, C., & Shaver, P. (1987). Romantic love conceptualized as an attachment process. *Journal of Personality and Social Psychology, 52,* 511–524.

Heiman, J. R. (1975). The physiology of erotica: Women's sexual arousal. *Psychology Today, 8*(11), 90–94.

Hendrick, C., & Hendrick, S. S. (1989). Research on love: Does it measure up? *Journal of Personality and Social Psychology, 56*, 784–794.

Hite, S. (1976). *The Hite report.* New York: Macmillan.

Hite, S. (1981). *The Hite report on male sexuality.* New York: Knopf.

Hochschild, A. (1983). *The managed heart: Commercialization of human feeling.* Berkeley: University of California Press.

Jupp, J. J., & McCabe, M. (1989). Sexual desire, general arousability, and sexual dysfunction. *Archives of Sexual Behavior, 18*, 509–516.

Kaplan, H. S. (1979). *Disorders of sexual desire.* New York: Simon & Schuster.

Katz, R. C., Gipson, M. T., Kearl, A., & Kriskovich, M. (1989). Assessing sexual aversion in college students: The Sexual Aversion Scale. *Journal of Sex and Marital Therapy, 15*, 135–140.

Kilmann, P. R., et al. (1984). The sexual interaction of women with secondary orgasmic dysfunction and their partners. *Archives of Sexual Behavior, 13*, 41–49.

Knoth, R., Boyd, K., & Singer, B. (1988). Empirical tests of sexual selection theory: Predictions of sex differences in onset, intensity, and time course of sexual arousal. *Journal of Sex Research, 24*, 73–89.

Lazarus, R. S. (1982). Thoughts on the relations between emotion and cognition. *American Psychologist, 37*, 1019–1024.

Leventhal, H. (1980). Toward a comprehensive theory of emotion. In L. Berkowitz (Ed.), *Advances in experimental social psychology* (Vol. 13, pp. 139–207). New York: Academic Press.

Leventhal, H. (1984). A perceptual-motor theory of emotion. In L. Berkowitz (Ed.), *Advances in experimental social psychology* (Vol. 17, pp. 117–182). New York: Academic Press.

Leventhal, H., & Scherer, K. (1987). The relationship of emotion to cognition: A functional approach to a semantic controversy. *Cognition and Emotion, 1*, 3–28.

MacCorquodale, P. (1989). Gender and sexual behavior. In K. McKinney and S. Sprecher (Eds.), *Human sexuality: The societal and interpersonal context* (pp. 91–112). Norwood, NJ: Ablex.

Mandler, G. (1984). *Mind and body: Psychology of emotion and stress.* New York: Norton.

McCarthy, E. D. (1990). Emotions are social things: An essay in the sociology of emotions. In D. D. Franks & E. D. McCarthy (Eds.), *The sociology of emotions: Original essays and research papers* (pp. 51–72). Greenwich, CT: JAI Press.

Metts, S., & Cupach, W. R. (1989). The role of communication in human sexuality. In K. McKinney and S. Sprecher (Eds.), *Human sexuality: The societal and interpersonal context* (pp. 139–161). Norwood, NJ: Ablex.

Mosher, D. L., Barton-Henry, M., & Green, S. E. (1988). Subjective sexual arousal and involvement: Development of multiple indicators. *Journal of Sex Research, 25*, 412–425.

Newsweek (1987, Oct. 26). Not tonight, dear. Pp. 64–66.

Norton, G. R., & Jehn, D. (1984). The role of anxiety in sexual dysfunctions: A review. *Archives of Sexual Behavior, 13*, 165–183.

Oatley, K., & Johnson-Laird, P. N. (1987). Towards a cognitive theory of emotions. *Cognition and Emotion, 1*, 29–50.

Orbuch, T. L. (1989). Human sexuality education. In K. McKinney & S. Sprecher (Eds.), *Human sexuality: The societal and interpersonal context* (pp. 438–462). Norwood, NJ: Ablex.

Pinney, E. M., Gerrard, M., & Denney, N. W. (1987). The Pinney sexual satisfaction inventory. *Journal of Sex Research, 23*, 233–251.

Reiss, I. L. (1986). *Journey into sexuality: An exploratory voyage.* Englewood Cliffs, NJ: Prentice Hall.

Reiss, I. L., & Lee, G. R. (1988). *Family systems in America* (4th ed.). New York: Holt, Rinehart, & Winston.

Reynolds, C. F., Frank, E., Thase, M. E., Houck, P. R., Jennings, J. R., Howell, J. R., Lilienfeld, S. O., & Kupfer, D. J. (1988). Assessment of sexual function in depressed, impotent, and healthy men: Factor analysis of a brief sexual function questionnaire for men. *Psychiatry Research, 24,* 231–250.

Rook, K. S., & Hammen, C. L. (1977). A cognitive perspective on the experience of sexual arousal. *Journal of Social Issues, 33*(2), 7–29.

Rosen, R. C., & Leiblum, S. R. (1987). Current approaches to the evaluation of sexual desire disorders. *Journal of Sex Research, 23,* 141–162.

Schachter, S. (1964). The interaction of cognitive and physiological determinants of emotional state. In L. Berkowitz (Ed.), *Advances in experimental social psychology* (Vol. 1, pp. 49–80). New York: Academic Press.

Schwartz, J. C., & Shaver, P. (1987). Emotions and emotion knowledge in interpersonal relations. In W. H. Jones and D. Perlman (Eds.), *Advances in personal relationships* (Vol. 1, pp. 197–241). Greenwich, CT: JAI Press.

Shaver, P., Schwartz, J., Kirson, D., & O'Connor, C. (1987). Emotion knowledge: Further exploration of a prototype approach. *Journal of Personality and Social Psychology, 52,* 1061–1086.

Shott, S. (1979). Emotion and social life: A symbolic interactionist analysis. *American Journal of Sociology, 84,* 1317–1334.

Simon, R. W. (1989). The development of feeling rules underlying romantic love among adolescent females. Paper presented at Midwest Sociological Society meetings, St. Louis.

Singer, B., & Toates, F. M. (1987). Sexual motivation. *Journal of Sex Research, 23,* 481–501.

Sprague, J., & Quadagno, D. (1989). Gender and sexual motivation: An exploration of two assumptions. *Journal of Psychology and Human Sexuality, 2,* 57–76.

Sprecher, S. (1989). Influences on choice of a partner and on sexual decision making in the relationship. In K. McKinney, & S. Sprecher (Eds.), *Human sexuality: The societal and interpersonal context* (pp. 438–462). Norwood, NJ: Ablex.

Stanislaw, H., & Rice, F. J. (1988). Correlation between sexual desire and menstrual cycle characteristics. *Archives of Sexual Behavior, 17,* 499–508.

Sternberg, R. J. (1986). A triangular theory of love. *Psychological Review, 93,* 119–135.

Stone, L. (1988). Passionate attachments in the west in historical perspective. In W. Gaylin & E. Person (Eds.), *Passionate attachments: Thinking about love* (pp. 15–26). New York: Free Press.

Strongman, K. T. (1987). *The psychology of emotion* (3rd ed.). New York: Wiley.

Stuart, F. M., Hammond, D. C., & Pett, M. A. (1987). Inhibited sexual desire in women. *Archives of Sexual Behavior, 16,* 91–106.

Tavris, C., & Sadd, S. (1978). *The Redbook report on female sexuality.* New York: Dell.

Thorne, B., & Luria, Z. (1986). Sexuality and gender in children's daily worlds. *Social Problems, 33,* 176–190.

Victor, J. S. (1980). *Human sexuality: A social psychological approach.* Englewood Cliffs, NJ: Prentice Hall.

Viederman, M. (1988). The nature of passionate love. In W. Gaylin and E. Person (Eds.), *Passionate attachments: Thinking about love* (pp. 1–14). New York: Free Press.

White, G. L., Fishbein, S., & Rutstein, J. (1981). Passionate love and the misattribution of arousal. *Journal of Personality and Social Psychology, 41,* 56–62.

4

Personality and Sexuality: Empirical Relations and an Integrative Theoretical Model

Jeffry A. Simpson
Texas A & M University

Steven W. Gangestad
University of New Mexico

Nearly a century ago, Sigmund Freud began formulating a theoretical account of the relation between personality and sexuality—the most ambitious and comprehensive one ever proposed. Central to Freud's theory was the notion that individual differences in personality stem from more basic processes underlying sex and sexuality. According to Freud, individual differences in personality were the product of biologically based sex drive in conjunction with the particular sexual learning history and/or early experiences to which an individual had been exposed. For Freud, the causal order was clear: Personality can be understood in terms of sexuality.

In recent years, personality theorists have questioned this basic premise. Both Eysenck (1976) and Zuckerman (1983) have claimed that individual differences in sex and sexuality can be understood as the by-product of biologically based individual differences in personality processes. Eysenck, for example, has suggested that extraverted individuals, relative to introverts, typically engage in more frequent and/or diverse sexual activity in order to raise their habitually dampened levels of cortical arousal to an optimal level. Similarly, Zuckerman has argued that individuals high in sensation seeking, compared to those low on this dimension, are inclined to engage in diverse sexual activities in order to raise their normally suppressed arousal levels. According to these theorists, individual differences in sexuality can be understood in terms of personality.

Contemporary theoretical and empirical work suggests that Freud may have been partially correct—an understanding of the factors underlying sexuality *may* shed light on personality processes—but he was correct for the wrong theoretical reasons. Various theorists (e.g., Draper & Harpending, 1982; Gangestad & Simpson, 1990, in press, b; Harpending & Draper, 1986) have recently developed models of mating propensities that examine the relations between several major dimensions of personality and one prominent dimension of sexuality—sociosexuality—from evolutionary perspectives. These models contend that the variance underlying several major personality traits may actually reflect differences in more basic reproductive propensities that could have been selected during evolutionary history.

In the first section of this chapter, we briefly review some of the major individual difference dimensions presumed to underlie heterosexual sexuality within close relationships confined to behavior among normal (i.e., nonpathological) individuals. We then describe a newly developed measure—the Sociosexual Orientation Inventory (SOI) (Simpson & Gangestad, in press, a)—that taps individual differences in willingness to engage in uncommitted sexual relations. The SOI accounts for a large proportion of the variability underlying many facets of sexuality, and it covaries with several trait measures associated with sexual attitudes and behaviors (e.g., extraversion, disinhibition, self-monitoring, dominance-feeling, and so on). In the second section, we review past research on the relation between attitudinal and behavioral indicators of sociosexuality and two broad dimensions of personality known to correlate with them, namely, extraversion and lack of constraint. We then discuss how past theoretical approaches have attempted to explain these empirical relations, and we note their deficiencies. In section three, we present an evolutionary framework within which individual differences in sociosexual orientation may be understood. We discuss our own specific model and present empirical evidence in support of it. Finally, we discuss implications of the model for understanding relationship initiation, maintenance, and dissolution.

INDIVIDUAL DIFFERENCES IN SEXUALITY

Eysenck (1976) has suggested that two relatively orthogonal dimensions—libido and sexual satisfaction—account for much of the variability underlying many heterosexual attitudes and behaviors. Libido reflects an individual's absolute frequency of sexual activity or his or her general interest in sex per se, whereas satisfaction represents the degree to which sex is found pleasurable and gratifying. Broadly speaking, past research on the relation between personality/individual differences and sexuality can be loosely placed within the framework of Eysenck's two-factor model.

Individual Differences in Frequency of Sex

A variety of personality and individual difference measures are known to covary with absolute frequency of sexual activity. Individuals who score high on the measures of extraversion (Eysenck, 1974, 1976), disinhibition (Zuckerman,

Bone, Neary, Mangelsdorff, & Brustman, 1972; Zuckerman, Tushup, & Finner, 1976), self-monitoring (Snyder, Simpson, & Gangestad, 1986), psychoticism (Eysenck, 1974, 1976), and dominance-feeling (Maslow, 1942) all tend to engage in sex more frequently and/or with more partners. Individuals who engage in frequent sex also tend to possess more positive attitudes toward impersonal sex, aggressive sex, pornography, and sexual permissiveness (see Eysenck, 1976; Wilson, 1981). They also are more inclined to be less religious (Byrne, 1983; Kinsey, Pomeroy, & Martin, 1948; Kinsey, Pomeroy, Martin, & Gebhard, 1953; Reiss, 1967; Zuckerman et al., 1976), less socially and politically conservative (Curran, Neff, & Lippold, 1973; D'Augelli & Cross, 1975; Eysenck, 1976; Griffit, 1973), and better educated (Alston & Tucker, 1973; Hunt, 1974).

Individual Differences in Sexual Satisfaction

Several individual difference measures appear to reflect the extent to which individuals typically find sex to be pleasurable and satisfying. Global satisfaction with sex is known to correlate with erotophobia (i.e., the extent to which individuals possess extremely negative attitudes toward sex in general: Byrne & Sheffield, 1965; Gerrard, 1980; Gerrard & Gibbons, 1982), sex guilt (Mosher, 1979; O'Grady, Janda, & Gillen, 1979), and social/sexual anxiety (Leary & Dobbins, 1983). Moreover, individuals who score high on indices of neurotic sex, sexual shyness, sexual disgust, and prudishness also tend to be more dissatisfied with sex in general (Eysenck, 1976).

Some of the measures that tap global satisfaction with sex correlate moderately with measures reflecting absolute frequency of sexual activity (see Eysenck, 1976). Extraverted individuals, for instance, usually display less sexual anxiety, less guilt, and less shyness than do introverts. Nonetheless, Eysenck has provided strong evidence that libido and sexual satisfaction are distinct, relatively independent dimensions.

Individual Differences in Sociosexuality

One of the primary problems with past research is that individual differences in the tendency to engage in frequent sex within exclusive relationships often have been theoretically and empirically confounded with individual differences in the propensity to engage in frequent sex with multiple partners. Although individuals who differ on these two dimensions may engage in the same absolute amount of sexual activity, those who frequently engage in sex but only within single, exclusive relationships are likely to be very different sexual and psychological beings from those who frequently have sex with several partners. The former individuals probably vary according to their general level of sex drive or interest in sex per se, whereas the latter ones are likely to differ in the extent to which they are willing to engage in sex without emotional closeness and commitment.

Past research indicates that individuals vary widely on several sociosexual variables including number of past sexual partners, number of partners expected in the future, number of one-night stands, and attitudes toward engaging in casual, uncommitted sex (see Eysenck, 1976; Hunt, 1974). All of these dimensions, although operationally distinct, strongly covary (Simpson & Gangestad, 1990a). Considered together, these variables appear to tap an individual difference dimension reflecting *sociosexual orientation* (Gangestad & Simpson, 1990a). We have recently developed and validated a self-report measure (the Sociosexual Orientation Inventory) that assesses this dimension. The SOI consists of five components that tap aspects of an individual's past overt sexual behavior (e.g., number of sex partners in the past year, number of one-night stands), their future overt sexual behavior (e.g., number of partners foreseen in the next 5 years), their current sexual thoughts (e.g., frequency of sexual fantasies about partners other than the current one), and their current attitudes toward engaging in casual, uncommitted sex.

Individuals who possess a *restricted sociosexual orientation* (those who score below the median within their gender on the SOI) require greater closeness and commitment in a relationship prior to engaging in sex with a romantic partner. Restricted individuals, for example, indicate that they have had sex with fewer partners in the past year, they foresee fewer partners in the next 5 years, they have rarely had sex with partners on one and only one occasion (if ever), they infrequently fantasize about having sex with someone other than their current (or most recent) dating partner, and they hold less permissive attitudes about engaging in uncommitted sex. Conversely, individuals who possess an *unrestricted sociosexual orientation* (those who score above the median within their gender) require less closeness and commitment prior to having sex. Unrestricted individuals report that they have had sex with a larger number of partners in the past year, they foresee a greater number of partners in the next 5 years, they typically have had sex with someone on one and only one occasion at least once, they often fantasize about having sex with someone other than their current (or most recent) dating partner, and they possess more permissive attitudes about casual sex.

According to information provided by their romantic partners, unrestricted individuals, relative to restricted ones, tend to engage in sex at an earlier point in their relationships, they are more likely to engage in concurrent sexual affairs with more than one partner at a time, and they tend to be involved in relationships characterized by less commitment, less investment, less love, and less psychological and emotional dependency (Simpson & Gangestad, in press, a). This convergent validation evidence is complemented by discriminant evidence indicating that sociosexuality does not correlate appreciably with indicators of either sex drive or sexual satisfaction. Among sexually active dating couples, restricted and unrestricted men and women do not differ in the absolute frequency of sex that has recently occurred in their relationships. Moreover, they do not differ in their global level of sexual satisfaction, anxiety, or guilt (Simpson & Gangestad, 1990a). Viewed together, these results indicate that sociosexuality taps an important interpersonal component underlying sexuality, namely, individual differences in willingness to engage in uncommitted sexual relations, and it is distinct from frequency of sexual activity within ongoing relationships.

SOCIOSEXUALITY AND PERSONALITY

Personality Correlates of Sociosexual Behavior

Two major clusters of personality measures correlate highly with indicators of sociosexuality: measures related to extraversion and those related to lack of constraint. One of the most reliable and widely studied correlates of sociosexuality is extraversion/introversion (Eysenck & Eysenck, 1964, 1975). Extraverts, relative to introverts, typically have sexual intercourse at a younger age, engage in sex more frequently and with more partners, and possess more permissive attitudes toward premarital and casual sex (e.g., Bynner, 1969; Eysenck, 1972, 1973, 1974, 1976; Giese & Schmidt, 1968; Schofield, 1968). Several measures known to covary with extraversion also correlate with sociosexuality. The Self-Monitoring Scale (Gangestad & Snyder, 1985; Snyder, 1974; Snyder & Gangestad, 1986), for instance, correlates positively with both Eysenck's measure of extraversion (Briggs & Cheek, 1988) as well as with sociosexuality (Snyder et al., 1986). In addition, Maslow's (1942) index of dominance-feeling correlates positively with both extraversion and markers of sociosexuality.

A second cluster of personality measures known to be associated with sociosexuality assess lack of constraint. Zuckerman's (1971) measure of disinhibition, one component of the Sensation-Seeking Scale (Zuckerman, Kolin, Price, & Zoob, 1964), is a central marker of this broad dimension. Highly disinhibited persons typically seek thrills and adventure; enjoy novel, spontaneous, and atypical experiences; and engage in uninhibited forms of social behavior (Zuckerman, 1974). They also exhibit more unrestricted forms of sociosexual behavior (Daitzman & Zuckerman, 1980; S. Fisher, 1973; Husted & Edwards, 1976; Zuckerman, 1983; Zuckerman et al., 1972, 1976). Psychoticism, a measure closely related to lack of constraint that taps tendencies to engage in deviant and antisocial forms of behavior, also is known to covary with sociosexuality (Eysenck & Eysenck, 1975, 1976). High scorers typically engage in sex more frequently and with more partners. They also adopt more permissive attitudes toward impersonal sex (Eysenck, 1971, 1972, 1974, 1976).

To explore the relations between sociosexuality and the general dimensions of extraversion and lack of constraint, we conducted a peer rating study involving 97 college dating couples (Simpson & Gangestad, 1990). Both members of each dyad first completed the SOI as well as measures of extraversion (Eysenck &

Eysenck, 1975) and disinhibition (Zuckerman, 1971). They then were rated on three markers of extraversion and lack of constraint by their dating partner. The three markers of extraversion included social potency (assessed by the adjectives *dominant, persuasive,* and *socially visible*), social closeness (assessed by *gregarious, people oriented,* and *affectionate*), and well-being (assessed by *cheerful, interested,* and *optimistic*). Markers of lack of constraint included lack of control (indexed by *freewheeling, non-level headed,* and *nonplanful*), lack of harm-avoidance (indexed by *adventurous, thrill seeking,* and *lack of safety-consciousness*), and aggression (indexed by *aggressive, tough,* and *nonconciliatory*). We then factor-analyzed all of these measures, and two factors emerged. The first one reflected extraversion, and the second one represented lack of constraint. As anticipated, the SOI loaded highly on both factors. In fact, it loaded *higher* on the extraversion and lack of constraint factors than did the self-report measures of extraversion and disinhibition themselves. Sociosexuality, therefore, correlates very highly with, and appears to be central to, both of these major personality dimensions.

Past Accounts of Personality Correlates and Conceptual Problems with Them

Both Eysenck (1976) and Zuckerman (1983) have suggested that individual differences in sexuality stem from biologically based individual differences underlying personality. Their respective theories share two central features. First, they both posit that sexual behavior represents only one behavior among a larger equivalence class of actions that are functionally synonymous in that they all fulfill a particular motive—to maintain optimal arousal. Parachuting, eating exotic foods, or entering an occupation that requires incessant contact with different people, for example, can satisfy the motives underlying sensation seeking or extraversion just as adequately as does having sex with several partners. Second, these approaches claim that the general motive(s) underlying individual differences in many aspects of sexual behavior are substantially heritable. Estimated heritabilities of extraversion and disinhibition are about .50 or greater in Western populations (Eaves & Eysenck, 1975; Floderus-Myrhed, Pederson, & Rasmusser, 1980; Fulker, Eysenck, & Zuckerman, 1980; Gangestad & Simpson, 1990c; Loehlin, Willerman, & Horn, 1988; Pederson, Plomin, McClearn, & Friberg, in press; Tellegen, Lykken, Bouchard, Wilcox, Segal, & Rich, 1988). As a result, the genetic variance underlying many aspects of sexuality has been presumed to be attributable to genetic variance underlying more basic personality motives (see Eysenck, 1976).

One disconcerting aspect of these perspectives is that they are neither sensitive nor responsive to the concerns of either evolutionary biology or population genetics. Any account of variation in sexual behavior—especially *genetic* variation—should address evolutionary principles. Needless to say, sex is closely tied to reproduction, reproduction strongly relates to inclusive fitness, and inclusive fitness relates to future genetic representation. Hence, if selection has operated on *any* form of social behavior, it ought to have operated on sexual behavior. Neither Eysenck nor Zuckerman has devoted much attention to the question of why genetic variation underlies their respective personality dimensions. Moreover, the single feature that gives sociosexuality a special status within population genetics—its relation to reproduction—does not even figure into the accounts provided by either Eysenck (1976) or Zuckerman (1983). Past approaches, therefore, have not dealt with the concerns of evolutionary biology. If they are not wrong, these theories are likely to be incomplete.

Scale Zeta and the Genetic Variation Underlying Sociosexuality

Is sociosexual variation as peripheral to its genetic origins as Eysenck and Zuckerman have implicitly suggested? Recent research has suggested that the Self-Monitoring Scale possesses considerable genetic variation (Gangestad, 1986). Specifically, monozygotic (MZ, or identical) pairs of twins tend to be highly concordant in their responses to Self-Monitoring Scale items, whereas dizygotic (DZ, or fraternal) twin pairs tend to display considerably less concordance. To understand this genetic variation more fully, we constructed a better measure of it (Gangestad & Simpson, 1990c). We initially identified items on the Multidimensional Personality Questionnaire (MPQ) (Tellegen, 1982) that possessed high MZ twin cross-correlations with the Self-Monitoring Scale (items for which, across all MZ twin pairs, Twin A's response to a given MPQ item was highly correlated with Twin B's response to a given Self-Monitoring item, and vice versa). We then factor-analyzed these cross-correlations to select a subset of items that reflected a single, genetically homogeneous dimension. Following this, we incorporated the 11 items on the Self-Monitoring Scale that optimally tap the genetic variation underlying it (Gangestad, 1986). The resultant scale, which we refer to as Zeta, possessed a cross-validated MZ twin intraclass correlation of .76, higher than any existing self-report measure with which we are familiar. The DZ twin correlation was only .16, indicating that the high MZ twin correlation is probably attributable to genetic as opposed to common environmental variance. Additional analyses revealed that the averaged MZ twin pair scores on Scale Zeta were bimodally distributed, suggesting that two quasi-discrete genetic classes may underlie the measure.

Scale Zeta correlates with several MPQ measures, including social potency (r = .67), absorption (.34), harm-avoidance ($-.29$), aggression (.26), well-being

(.22), stress-reaction (−.19), and control (−.16). With the exception of stress-reaction, all of these measures are markers of either extraversion or lack of constraint. Scale Zeta, therefore, appears to tap the genetic variance that extraversion and lack of constraint share.

If the genetic variation reflected in Scale Zeta is common to both extraversion and lack of constraint, it should account for much of the covariation that exists between these two dimensions. Accordingly, we sought to identify an axis placement that would maximize the correspondence between the factor loadings for the six MPQ measures and the MZ cross-correlations between these six variables and Scale Zeta. The criterion we maximized to locate this axis was the correlation between the factor loadings and the MZ cross-correlations with Scale Zeta. This correlation turned out to be extremely high ($r = .95$), implying that an axis closely corresponding to the genetic variation underlying Zeta could be identified. As displayed in Fig. 4.1, this axis was located *right through* sociosexuality. Indeed, sociosexuality and social potency proved to be primary markers of this axis. The self-report measures of extraversion and disinhibition possessed smaller factor loadings, suggesting that sociosexuality has more to do with the genetic variation underlying Scale Zeta than do the dimensions of either extraversion or lack of constraint. This finding could not have been anticipated by existing theories of sociosexual variation, and it highlights the need to view sociosexuality within an evolutionary context.

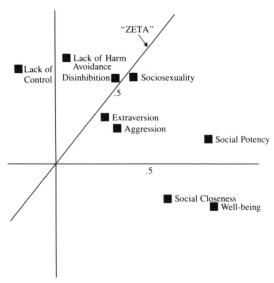

FIG. 4.1.   Factor analysis of self-report and other-report measures of Extraversion, Lack of Constraint, and Sociosexuality.

SOCIOSEXUALITY: AN INTEGRATIVE
THEORETICAL MODEL

Evolutionary Considerations in Formulating
a Model of Sociosexuality

Evolutionary theorists (e.g., Trivers, 1972) suggest that at least three factors should be taken into consideration when developing a model of reproductive orientations in a species whose offspring require substantial parental care:

1. *Parental investment.* All else being equal, an individual should opt to reproduce with a mate who can and will invest in his or her offspring, thereby increasing its chances of survival.

2. *Fitness of the potential mate.* Everything else being equal, an individual should choose to reproduce with a mate who possesses characteristics that are related to reproductive success, independent of the mate's ability to invest in offspring. These characteristics may reveal something about his or her genetic make-up, which will be passed onto the offspring of anyone who selects him or her as a mate (R. A. Fisher, 1958).

3. *Certainty of parenthood.* All else being equal, an individual should choose to reproduce with a mate whose offspring are certain to be his or her own.

Clearly, this last factor is a consideration for males but not for females. Females are certain the offspring they produce are their own, whereas males may not necessarily be. Different considerations also may exist for the two sexes with regard to the other two factors. Females must initially make greater investments in offspring than males, given that they must actually carry and bear them. Male investment, therefore, may be less certain than female investment, and finding a mate who will invest may be of greater concern for females than for males. The reproductive fitness of potential mates also may be a more salient consideration for females given that the variation in individual fitness tends to be greater for males than for females within mammalian species (Alexander, Hoogland, Howard, Noonan, & Sherman, 1979; Trivers, 1972). Because each of these factors should be of differential importance to females and males, the different mating propensities of the sexes should be addressed separately.

Several models of individual differences in human mating propensities have been proposed in the past decade, each of which may shed light on the relation between sexuality and personality (e.g., Draper & Harpending, 1982; Gangestad & Simpson, 1990a, 1990b; Harpending & Draper, 1986; Rushton, 1985). We focus on our own model in the following discussion. After presenting our model, we discuss one alternate perspective proposed by Draper and Harpending (1982).

A Model of Female Mate Choice

An evolutionary model of female mating propensities should focus on issues of parental investment and fitness of potential mates. Females should prefer mates who can and will invest in their offspring and, at the same time, who are likely to produce offspring with reproductively advantaged genetic make-ups.

Various theorists (e.g., Symons, 1979; Trivers, 1972; Wilson, 1978) have suggested one means by which a female can increase the chances of her mate investing heavily in her offspring: She can be restricted in her sexual behavior, thereby forcing her mate to make a substantial initial investment in her offspring and concurrently demonstrating that no other male could be their father. Restricted sexual behavior, therefore, should enhance paternal investment and increase either the survival rate of the female's offspring or the rate at which she can bear future offspring (cf. Dorjahn, 1954; Muhsam, 1956; Ukaegbu, 1977).

Because restricted sexual behavior in females should promote paternal investment, restricted sociosexuality ought to have been exclusively selected for within women during evolutionary history (Wilson, 1978). Empirical evidence (Gangestad & Simpson, 1990a; 1990b), however, suggests that it has not, because genetic variation appears to underlie sociosexuality within both men *and* women. Moreover, from a conceptual standpoint, a second factor also should strongly influence female mate choice—the fitness of the mate. Females should benefit by reproducing with males who have the potential to be reproductively successful, for the genes of these males will be passed onto their offspring. To the extent that additive genetic variance (i.e., genetic variance transmitted across generations) exists on characteristics that promote male reproductive success, the transmission of these genes should benefit their offspring and *particularly* their sons, given the greater variance in male reproductive success in our evolutionary past (Clutton-Brock & Iason, 1986).

If unrestricted females exist in a population, restricted sexual behavior will not promote a female's chances of reproducing with highly successful males. By definition, unrestricted females do not force males to wait long periods of time prior to engaging in sex with them. Hence, they may secure a competitive advantage when it comes to mating with males who are most reproductively successful. As it turns out, the very benefit restricted sexual behavior confers—gaining paternal investment—may preclude restricted females from mating with males who possess characteristics related to reproductive success because such males should have been less likely to exclusively invest in offspring.

We have recently developed an evolutionary-based model of mating propensities (Gangestad & Simpson, 1990a, 1990b). The model posits that, in our ancestral past, two global mating propensities might have evolved and been maintained through frequency-dependent selection for genetic polymorphism within women. Frequency-dependent selection operates when the fitnesses of two or more different genotypes vary according to their relative frequencies within a population (Crow, 1986). Given that the genetic variation underlying Scale Zeta strongly reflects the genetic variation in sociosexuality coupled with the observation that two genotypic classes appear to underlie Zeta, we have proposed that restricted and unrestricted sociosexual orientations may reflect two different mating propensities, both of which might have promoted reproductive fitness in our evolutionary past. The restricted orientation may have been designed to enhance paternal investment in offspring, while the unrestricted orientation may have served to promote the reproductive abilities of surviving offspring, particularly males. (For a detailed discussion of the model, of frequency-dependent selection, and of the assumptions behind both, see Gangestad & Simpson, 1990b).

Empirical Tests of the Model

How might we provisionally test this evolutionary model? The model suggests that variants in female sociosexuality have or once had adaptive value. The hallmark of adaptive value is special design, whereby certain physical features and/or behavioral propensities specifically exist to promote adaptation and reproductive fitness (see Tooby & Cosmides, 1990; Williams, 1966). Two clear predictions can be derived from our model concerning how restricted and unrestricted female sociosexuality might have been specially designed from an evolutionary standpoint.

Prediction 1: Characteristics of desired partners.   According to our model, females who differ in sociosexual nature should seek out different types of romantic partners. Restricted females should prefer males who are likely to commit themselves exclusively to a single relationship and who will be good "investors" in their offspring. By contrast, unrestricted females should prefer males who possess characteristics that would have allowed them, in an evolutionary state, to produce many offspring. Although we do not know exactly what these characteristics are, they probably include physical and sexual attractiveness (cf. Hamilton & Zuk, 1982). Do restricted females prefer prospective mates who are stable and likely to be faithful? Do unrestricted females prefer mates who are physically and sexually attractive? To answer these questions, we conducted three studies (see Simpson & Gangestad, 1990c).

As part of Study 1, we asked 252 college women what characteristics they desired in a mate. Specifically, they rated 15 attributes in terms of what they looked for in a romantic partner. Factor analysis of these attributes yielded two major factors: concern for physical attractiveness/social visibility and concern for good personal/parenting qualities. Attributes that loaded on the first factor included physical attractiveness, sex appeal, and social status. Those loading on the second factor included faithfulness/loyalty, responsibility, and qualities of a good parent. Based on these loadings, we constructed two aggregated mate preference indices, one reflecting each dimension. We then correlated each index with scores on the SOI. Results revealed that unrestricted women rated attributes pertaining to attractiveness and social visibility as relatively more important in selecting a mate than did restricted women. Restricted women, on the other hand, rated attributes dealing with personal/parenting qualities as more important than did unrestricted ones.

Based on the findings of Study 1, we created two vignettes that described characteristics possessed by two prospective romantic partners in Study 2. One partner was described as physically attractive, sexy, and charismatic, but not very responsible and known for being unfaithful. The second partner was described as stable, responsible, caring, and faithful, but of average physical attractiveness. Two hundred college women were asked to indicate which partner most closely resembled their current or most recent romantic partner, which one represented the type of person they ideally would prefer to be involved with, and which one they found themselves most attracted to. As anticipated, unrestricted women, relative to restricted ones, claimed their current partner more closely resembled the highly attractive prototype rather than the highly faithful one. Unrestricted women also found themselves more attracted to the attractive prototype rather than the faithful one. Although unrestricted and restricted women did not reliably differ in their preference of whom they ideally would like to be involved with, an aggregated measure composed of all three items reliably distinguished between unrestricted and restricted women.

Studies 1 and 2 examined what women report they want in a mate. Study 3 was conducted to discover what they actually acquire. Both partners of 241 college dating couples independently completed several measures, including Rubin's Love Scale (Rubin, 1970) and the SOI (Simpson & Gangestad, in press, a). The Love Scale assesses self-reported love, care, and concern for a partner. In addition, the physical attractiveness of participants was unobtrusively rated by independent observers. As predicted, unrestricted women were romantically involved with more attractive partners. Restricted women, on the other hand, were involved with partners who displayed greater love for them (revealed by their higher scores on Rubin's Love Scale). These effects held even when length of relationship was partialled out. When female attractiveness was partialled out, unrestricted women continued to be involved with more attractive men. Similarly, when female Love Scale scores were statistically controlled for, restricted women still were involved with men who scored higher on the Love Scale.

We also examined the relation between females' sociosexuality and their male partners' number of previous sexual partners. As predicted, male partners of unrestricted females, compared to those of restricted females, reported significantly more lifetime sexual partners and more partners in the past year. Moreover, they projected they would have sex with significantly more partners within the next 5 years, and they scored significantly higher on the full measure of sociosexuality.

These findings, of course, are correlational in nature. Different patterns of female mate choice may not necessarily be solely responsible for them. Nonetheless, these results do conform to predictions derived from our model. Let us now turn to some more compelling empirical evidence in support of the model.

Prediction 2: Sex ratio of offspring. Our model also contends that, in an evolutionary sense, male and female offspring should have been of differential value to restricted and unrestricted women. According to the model, unrestricted women should have benefited from mating with reproductively successful men because the characteristics that allowed these males to produce many offspring would have been passed onto their own progeny. These characteristics, however, would not have benefited their daughters and sons equally (e.g., Weatherhead & Robertson, 1979, 1981). Sons should have benefited more because males tend to exhibit greater variability in total number of offspring produced than do females. Consequently, reproductively successful males tend to produce more offspring than do reproductively successful females (Clutton-Brock & Iason, 1986). As a result, unrestricted women should have benefited from having relatively more sons, whereas restricted women should have benefited from having more daughters. After all, their sons would be at a disadvantage competing with the reproductively more successful sons of unrestricted women. To the extent that evolutionary pressures can affect sex ratios (see Trivers, 1972), the offspring sex ratio of restricted and unrestricted women should systematically differ, such that unrestricted women should bear more sons, whereas restricted women should have more daughters. Three convergent studies were conducted to test this prediction (see Gangestad & Simpson, 1990; Gangestad, Simpson, & Thomsen, 1987).

Study 1 tested this hypothesis on archival data. Markers of the genetic variation underlying sociosexuality include the general personality dimensions of extraversion and lack of constraint. The periodical *Who's Who in American Women* contains brief biographical information on women who have distinguished themselves in their careers, including information on their occupations and a listing of their children. Because occupation reliably covaries with features of personality (e.g., Myers & McCaulley, 1985), it should serve as an indirect marker of extraversion, lack of constraint, and, thus, the genetic variation underlying sociosexuality. Accordingly, we identified 19 occupations listed in *Who's Who* for which reliable norms on the Myers–Briggs Type Indicator are available (Myers & McCaulley, 1985). Almost 80% of the women sampled could be placed within one of these occupations.

We then sampled every fifth page of the periodical, identifying members of the 19 occupational categories. The number of male and female progeny possessed by each of 2,002 women was recorded. Within each occupation, we averaged the individual offspring sex ratios. The Myers–Briggs taps several widely recognized dimensions of personality, including extraversion and lack of constraint (McCrae & Costa, 1989). Based on information provided by the Myers–Briggs manual, one can calculate the percentage of workers in various occupations who typically score high on both dimensions. Results revealed that members of occupations associated with relatively higher standing on extraversion and lack of constraint (e.g., marketing and sales persons, performing artists) had reliably more sons relative to daughters than did members of occupations associated with relatively lower standing on these two dimensions (e.g., bank officers, educational administrators).[1]

To examine a more direct marker of the personality features associated with sociosexuality, we conducted Study 2. Participants were 308 mothers of undergraduate students. Each mother had at least two children. Rather than asking them to reveal their sexual history, we assessed the genetic variation underlying sociosexuality with personality items known to be good markers of it, namely eight items on the Self-Monitoring Scale (Gangestad & Snyder, 1985). Based on their responses to these eight items, we classified mothers as unrestricted if they were judged to be at least 90% probable of belonging to the high self-monitoring class. Mothers were classified as being restricted if they were judged to be at least 90% probable of belonging to the low self-monitoring class. Twin research has shown that the eight-item index is a good marker of the genetic variation underlying the Self-Monitoring Scale (Gangestad, 1986), which, in turn, taps genetic variation underlying sociosexuality (Gangestad & Simpson, 1990). The results supported our predictions. Probable unrestricted women had significantly more male offspring than did their restricted counterparts.

We employed a more direct marker of sociosexuality in Study 3. During the 1930s and 1940s, Kinsey and his colleagues (Kinsey et al., 1948, 1953) collected a massive amount of data on various aspects of sociosexual behavior. Besides inquiring about sexual behavior, they also gathered information about respondents' offspring. To determine whether offspring sex ratio was related to sociosexuality, we first identified the most direct behavioral marker of sociosexuality in the Kinsey data—number of premarital sex partners. We then correlated offspring sex ratio with number of premarital partners for 1,461 individuals who had at least two children. The number of premarital sexual partners was reliably associated with offspring sex ratio. Specifically, women and men who had a larger number of premarital sex partners were significantly more likely to have male offspring relative to those who had fewer partners.[2]

---

[1]Because many women may establish careers after they have children, it might be argued that sex of offspring could influence occupational choice. While this alternate explanation is possible, it is not highly plausible. Although the existence of children *in general* may affect what types of careers women enter, it is difficult to believe that the *specific sex* of offspring would systematically influence career choices. Furthermore, data from two additional studies (described below) relying on markers of sociosexuality other than occupation choice produced similar findings.

[2]Males were included in this analysis because our model suggests that males who have had many previous sexual partners also should have more sons. Because males with many previous partners typically should mate with females with many partners (as evidence reported earlier corroborates), both should have relatively more sons.

It might be argued that this set of differential sex ratio predictions and findings is implausible because males determine the sex of offspring at conception. However, this is not entirely true; inter-

The Case of Male Mate Choice

According to our model, female sociosexual variation exists because, in an evolutionary-relevant state, males varied considerably in reproductive success. Unrestricted women benefited from passing the genes of those men who possessed greater reproductive potential onto their own offspring. Conversely, restricted women benefited from the relatively greater investment of men who limited their reproductive efforts to her own. Given this scenario, how could males have best benefited reproductively? On the face of it, the answer may seem obvious. If unrestricted women were as reproductively successful as restricted ones, males who reproduced with several females would have been more reproductively successful. It might seem, then, that males should have been uniformly selected to be unrestricted (see Symons, 1979; Wilson, 1978).

The problem with this analysis is that not all males could succeed by adopting an unrestricted strategy. Obviously, if some males had several mates, some males would have no mates. Among those males who could not succeed, those adopting a restricted strategy may have been more successful, for they would have offered paternal care to the offspring of any mate who would have selected them (presumably, restricted females). One explanation for male sociosexual variation, therefore, is that as frequency-dependent selection produced female variation in mating strategies, the possibility for variation in male strategy was created. If the genetic factors that underlie female sociosexuality also existed within males, variability in males would have been created and not selected against.

This conceptualization, however, may not be an entirely tenable one. If surveyance of the local environment could have resulted in the choice of a more adaptive reproductive strategy, strategy choice based on environmental circumstances might have been more optimal (cf. Tooby & Cosmides, 1990). For females, surveyance of local circumstances may not have been extremely beneficial (see Gangestad & Simpson, 1990b). For males, however, ecologically contingent strategy choice often may have resulted in the selection of a more optimal orientation (Trivers, 1972).[3] Thus, the choice of sociosexual orientation among males might have been more efficient if it were at least partly ecologically contingent, with males who did not succeed under an unrestricted orientation eventually becoming more restricted.

---

uterine environment also can influence offspring sex ratio. In fact, several different proximate mechanisms may mediate offspring sex ratio within women, including individual differences in cervical mucus (Guerrero, 1974; Roberts, 1978), hormonal levels (James, 1986), immune response systems (Gualtieri & Hicks, 1985), and timing of intercourse within the reproductive cycle (Harlap, 1979).

Finally, it should be noted that for all six studies, we also collected data on males. Across all six studies, effects for males closely paralleled those we report for females.

[3]Specifically, a design allowing for the adoption of an unrestricted strategy first, followed by the adoption of a restricted one *only if* the former one failed, could have evolved. Moreover, a design permitting facultative unrestricted sociosexuality under certain circumstances also may have emerged (cf. Maynard Smith, 1982; Trivers, 1972).

Available data support this tentative conjecture. If male sociosexuality and mate choice are partly contingent upon reproductive success with females, both should be associated with male attractiveness. Recent research has confirmed that female physical and sexual attractiveness (as rated by independent observers) do not reliably correlate with either sociosexuality or preferences for a highly attractive versus a faithful mate (Simpson & Gangestad, 1990). Male attractiveness, however, does reliably covary with both sociosexuality as well as these mate preference dimensions.

The Relation Between Sociosexuality and Personality

How can the personality correlates discussed earlier be understood within our model? One possibility is that features of personality are adaptive aspects of female mating propensities, such that women who tend to be disinhibited, extraverted, attention seeking, socially potent, and aggressive are more successful at enacting an unrestricted orientation. In order to induce males to invest in their offspring, for instance, unrestricted women frequently may have engaged in pretense and deceit (cf. Harpending & Draper, 1986), facets tapped by the Self-Monitoring Scale that strongly covary with sociosexuality (Snyder et al., 1986).

At least two other viable explanations also exist. First, disinhibition, extraversion, attention seeking, social potency, and aggressivity may be precisely the characteristics that unrestricted women preferentially seek out in men, whereas the reverse may be true of restricted women. If so, these characteristics may have become genetically linked to unrestricted sexual behavior in females over time (R. A. Fisher, 1958). Second, the same biological factor that underlies female sociosexuality also may underlie extraversion, disinhibition, attention seeking, aggressivity, and the like. That is, perhaps the characteristics that covary with sociosexuality were not selected *for* but rather they were selected *with* unrestricted sociosexuality (see Gould & Lewontin, 1974; Sober, 1984).

Possible Alternate Explanations of Female Sociosexual Variation

Several investigators have attempted to formulate evolutionary theories of human sexuality (e.g., Buss, 1987, 1989; Rushton, 1985; Wilson, 1978). Although our approach is distinct in its attempt to explain variability in sociosexual attitudes and behavior that exists *within* the sexes, it is by no means the first one to do so. One of the leading alternate accounts, in fact, views individual differences in female sociosexuality as stemming from adaptations to specific environmental circumstances. Let us briefly consider this alternate explanation.

We have suggested that the genetic variation underlying female sociosexuality may represent alternate mating orientations. The vast majority of alternate mating propensities, however, probably are ecologically contingent. Under these circumstances, individuals adopt a specific strategy once they have identified which one is optimal in light of local environmental factors (e.g., Dunbar, 1982). More often than not, ecologically contingent strategy choice should supplant frequency-dependent selection if environmental cues signaling optimal strategy choice exist (see Tooby & Cosmides, 1990). Yet, as noted earlier, female strategy choice may not have been greatly facilitated by environmental cues in our ancestral past (see Gangestad & Simpson, 1990b). Furthermore, ecologically-contingent strategy choice does not produce genetic variation, and, thus, it cannot account for the genetic variation that underlies sociosexuality and related traits.

Nevertheless, certain aspects of female mate choice can be explained by ecologically contingent models. Draper and Harpending (1982), for instance, have argued that father-absence may be one environmental variable upon which strategy choice might critically depend. They suggest that females who experienced long periods of father-absence in evolutionary history could have come to anticipate both lack of paternal care as well as intense reproductive competition among males. According to their model, females faced with these circumstances should have adopted a reproductive orientation similar to unrestricted women. Since this model does not account for the genetic variability in sociosexuality, it is not a complete alternative to our own. In fact, as Harpending and Draper (1986) have noted, ecologically contingent models that attempt to explain the variability underlying human sexuality may complement genetic models. Because environmental and cultural factors undoubtedly have a profound impact on the development and expression of sociosexual behavior, future research must address how environmental and genetic factors interact to generate individual variability in sociosexuality.

IMPLICATIONS OF THE MODEL
FOR UNDERSTANDING RELATIONSHIPS

The study of individual differences in sociosexuality has the potential to advance our knowledge of how and why relationships are initiated, develop, and deteriorate. In this final section, we first discuss whether sociosexuality is a stable, traitlike dimension. We then briefly raise some implications that our model may have for understanding processes of relationship initiation, maintenance, and dissolution.

Do individual differences in sociosexuality reflect a stable, traitlike dimension? Or do they represent a transient individual difference variable whose effects are witnessed mainly during one stage of life (the dating years)? Despite the fact that the SOI appears to have heritable origins and high 2-month test-retest reliability (Simpson & Gangestad, in press, a), definitive answers to these questions are not yet available. Nevertheless, even if sociosexuality does exhibit traitlike qualities, its phenotypic manifestations may change across the life span. During the dating years, for example, individual differences in sociosexuality might be most clearly revealed in differential willingness to engage in sex prior to the development of strong commitment and enduring emotional bonds. During the marital years, however, sociosexuality might be most clearly evident in either differential willingness to remain in unsatisfactory marriages (cf. Newcomb & Bentler, 1981) and/or differential susceptibility to being drawn out of such relationships by attractive alternative partners (e.g., extramarital affairs: Kelley & Thibaut, 1978). In particular, unrestricted individuals, relative to restricted ones, may be more inclined to terminate unsatisfactory marital relationships and be more easily drawn out of positive ones. Future research must explore whether and how the phenotypic manifestations of sociosexuality change over the life span.

As we have demonstrated, restricted and unrestricted individuals typically rely on different sorts of criteria when choosing dating partners (Simpson & Gangestad, 1990c). Restricted individuals tend to place relatively more emphasis on attributes such as the partner's loyalty and faithfulness, their personal compatibility, and their responsibility, characteristics that should facilitate the development of relatively stable, committed, and long-term relationships. Unrestricted individuals, on the other hand, tend to focus on attributes such as physical/sexual attractiveness and social visibility, dimensions that may not necessarily foster long-term stability and commitment.

Recent longitudinal research has documented that the dating relationships of restricted individuals are significantly less vulnerable to dissolution over time. Simpson (1987) surveyed 234 individuals involved in ongoing dating relationships about their sociosexual orientation as well as the nature of their current dating relationships on several dimensions. Three months later, nearly 95% of these individuals were telephoned and asked whether they still were dating the same partner. Unrestricted individuals, relative to restricted ones, were significantly more likely to have experienced relationship dissolution during the preceding 3 months. This effect remained reliable even when relationship length, closeness, satisfaction, and the perceived quality of alternative partners, all of which had been assessed 3 months earlier, were controlled for. These results suggest that the criteria by which restricted and unrestricted individuals select romantic partners may affect the long-term stability of their romantic involvements more strongly than the quality of their relationships per se.

Reliance on these different mate selection criteria also might systematically influence relationship satisfaction and the grounds for dissolution. For unrestricted individuals, long-term satisfaction with a romantic partner may depend more heavily on the extent to which the partner is highly attractive and possesses high social visibility. Decisions to either continue or terminate a relationship also may be more contingent on changes—and particularly precipitous declines—in the partner's level of physical attractiveness or social status with the passage of time. For restricted individuals, satisfaction may depend more directly on the degree to which the partner is loyal, responsible, and faithful. Similarly, decisions to remain in or leave a relationship may hinge on the extent of loyalty and commitment the partner displays during the course of the relationship. Future research must determine whether or not these conjectures are accurate reflections of the romantic lives of restricted and unrestricted persons.

During the past decade, two prominent themes have emerged within the field of interpersonal relations. First, researchers have begun to recognize the important role that individual difference orientations assume in affecting the formation, maintenance, and dissolution of romantic relationships (Clark & Reis, 1988). Second, it has become apparent that sex and sexuality can and do appreciably influence the nature and course of romantic involvements. Our theoretical and empirical work represent a synthesis of these two recent themes from an evolutionary perspective. Future research must determine the extent to which our evolutionary model can advance our understanding of the relations between personality, sexuality, and close relationships.

REFERENCES

Alexander, R. D., Hoogland, J. L., Howard, R. D., Noonan, K. M., & Sherman, P. W. (1979). Sexual dimorphisms and breeding systems in pinnepeds, ungulates, primates, and humans. In N. Chagnon & W. Irons (Eds.), *Evolutionary biology and human social behavior: An anthropological perspective*. North Scituate, MA: Duxbury.

Alston, J. P., & Tucker, F. (1973). The myth of sexual permissiveness. *Journal of Sex Research, 9*, 34–40.

Briggs, S. R., & Cheek, J. M. (1988). On the nature of self-monitoring: Problems with assessment, problems with validity. *Journal of Personality and Social Psychology, 54*, 663–678.

Buss, D. M. (1987). Sex differences in human mate selection criteria: An evolutionary perspective. In C. B. Crawford, M. F. Smith, & D. L. Krebs (Eds.), *Sociobiology and psychology*. Hillsdale, NJ: Erlbaum.

Buss, D. M. (1989). Sex differences in human mate preference: Evolutionary hypotheses tested in 37 cultures. *Behavioral and Brain Sciences, 12*, 1–14.

Bynner, J. M. (1969). *The association between adolescent behaviour and attitudes as revealed by a new social attitude inventory*. Unpublished doctoral dissertation, University of London.

Byrne, D. (1983). The antecedents, correlates, and consequents of erotophobia-erotophilia. In C. M. Daniels (Ed.), *Challenges in sexual science* (pp. 53–75). Philadelphia: Society for the Scientific Study of Sex.

Byrne, D., & Sheffield, J. (1965). Response to sexually arousing stimuli as a function of repressing and sensitizing defenses. *Journal of Abnormal Psychology, 70*, 114–118.

Clark, M. S., & Reis, H. T. (1988). Interpersonal processes in close relationships. *Annual Review of Psychology, 39*, 609–672.

Clutton-Brock, T. H., & Iason, G. R. (1986). Sex ratio variation in mammals. *The Quarterly Review of Biology, 61*, 339–374.

Crow, J. F. (1986). *Basic concepts in population, quantitative, and evolutionary genetics*. New York: Freeman.

Curran, J. P., Neff, S., & Lippold, S. (1973). Correlates of sexual experience among university students. *Journal of Sex Research, 9,* 124–131.

Daitzman, R. J., & Zuckerman, M. (1980). Disinhibitory sensation seeking, personality, and gonadal hormones. *Personality and Individual Differences, 1,* 103–110.

D'Augelli, J. F., & Cross, H. J. (1975). Relationship of sex guilt and moral reasoning to premarital sex in college women and in couples. *Journal of Consulting and Clinical Psychology, 43,* 40–47.

Dorjahn, V. R. (1954). The factor of polygyny in African demography. In W. Bascom & M. H. Herkovits (Eds.), *Continuity and change in African cultures.* Chicago: University of Chicago Press.

Draper, P., & Harpending, H. (1982). Father absence and reproductive strategy: An evolutionary perspective. *Journal of Anthropological Research, 38,* 235–243.

Dunbar, R. I. M. (1982). Intraspecific variations in mating strategy. In P. P. G. Bateson & P. H. Klopfer (Eds.), *Perspectives in ethology* (Vol. 5, pp. 385–431). New York: Plenum.

Eaves, L., & Eysenck, H. J. (1975). The nature of extraversion: A genetical analysis. *Journal of Personality and Social Psychology, 32,* 102–112.

Eysenck, H. J. (1971). Hysterical personality and sexual adjustment, attitudes and behaviour. *Journal of Sexual Research, 7,* 274–281.

Eysenck, H. J. (1972). Personality and sexual behaviour. *Journal of Psychosomatic Research, 16,* 141–152.

Eysenck, H. J. (1973). Personality and attitudes to sex in criminals. *Journal of Sexual Research, 9,* 295–306.

Eysenck, H. J. (1974). Personality, premarital sexual permissiveness, and assortative mating. *Journal of Sexual Research, 10,* 47–51.

Eysenck, H. J. (1976). *Sex and personality.* London: Open Books.

Eysenck, H. J., & Eysenck, S. B. (1964). *Manual of the EPI.* London: University of London Press.

Eysenck, H. J., & Eysenck, S. B. (1975). *Manual of the E.P.Q. (Eysenck personality questionnaire).* London: University of London Press.

Eysenck, H. J., & Eysenck, S. B. (1976). *Psychoticism as a dimension of personality.* London: University of London Press.

Fisher, R. A. (1958). *The genetical theory of natural selection* (2nd ed.). Oxford: Clarendon.

Fisher, S. (1973). *The female orgasm.* London: Allen Lane.

Floderus-Myrhed, B., Pederson, N., & Rasmussen, I. (1980). Assessment of heritability for personality based on a short form of the Eysenck Personality Inventory: A study of 12,898 twin pairs. *Behavior Genetics, 10,* 153–162.

Fulker, D. W., Eysenck, S. B. G., & Zuckerman, M. (1980). The genetics of sensation-seeking. *Journal of Personality Research, 14,* 261–281.

Gangestad, S. W. (1986). *On the etiology of expressive self-control: Testing the case of strong genetic influence.* Unpublished doctoral dissertation, University of Minnesota, Minneapolis.

Gangestad, S. W., & Simpson, J. A. (1990a). Toward an evolutionary history of female sociosexual variation. *Journal of Personality, 58,* 69–96.

Gangestad, S. W., & Simpson, J. A. (1990b). *On human sociosexual variation: An evolutionary model of mating propensities.* Manuscript submitted for publication.

Gangestad, S. W., & Simpson, J. A. (1990c). *On assessing a genetic factor underlying personality: Development and validation of Scale Zeta.* Manuscript submitted for publication.

Gangestad, S. W., Simpson, J. A., & Thomsen, C. (1987). *Personality and sex ratio of offspring.* Unpublished data, University of Minnesota, Minneapolis.

Gangestad, S., & Snyder, M. (1985). To carve nature at its joints: On the existence of discrete classes in personality. *Psychological Review, 92,* 317–349.

Gerrard, M. (1980). Sex guilt and attitudes toward sex in sexually active and inactive female college students. *Journal of Personality Assessment, 44,* 258–261.

Gerrard, M., & Gibbons, F. X. (1982). Sexual experience, sex guilt, and sexual moral reasoning. *Journal of Personality, 50,* 345–359.

Giese, H., & Schmidt, A. (1968). *Studenten sexualitat.* Hamburg: Rowohlt.

Gould, S. J., & Lewontin, R. C. (1974). The spandrels of San Marco and the panglossian paradigm:

A critique of the adaptationist programme. *Proceedings of the Royal Society of London, B205*, 581–598.

Griffit, W. (1973). Response to erotica and the projection of response to erotica in the opposite sex. *Journal of Experimental Research in Personality, 6*, 330–338.

Gualtieri, T., & Hicks, R. E. (1985). An immunoreactive theory of selective male affliction. *Behavioral and Brain Sciences, 8*, 427–441.

Guerrero, R. (1974). Association of the type and time of insemination within the menstrual cycle with the human sex ratio at birth. *New England Journal of Medicine, 291*, 1056–1059.

Hamilton, W. D., & Zuk, M. (1982). Heritable true fitness and bright birds: A role for parasites. *Science, 218*, 384–387.

Harlap, S. (1979). Gender of infants conceived on different days of the menstrual cycle. *New England Journal of Medicine, 300*, 1445–1448.

Harpending, H., & Draper, P. (1986). Selection against human family organization. In B. J. Williams (Ed.), *On evolutionary anthropology: Essays in honor of Harry Hoijer*. Malibu, CA: Undena.

Hunt, M. (1974). *Sexual behavior in the 1970s*. New York: Dell.

Husted, J. R., & Edwards, A. E. (1976). Personality correlates of male sexual arousal and behavior. *Archives of Sexual Behavior, 5*, 149–156.

James, W. H. (1986). Hormonal control of sex ratio. *Journal of Theoretical Biology, 118*, 427–441.

Kelley, H. H., & Thibaut, J. W. (1978). *Interpersonal relations: A theory of interdependence*. New York: Wiley.

Kinsey, A. C., Pomeroy, W. B., & Martin, C. E. (1948). *Sexual behavior in the human male*. Philadelphia: Saunders.

Kinsey, A. C., Pomeroy, W. B., Martin, C. E., & Gebhard, P. H. (1953). *Sexual behavior in the human female*. Philadelphia: Saunders.

Leary, M. R., & Dobbins, S. E. (1983). Social anxiety, sexual behavior, and contraceptive use. *Journal of Personality and Social Psychology, 45*, 1347–1354.

Loehlin, J. C., Willerman, L., & Horn, J. M. (1988). Human behavior genetics. *Annual Review of Psychology, 38*, 101–133.

Maslow, A. H. (1942). Self-esteem (dominance-feeling) and sexuality in women. *Journal of Social Psychology, 16*, 259–294.

Maynard Smith, J. (1982). *Evolution and theory of games*. New York: Cambridge University Press.

McCrae, R. R., & Costa, P. T. (1989). Reinterpreting the Myers–Briggs Type Indicator from the perspective of the five-factor model of personality. *Journal of Personality, 57*, 17–42.

Mosher, D. L. (1979). Sex guilt and sex myths in college men and women. *Journal of Sex Research, 15*, 224–234.

Muhsam, M. V. (1956). Fertility of polygamous marriages. *Population studies, 10*, 3–16.

Myers, I. B., & McCaulley, M. H. (1985). *Manual: A guide to the development and use of the Myers-Briggs Type Indicator*. Palo Alto, CA: Consulting Psychologists Press.

Newcomb, M. D., & Bentler, P. M. (1981). Marital breakdown. In S. Duck & R. Gilmour (Eds.), *Personal relationships 3: Personal relationships in disorder* (pp. 57–94). London: Academic.

O'Grady, K. E., Janda, L. H., & Gillen, H. B. (1979). A multidimensional scaling analysis of sex guilt. *Multivariate Behavioral Research, 14*, 415–434.

Pederson, N. L., Plomin, R., McClearn, G. C., & Friberg, L. (in press). Neuroticism, extraversion and related traits in adult twins reared apart and reared together. *Journal of Personality and Social Psychology*.

Reiss, I. L. (1967). *The social context of premarital sexual permissiveness*. New York: Holt, Rinehart & Winston.

Roberts, A. M. (1978). The origins of fluctuations in the human secondary sex ratio. *Journal of Biosocial Science, 10*, 169–182.

Rubin, Z. (1970). Measurement of romantic love. *Journal of Personality and Social Psychology, 16*, 265–273.

Rushton, J. P. (1985). Differential K Theory: The sociobiology of individual and group differences. *Personality and Individual Differences, 6*, 441–452.

Schofield, M. (1968). *The sexual behaviour of young people*. Harmondsworth: Penguin Books.

Simpson, J. A. (1987). The dissolution of romantic relationships: Factors involved in relationship stability and emotional distress. *Journal of Personality and Social Psychology, 53*, 683–692.

Simpson, J. A., & Gangestad, S. W. (1990). *Personality and sociosexuality: A peer rating study*. Unpublished manuscript, Texas A & M University, College Station.

Simpson, J. A., & Gangestad, S. W. (in press, a). *Individual differences in sociosexuality: Evidence for convergent and discriminant validity*. Journal of Personality and Social Psychology.

Simpson, J. A., & Gangestad, S. W. (in press, b). *Sociosexuality and romantic partner choice*. Manuscript submitted for publication.

Sober, E. (1984). *The nature of selection*. Cambridge, MA: MIT Press.

Snyder, M. (1974). The self-monitoring of expressive behavior. *Journal of Personality and Social Psychology, 30*, 526–537.

Snyder, M., & Gangestad, S. (1986). On the nature of self-monitoring: Matters of assessment, matters of validity. *Journal of Personality and Social Psychology, 51*, 125–139.

Snyder, M., Simpson, J. A., & Gangestad, S. (1986). Personality and sexual relations. *Journal of Personality and Social Psychology, 51*, 181–190.

Symons, D. (1979). *The evolution of human sexuality*. New York: Oxford University Press.

Tellegen, A. (1982). *A short manual for the Differential Personality Questionnaire*. Unpublished manuscript, University of Minnesota, Minneapolis.

Tellegen, A., Lykken, D. T., Bouchard Jr., T. J., Wilcox, K. J., Segal, N. L., & Rich, S. (1988). Personality similarity in twins reared apart and together. *Journal of Personality and Social Psychology, 54*, 1031–1039.

Tooby, J., & Cosmides, L. (1990). On the universality of human nature and the uniqueness of the individual: The role of genetics and adaptation. *Journal of Personality, 58*, 17–67.

Trivers, R. (1972). Parental investment and sexual selection. In B. Campbell (Eds.), *Sexual selection and the descent of man, 1871–1971* (pp. 136–179). Chicago: Aldine.

Ukaegbu, A. O. (1977). Fertility of women in polygynous unions in rural Eastern Nigeria. *Journal of Marriage and the Family, 39*, 397–404.

Weatherhead, P. J., & Robertson, R. J. (1979). Offspring quality and the polygyny threshold: The "sexy son" hypothesis. *American Naturalist, 113*, 201–208.

Weatherhead, P. J., & Robertson, R. J. (1981). In defense of the "sexy son" hypothesis. *American Naturalist, 117*, 349–356.

Williams, G. C. (1966). *Adaptation and natural selection: A critique of some current evolutionary thought*. Princeton, NJ: Princeton University Press.

Wilson, E. O. (1978). *On human nature*. Cambridge, MA: Harvard University Press.

Wilson, G. (1981). Personality and sex. In R. Lynn (Ed.), *Dimensions of personality: Papers in honour of H J Eysenck* (pp. 355–375). New York: Pergamon Press.

Zuckerman, M. (1971). Dimensions of sensation seeking. *Journal of Consulting and Clinical Psychology, 36*, 45–52.

Zuckerman, M. (1974). The sensation seeking motive. In B. A. Maher (Ed.), *Progress in experimental personality research* (Vol. 7). New York: Academic Press.

Zuckerman, M. (1983). *Biological bases of sensation seeking, impulsivity, and anxiety*. Hillsdale, NJ: Erlbaum.

Zuckerman, M., Bone, R. N., Neary, R., Mangelsdorff, D., & Brustman, B. (1972). What is the sensation seeker? Personality trait and experience correlates of the Sensation Seeking Scales. *Journal of Consulting and Clinical Psychology, 39*, 308–321.

Zuckerman, M., Kolin, E. A., Price, L., & Zoob, I. (1964). Development of a Sensation-Seeking Scale. *Journal of Consulting Psychology, 28*, 477–482.

Zuckerman, M., Tushup, R., & Finner, S. (1976). Sexual attitudes and experience: Attitude and personality correlates and changes produced by a course in sexuality. *Journal of Consulting and Clinical Psychology, 44*, 7–19.

5 Sexuality and Communication in Close Relationships

William R. Cupach
Sandra Metts
Illinois State University

It is widely proclaimed that good communication is essential to good sexual relations. However, the association between communication and sexuality is not necessarily simple or direct. The purpose of this chapter is to explore the ways in which individuals use communication to achieve sexual goals, while simultaneously pursuing other subjectively important goals (such as maintaining a relationship or preserving a partner's self-esteem). In particular, we consider the role of communication in the enactment and interpretation of sexual episodes within various types of heterosexual interpersonal relationships.

Research documenting the role of communication in intimate relationships substantiates two generalizations. First, the quality of communication and the quality of the relationship are closely linked. Communication is both constrained by and defines the nature and quality of an interpersonal relationship. When communication is incompetent, the quality of the relationship suffers. Of course, causality can manifest itself in the other direction as well; relational problems can trigger disenchantment with one's partner and one's relationship, thereby diminishing the effort devoted to effective communication. In either case, sexual satisfaction and relationship satisfaction are clearly interconnected (e.g., Blumstein & Schwartz, 1983; Hudson, Harrison, & Crosscup, 1981; Perlman & Abramson, 1982; Snyder, 1979), and both are affected by the ability and willingness of partners to interact effectively with one another (e.g., Banmen & Vogel, 1985; Chesney, Blakeney, Cole, & Chan, 1981; Fay, 1977; Fowers & Olson, 1989; Schenk, Pfrang, & Rausche, 1983; Zimmer, 1983). Consequently, communication skills that facilitate the development and maintenance of close relationships are an important component of sexual competence (D'Augelli & D'Augelli, 1985).

A second conclusion indicates that the ability to communicate about sex in particular is instrumental in maintaining sexual and relational satisfaction (Banmen & Vogel, 1985; Baus, 1987; Cupach & Comstock, 1990; Masters, Johnson, & Kolodny, 1986). Sex talk allows partners to communicate desires and preferences to each other, to coordinate meanings for sexual behaviors, and to negotiate a dyadic sexual script (Metts & Cupach, 1989). Sexual communication decreases uncertainty about a partner's expectations and about sexuality in general. Such knowledge can promote sexual satisfaction (Perlman & Abramson, 1982; Sarver & Murry, 1981).

In the following sections, we consider negotiation of the occurrence of sexual activity in various types of heterosexual relationships. First, we address the issue of managing sexual attraction in cross-sex friendships. Then we discuss the dynamics of sexual negotiation episodes in potentially sexual relationships, such as dating, and in developed sexual relationships, such as marriage and cohabitation. We close the chapter with suggestions for additional research. (Readers are referred to chapter 6 for a review of issues concerning sexual decision making.)

SEXUAL ATTRACTION
IN CROSS-SEX FRIENDSHIPS

Although scholars typically distinguish romantic relationships from other relationships on the basis of sexual involvement, in actual practice the attraction between friends is sometimes manifested as sexual desire or even sexual involvement. This possibility makes the management of cross-sex friendship particularly difficult.

Sexual tension complicates an already-difficult type of relationship. Friendship in general has fewer guidelines in terms of rules and role expectations than culturally institutionalized relationships such as marriage and kinship (Hays, 1988). Even same-sex friends must manage the placement of their friendship within their social network, and adjust its position when circumstances change (e.g., getting married, getting divorced, and entering the work force; Sapadin, 1988). Cross-sex friends must likewise place their relationship within their social network, but must recognize the potential jealousy of romantic partners (O'Meara, 1989) and the prevailing social suspicion of nonsexual cross-sex relationships (Rawlins, 1982). Thus, communication for the persons involved in a cross-sex friendship becomes critically important in managing both the private relationship between partners and the public relationship as situated within its social network.

Managing Private Aspects of Cross-Sex Friendship

Communication plays an important role in how a couple manages the potential for sexual involvement. If sexual attraction is simply not present, cross-sex friends will enjoy a relatively uncomplicated and open relationship (although they may exert considerable energy convincing the social network). However, when sexual attraction is present, couples must draw on one or a combination of strategies for managing it.

Management strategies are direct or indirect, long term or short, serious or light-hearted. For some friendship pairs, sexual bantering and teasing add a playful component to the relationship that both partners find comfortable and nonthreatening. For other friendship pairs, sexual attraction may be too intense or too threatening to treat indirectly and/or playfully. In such cases, explicit discussion of sexual attraction may allow partners to confront relevant issues and to make informed decisions about the future of the relationship.

Obviously, explicit revelation of sexual attraction, like other types of self-disclosure, may have unexpected consequences. Revealing sexual attraction, if not previously perceived by the partner, may function to increase his or her level of uncertainty (Planalp, Rutherford, & Honeycutt, 1988) and possibly feelings of being exploited (Sapadin, 1988). Revealing sexual attraction, if not reciprocated by the partner, may result in face loss for the initiating partner, although friends appear to be less embarrassed by sexual rejection than are dating partners (Metts, Cupach, & Imahori, 1989). In fact, even when sexual attraction is mutual, overt discussion can demystify and reify what might have been elements of a fantasy. This consequence will be perceived as good or bad depending upon the goals and needs of the couple.

In sum, although no particular strategy fits the needs of all couples, when sexual attraction is present for at least one person, it carries implications for the relationship. Failure to acknowledge and manage sexual attraction may result in relational tension or interactional awkwardness that partners attribute to other causes (e.g., decreased affection, trust, or commitment) (Rawlins, 1982).

If sexual attraction leads to sexual involvement, then communication is also critically important. Because sexual involvement is usually interpreted as a "turning point" in the status or trajectory of the relationship (i.e., from friends to dating partners), friends who become sexually involved must clarify the expectations they have for their relationship (Baxter, 1987; Baxter & Bullis, 1986).

Communication enables couples to interpret their sexual involvement and judge whether it is consistent or inconsistent with the norms of friendship as they currently practice it. If sexual involvement is inconsistent, couples can redefine either the sexual involvement or the relationship. For example, a couple may treat isolated sexual events as anomalous in an otherwise platonic relationship, or they may treat sexual events as signals that a romantic relationship has emerged from the friendship. Couples sometimes attempt to maintain the relationship as a friendship, characterized by openness and autonomy, but to also incorporate a sexual component into the general framework. Rawlins (1982) refers to this type of relationship as "friendship-love," but notes its general instability as partners alternate between the roles of friend and lover, and the emotional and sexual expression of affection. These relationships seem particularly difficult for women to maintain (R. R. Bell, 1981). For example, Sapadin (1988) found that professional women reported significantly less agreement than men with the statement "Having a sexual relationship adds deeper feelings and closeness to friendship."

Managing Public Aspects of Cross-Sex Friendship

Communication also aids cross-sex friends in their efforts to situate the friendship comfortably in their social network. Perhaps most difficult, friends need to assure romantic partners that the cross-sex friendship is not a threat. Jealousy is a common reaction to cross-sex friendships and probably explains why existing friendships diminish at the time of marriage and why almost no new ones begin after marriage (O'Meara, 1989).

Reassuring one's romantic partner that a friend of the opposite sex is not a threat to the relationship may become more difficult under certain circumstances. For example, when sexual attraction is present in the friendship, it may be more awkward to discuss with a romantic partner. Also, to the extent that men generally view interactions as sexual (Abbey, 1982) and see sex as fundamental to opposite-sex relationships (R. R. Bell, 1981), it may be relatively more difficult for a woman to convince her male partner that her friendship is platonic than it would be for a man to convince his female partner. Thus, the meanings and understandings negotiated within the friendship cannot be separated from the individuals' social network.

In addition, cross-sex friends must offer to the larger social network an accounting for the nontraditional mode of their relationship. Male/female friendship pairs are subject to outside attributions of hidden sexual agendas, lack of awareness of their own sexual attraction, or even inferences that one or both partners are homosexual (O'Meara, 1989). If the couple is unable to neutralize or ignore these attributions, the friendship may eventually become a more conventional romantic relationship, diminish in its importance, or terminate.

SEXUAL EPISODES IN DEVELOPING
ROMANTIC RELATIONSHIPS

Although sexual attraction may be more easily assimilated into a romantic relationship than a friendship, managing sexual involvement is still a communicative challenge. Sexual episodes are microcosms of the broader interpersonal relationship in which they occur. They represent encounters in which partners negotiate the time, place, manner, and meaning of sexual interaction. In the next section, we specifically consider the moves that relational partners make to initiate, resist, and direct sexual activity.

Initiation of Sexual Activity

At early stages of intimacy, the negotiation of sexual activity can be a particularly difficult accomplishment. Individuals attempt to meet multiple goals related to the situation, including impression management and relationship definition. These attempts are complicated by the fact that partners may possess different sexual experiences and standards. Partners also frequently differ in their sexual vocabularies (e.g., Sanders, 1978; Sanders & Robinson, 1979; Simkins & Rinck, 1982; Wells, 1989). Moreover, partners lack breadth and depth of information about each other.

In the absence of detailed and intimate knowledge about each other, partners rely on generalized cultural scripts for guidance regarding how relationships ought to progress, and what actions would be appropriate to escalate and restrain relationship development (Baxter, 1987). "Scripts are hypothesized cognitive and performative structures which organize a person's comprehension of situated events and guide a person's performance of a situated set of actions" (Ginsburg, 1988, p. 29). Initiation of sexual activity in heterosexual relationships is consistent with the sociobiological theory that men seek to propagate widely, whereas women seek to propagate wisely (Hinde, 1984). The traditional stereotype holds that men perform the role of sexual initiation and that women control the occurrence of sexual activity (LaPlante, McCormick, & Brannigan, 1980; McCormick, 1979; Peplau, Rubin, & Hill, 1977).

Attempts to initiate sexual activity are typically subtle and indirect. Indeed, the very nature of what constitutes sexual initiation is often ambiguous in actual interaction. Evidence exists that women engage in "proceptive" behaviors such as extended eye gaze and physical closeness to indicate sexual interest and perhaps to evoke arousal in a man (Moore, 1985; Perper & Weis, 1987). Sometimes this proceptivity is intended to communicate an immediate interest in sexual activity, and thereby encourage the man to initiate. However, sometimes the same cues may be used to evoke the partner's interest without intending to engage in sexual behavior until a later time. Women may also use such cues to garner attention and create interest, even when they have no intention whatsoever to engage in sexual activity.

Much of what contributes to the complexity of the sexual negotiation episode is actually a reflection of the general predisposition in developing relationships for partners to be circumspect and indirect. As Baxter (1987) notes, "the typical relationship process is not dominated by open, direct relationship communication, but rather involves the construction of a web of ambiguity by which parties signal their relationship indirectly" (p. 194).

For the partner seeking sexual compliance, indirectness and ambiguity facilitate the accomplishment of two sequentially ordered goals: to gain sexual access and to avoid rejection. Although these goals may appear to be logical alternatives, they are not. Gaining sexual access is a task accomplishment, and avoiding rejection is a self-image or face-maintenance goal. Indirect strategies accomplish both goals. It is no surprise that college students report a strong preference for indirect methods of seeking sexual involvement (McCormick, 1979). Seduction, nonverbal posturing, and verbal innuendo signal sexual interest and, if responded to favorably by partner, can become sexual initiation acts. On the other hand, if partner does not respond positively, then these cues can go unacknowledged. Because explicit overture has not been made, refusal is not necessary and thus rejection has not occurred.

Of course, direct strategies are sometimes used to gain sexual access. When one is fairly confident of the partner's sexual interest and/or unconcerned about rejection, directness is probably more likely. On occasion, however, an individual may misjudge his or her partner's sexual interest. For example, when sexual initiation by males is rebuffed, they sometimes persist in their initiation attempts, escalating to more aggressive, direct, and forceful behavior (Christopher, 1988; Koss & Oros, 1982; also see chapter 8 in this volume).

Poorly coordinated sexual episodes may occur for several reasons. First, men and women are inclined to disagree about when sexual activity should first occur in a relationship. Men are frequently interested in physical intimacy regardless of the level of emotional involvement, whereas women sometimes defer sexual activity until some degree of emotional intimacy has developed (e.g., Roche, 1986). Second, men may be skeptical that women do not want sex when they resist, both because of misinterpreted proceptive cues, and because of gender-role expectations that women cannot say yes because they would appear promiscuous. Some men respond to the ambiguity in the early stages of involvement by being sexually coercive and tend to view the relationship principally in sexual terms; non-coercive males "approach relationships in terms of a broader spectrum of possibilities, including friendship, companionship, enjoyment, etc." (Craig, Kalichman, & Follingstad, 1989, p. 430). To the extent that the sexual component is emphasized over other aspects of the relationship, men may be biased in their processing of contextual cues in a fashion consistent with their goal for sexual activity. Consequently, men believe that women who say no may not mean it. Indeed, this belief is reinforced by the fact that women occasionally *do* offer token resistance to sexual advances (Muehlenhard & Hollabaugh, 1988). Although perhaps more importantly, media portrayals seem to exaggerate the token resistance phenomenon (Muehlenhard, 1988).

Third, by being indirect, women may fail to communicate clearly their disinterest in sexual activity. In general, women tend to exhibit more politeness and indirectness in compliance situations (Baxter, 1984; Falbo & Peplau, 1980). Further, women have been socialized to put men's needs above their own (Lewin, 1985). This may render women more vulnerable as men's expectations of success are tacitly reinforced. Murnen, Perot, and Byrne (1989) have demonstrated that an unwanted sexual advance is more likely to be thwarted to the extent that a exhibits a strong verbal and/or physical response. Similarly, Byers (1988) found that men become more compliant when a woman is persistent in her refusal of a sexual advance. Direct, verbal refusals are inversely related to the occurrence of sexual activity (Christopher & Frandsen, 1990).

Fourth, men are more inclined than women to interpret social behavior in a sexual way. Research by Abbey (1982; Abbey & Melby, 1986) and others (Muehlenhard & Linton, 1987) indicates that men may wear sex-colored glasses. Although both men and women will flirt for the purpose of friendliness, men are more inclined to flirt with a sexual intent (Montgomery, 1987). Consequently, it is not surprising that men are more likely to enter social interaction with the perception that flirtation signals sexual receptivity. Shotland and Craig (1988) found that, although males perceive both males and females as having more sexual interest than females perceive, both males and females can differentiate between friendly versus sexually interested behavior. As a result, Shotland and Craig (1988) argue that men and women possess different thresholds for the perception of sexual intent. They speculate that this gender difference may be associated with biological processes. Such an explanation, Shotland and Craig (1988) suggest, is compatible with findings that free testosterone in males increases during social interaction compared to baseline levels, especially in heterosexual interactions. Whether this factor is a cause or symptom of males' perceptions of sexual intent is unknown.

Resistance to Sexual Initiation

As with all individual goals, the goal of sexual activity may or may not be shared by both partners in a particular encounter. It is not surprising, therefore, that some sexual initiations gain quick compliance and that others are met with resistance. The partner resisting a sexual advance also has goals and metagoals that motivate strategic actions. In addition, the resister stands in the unique position of determining "when" and "that" a sexual rejection episode has begun. When the sexual overture is explicit, the rejection is likely to be equally direct (Jesser, 1978; McCormick, 1979). However, when the sexual overture is characteristically indirect, identifying it and formulating a response can be very difficult. The resister must infer the goals of the compliance seeker (e.g., kissing as intimacy vs. kissing as a prelude to intercourse) and then generate a response appropriate to these inferred goals. Even more challenging, the resister's message must also facilitate achievement of his or her own goals.

The remarkably instrumental and multifaceted resistance behaviors reported in the essays of American and Canadian women attest to the skill of some resisters in formulating action sequences that meet multiple goals. One particular set of behaviors was referred to by Perper and Weis (1987) as "Incomplete Rejection." This strategy represents a "kind of filter through which only men sensitive and respectful of the women's meanings and intentions can pass" (p.

477). Men who fail to recognize or respect the rejection message and persist in their attempts to gain sexual compliance can be rejected as long-term relational partners.

This interpretation is consistent with Muehlenhard and Hollabaugh's (1988) finding that some women offer token resistance to the sexual advances of their dates. Among the several justifications offered for token resistance, the researchers identified a strong instrumental theme. For women who perceived their partner to endorse the sexual double standard, token resistance allowed them to meet the competing goals of retaining the image of a "proper" woman while also meeting the ultimate goal of sexual (and relational) involvement.

Directing Sexual Activity

Sexual involvement during early stages of relationships has become particularly complicated in recent years by the AIDS epidemic. Responsible sexual partners now find themselves faced with the need to talk about safe-sex practices. Adelman (1988, 1989), for example, refers to the need to acquire a partner's sexual history, to ascertain his or her knowledge of safe-sex practices, and to discuss condom use. Gathering such information requires sensitivity to the implicit face threat in questions about previous sexual experience (e.g., homosexual partners, promiscuity, and so on) and current willingness to practice safe sex (Adelman, 1988). In addition, gaining a partner's compliance to engage in safe sex is not always easy. Edgar and Fitzpatrick (1988) identified several reasons why persons might refuse to engage in safe sex: lack of skills, fear of homosexual association, reluctance to discuss it (break the mood), and lack of personalization of risk.

Even when both partners agree on the need to practice safe sex, actually using a condom is a communicative accomplishment. As Adelman (1988, 1989) has noted, there is an inherent incongruence between the rational and pragmatic language of safe-sex talk and the erotic, passionate language of sexual arousal. In an analysis of safe-sex talk in simulated episodes among college couples, Adelman (1989) observed the skillful use of humor in a sort of improvisational reframing of the sexual encounter from a tense moment to a playful episode. For example, she observed several instances in which the female requested that her partner use a condom, and he responded with a bit of humor (e.g., "a raincoat [smiling], is that what you're driving at?" or "I also have these condoms that a friend of mine sent me from Tijuana that have those Goodyear radial ribs on them that will drive you *wild*."). Adelman concludes:

> Given the lack of media scripts for directly discussing condom usage and the awkwardness associated with its practice, humor provides a transformation of its "immodest" presence. . . . Yet the joking response can also function as a sexual tease, a type of verbal foreplay that hints at the physical pleasures to come. (p. 24)

Thus, in potentially sexual relationships, communication is used not only to influence the occurrence of sex but also to negotiate and direct the manner of sexual activity.

SEXUAL EPISODES IN DEVELOPED
SEXUAL RELATIONSHIPS

As relational partners interact over time and develop intimacy, they create and share a relational culture—"a privately transacted system of understandings that coordinate attitudes, actions, and identities of participants in a relationship" (Wood, 1982, p. 76). This emergent relational culture is manifested in the coalescence of individual sexual scripts into a shared dyadic script (Simon & Gagnon, 1986, 1987). As intimacy develops, the rules governing interaction become more idiosyncratic to the dyad (Knapp, 1984). Gender differences in vocabularies for talking about sexual matters are somewhat mitigated as relational partners come to share idioms for referring to sexual activities, preferences, and body parts (Bell, Buerkel-Rothfuss, & Gore, 1987; Cornog, 1986).

Initiation of Sexual Activity

Although the sequencing and meaning of sexual episodes are necessarily embedded in the larger frame of the relational culture in intimate relationships, gender-role prescriptions deriving from the cultural script continue to be manifested for many couples in their dyadic scripts. For example, men initiate sexual interaction in marital and cohabiting relationships more frequently than do women (e.g., Blumstein & Schwartz, 1983; Brown & Auerback, 1981; Byers & Heinlein, 1989). It is not entirely clear whether this pattern stems from the male sex drive being relatively greater, or whether the cultural sexual script is being reflected, or both.

Despite male predominance in overt initiation attempts, eventually women seem to become more comfortable in initiating sex with their spouses. Brown and Auerback (1981) discovered in their sample an increase of about one percent per year in the rate of initiations among wives. This could be due to the fact that men initiate less frequently over time as their sexual drive declines, whereas women's sexual drive escalates. It also seems plausible that some of a woman's reluctance to initiate sex during courtship is based on the need to keep herself marketable within the persistent confines of the sexual double standard. Thus, once the formal relationship commitment is made, she can assume that her sexual advances are evaluated as a positive attribute of the relationship (i.e., love) rather than a potentially negative attribute of her personality (i.e., promiscuity). It is also possible that a number of couples negotiate more egalitarian sex roles over the course of their relationships. There is some evidence to support the idea that role equality in the initiation of sexual activity is positively associated with sexual satisfaction (Blumstein & Schwartz, 1983).

As with less developed relationships, the manner in which sexual interaction is initiated in intimate relationships tends to be indirect and nonverbal (Byers & Heinlein, 1989). Brown and Auerback (1981), for example, report that the most common techniques they discovered among married couples included kissing, nongenital touching, and genital fondling, as well as other cues such as playing music, consuming alcohol, and reading sexually explicit material. The communication of sexual interest indirectly makes initiation ambiguous, thereby permitting the initiator to save face if rejected.

The ambiguity regarding who really initiates a particular sexual encounter is also characteristic of developed relationships. Women apparently continue to employ proceptive strategies in an effort to indicate a readiness for sexual activity. O'Brien (1981) reported that, in comparison to retrospective reports, multiple periodic interviews revealed that sexual initiation by wives is more common than originally thought. "The woman seemed to 'pace' the frequency of intercourse by subtly (or openly) signaling her readiness; then the husband 'initiated' the precoital behavior" (p. 117). Moreover, it seems plausible that men may exhibit the use of proceptive strategies as well (see Pillard & Weinrich, 1987). Unfortunately, research has yet to explore the manifestation of presexual behaviors that may frame a more overt sexual initiation in ongoing relationships.

More often than not, in long-term relationships sexual initiations are met with success (Byers & Heinlein, 1989). This is due to a number of factors. First, individuals will often respond positively to a partner's initiation, even if they are not in the mood. Having unwanted sex with the partner may occur if the individual lacks the knowledge or communicative skill to effectively reject the partner, or if he or she feels that the effort required for resistance or the consequences of resistance outweigh the desire not to have sex. In certain circumstances, a reluctant individual may decide to accommodate the partner because he or she feels guilty for creating inequity in the relationship, does not want to hurt the partner's feelings, or is willing to satisfy the partner's needs. Second, because partners may be familiar with each other's proceptive/presexual routines, they may be able to "psyche out" their potential for success before every making an explicit overture. When the partner is unresponsive to initial proceptive cues, initiation may simply be postponed until a more promising time, thereby averting overt rejection. Third, an individual who is uninterested in sexual interaction but senses that the partner is likely to initiate, can structure the environment to reduce the partner's opportunity to initiate. Nevertheless, there are times when one partner initiates sexual interaction and the other refuses. We now consider this circumstance.

Resistance to Sexual Initiation

Because women are more frequently in the role of receiving sexual initiations, they are also in a position to reject initiations more frequently. Blumstein and Schwartz (1983) speculate that the differential frequency of refusals for men and women tends to equalize the balance of power in a relationship. They assert that

> women's right to refuse has evolved hand in hand with the conventional belief that women have a weaker sex drive. It may be that it has been in their best interest to suppress sexual desire in order to become less dependent on sex, and therefore more powerful. Perhaps, then, the idea that women have fewer sexual needs has evolved as a counterbalance to their weaker position in their relationships. (p. 221)

Importantly, Byers and Heinlein (1989) found that women not only resisted sexual initiation more than men did, they also responded positively to initiation more often than men. When controlling for the number of initiations made, men and women did not differ in their likelihood of refusing initiation. Thus, contrary to the stereotype of women restricting sexual activity, "whether the man or the woman is the one who initiates sexual activity, his or her partner is likely to respond positively and is no more likely to respond negatively" (p. 227). Of course, the ratio of initiations to refusals within particular relationships probably varies considerably, and research could profitably examine how the ratio (rather than mere frequency) of initiations and refusals in relationships corresponds to sexual and relational satisfaction.

Byers and Heinlein (1989) found that positive responses to initiation were communicated nonverbally most of the time. Recipients of initiation messages generally communicated interest by beginning or continuing the sexual interaction. Refusals, however, tended to be communicated verbally. In general, direct verbal tactics are more effective for avoiding unwanted sex (Christopher & Frandsen, 1990; Murnen et al., 1989). In developed relationships (such as those studied by Byers & Heinlein, 1989), direct refusal is not as threatening to the relationship as it is perceived to be in undeveloped relationship. Directness seems to fulfill simultaneously the goals of averting unwanted persistence of initiation by the partner and of maintaining the face of the rejected individual by offering an account.

Byers and Heinlein (1989) found that, in most cases, the couple resolved negative responses to sexual initiation by agreeing not to have sex. In addition, the couple resolved disagreements about whether or not to have sex by arranging to have sex at another time or agreeing to disagree. At other times, reluctant individuals reported changing their minds because they were verbally convinced, got aroused, or decided to accommodate their partner. Individuals were more satisfied with the manner in which disagreements were resolved when the original initiations were made verbally. The authors inferred from this "that it is easier to either say 'No' or accept 'No' to a verbal request, than it is to say or accept 'No' to physical sexual advances" (p. 230).

Meanings for Sexual Behavior

Sexual behavior can produce rather divergent meanings for partners, even in highly developed relationships such as marriage and cohabitation. These meanings are a function of personal experience, relational history, relational culture, and sexual scripts. Gender roles also contribute to fundamental differences between partners in the meanings ascribed to shared sexual behavior. Men and women differ in a number of ways in their interpretations of sexual interaction and relationships. Metts and Cupach (1987) asked married individuals to depict the sexual aspect of their relationships. Women were more likely than men to mention the themes of comfort, responsiveness, specialness, and communication associated with the sexual component of the relationship. In contrast, men were more likely than women to identify themes of frequency and arousal. This may suggest that men view their sexual relationship in largely physical terms. Women, on the other hand, tend to see sexual fulfillment as more closely tied to overall relationship intimacy (e.g., Patton & Waring, 1985).

Hatfield, Sprecher, Pillemer, Greenberger, and Wexler (1988) similarly discovered gender differences in what men and women report they desire in a sexual relationship. In a study of both college students and married couples, Hatfield et al. found that men desired activities focusing on arousal aspects of sexual activity (such as variety and partner initiative) and that women desired sexual activities demonstrating love and intimacy. These findings seem to parallel the somewhat different motives men and women report for having sex. In a study of 50 marital couples, Brown and Auerback (1981) inquired about the primary reasons spouses had for initiating intercourse with their partner. They found that for men the release of sexual tension was the most common reason for initiating coitus, whereas for women "the most important reason was to receive love, intimacy, and holding" (p. 106). Brown and Auerback suggest that these patterns "support and perpetuate the cliche 'men give love to get sex, while women give sex to get love' " (p. 106).

Importantly, Sprague and Quadagno (1989) present evidence that age may moderate the association between gender and sexual motivation. In a survey of 179 adults aged 22 to 57, they found that the proportion of women endorsing a physical motive for intercourse increased with age and that the proportion of men endorsing this motive rose and then declined. Similarly, the proportion of women reporting a love motive for intercourse "changes with age from a strong majority to a minority" (p. 62). Thus, the authors conclude that, over time, gender differences in motives for intercourse may exhibit a reversal such that "people of older ages [cohorts over 35 years of age] may more resemble the literature's stereotypes of the sexual motivation patterns of the opposite gender than those associated with their own" (p. 72). This finding is consistent with biological differences over the life span, as well as diminished pressure from the sexual double standard in developed relationships.

These different interpretations of sex also seem to apply to sexual behavior of spouses outside of their marital relationships. For example, women are more likely than men to cite an extramarital affair as being a problem that contributed to the demise of their relationship (Cupach & Metts, 1986). Women also more frequently report that an extramarital affair is associated with a decrease in marital satisfaction; men often report that extramarital sex is instrumental in reducing boredom and tension, thereby enhancing their marital relationship (Glass & Wright, 1977). Thus, it would seem that women often see extramarital sex (whether their own or their husbands') as a direct threat to the marital relationship and as contradicting the meaning of a marital relationship. Men, on the other hand, seem inclined to interpret extramarital sex in personal or egotistical terms.

CONCLUSION

Good communication is fundamental to sexual competence in a diversity of interpersonal relationships ranging from cross-sex friendship to marriage. Through interaction, partners negotiate whether and under what circumstances to engage in sexual activity. Moreover, communication is integral to the alignment of meaning between partners for sexual behavior, and the implications of sexual involvement for the definition of the relationship.

In spite of the importance of communication, our understanding of its functioning in sexual episodes and relationships remains simplistic and limited. Additional conceptualization and research are needed to further our knowledge about how communication is used to manage sexuality in close relationships. For instance, although the focus in this chapter (and most extant research) has been exclusively on heterosexual relationships, it is clear that principles of sexual negotiation and interpretation are relevant to and should be explored in gay and lesbian relationships as well.

Research on sexual negotiation should also incorporate more sophisticated conceptualizations of sexual communication processes and outcomes. A common criterion for judging the quality of interaction within a relationship is the satisfaction with communication reported by participants (Hecht, 1978; Spitzberg & Cupach, 1984). Wheeless, Wheeless, and Baus (1984) suggest four general components of satisfaction with sexual communication: satisfaction with communication about sexual behavior, communication about which sexual behaviors are satisfying, satisfaction derived from what is communicated by certain sexual behaviors, and willingness to communicate about sex with one's partner. Future research might profitably consider how these and other dimensions of communication quality are achieved in sexually intimate relationships.

Research must also become more elaborate and clever in order to capture the complexity inherent in sexual negotiation. As we have tried to illustrate here, sexual interaction is not merely comprised of a single goal (i.e., the desire to have sex), translated into a simple initiation move, followed by either compliance or noncompliance. Rather, sexual negotiation is marked by multiple goals, held (but not necessarily shared) by both relational partners. These goals are pursued by multiple (often subtle) behaviors enacted in an interactive context and influenced by prior sexual episodes in the relationship as well as the broader relational culture. A more processual view of sexual negotiation episodes will advance beyond the study of single and simple strategies directed only at having or avoiding intercourse.

Finally, as our understanding of sexual negotiations becomes more complete, efforts should be directed at the application of knowledge to facilitate the communicative competence of individuals within relationships in which sexual activity is an issue. For example, sex therapy and enrichment programs often include a component designed to cultivate interpersonal communication skills (Chesney, Blakeney, Chan, & Cole, 1981; LoPiccolo & Miller, 1975; Maddock, 1977; Tullman, Gilner, Kolodny, Dornbush, & Tullman, 1981; Zilbergeld & Ellison, 1979). Similarly, programs should educate individuals regarding how to cope with sexual predicaments, such as avoiding unwanted sex or influencing a partner to practice safe sex. This will involve going beyond traditional sex education and beyond typical sex and marital therapy programs. It will require specific information about how to communicate one's sexual intentions in an effective yet appropriate manner. We must gain sufficient knowledge to help individuals develop a diverse repertoire of sexual negotiation behaviors. Individuals also need assistance in learning how to adapt their repertoires to the exigencies of sexual situations. Thus, the challenge of future research is twofold: to provide the necessary information for such training and to assess the effectiveness of programs designed to develop sexual communication competency.

REFERENCES

Abbey, A. (1982). Sex differences in attributions for friendly behavior: Do males misperceive females' friendliness? *Journal of Personality and Social Psychology, 42,* 830–838.

Abbey, A., & Melby, C. (1986). The effects of nonverbal cues on gender differences in perceptions of sexual intent. *Sex Roles, 15,* 283–298.

Adelman, M. B. (1988, November). *Sustaining passion: Eroticism and safe sex talk.* Paper presented at the Speech Communication Association convention, New Orleans, LA.

Adelman, M. B. (1989, November). *Play and incongruity: Framing safe-sex talk.* Paper presented at the Speech Communication Association convention, San Francisco, CA.

Banmen, J., & Vogel, N. A. (1985). The relationship between marital quality and interpersonal sexual communication. *Family Therapy, 12,* 45–58.

Baus, R. D. (1987, May). *Indicators of relationship satisfaction in sexually intimate relationships.* Paper presented at the Iowa Conference on Personal Relationships, Iowa City, IA.

Baxter, L. A. (1984). An investigation of compliance-gaining as politeness. *Human Communication Research, 10,* 427–456.

Baxter, L. A. (1987). Cognition and communication in the relationship process. In R. Burnett, P. McGhee, & D. Clarke (Eds.), *Accounting for relationships: Explanation, representation and knowledge* (pp. 192–212). London: Methuen.

Baxter, L. A., & Bullis, C. (1986). Turning points in developing romantic relationships. *Human Communication Research, 12,* 469–493.

Bell, R. A., Buerkel-Rothfuss, N. L., & Gore, K. E. (1987). "Did you bring the yarmulke for the cabbage patch kid?" The idiomatic communication of young lovers. *Human Communication Research, 14,* 47–67.

Bell, R. R. (1981). Friendships of men and women. *Psychology of Women Quarterly, 5,* 402–417.

Blumstein, P., & Schwartz, P. (1983). *American couples.* New York: Pocket Books.

Brown, M., & Auerback, A. (1981). Communication patterns in initiation of marital sex. *Medical Aspects of Human Sexuality, 15,* 105–117.

Byers, E. S. (1988). Effects of sexual arousal on men's and women's behavior in sexual disagreement situations. *Journal of Sex Research, 25,* 235–254.

Byers, E. S., & Heinlein, L. (1989). Predicting initiations and refusals of sexual activities in married and cohabiting heterosexual couples. *Journal of Sex Research, 26,* 210–231.

Chesney, A. P., Blakeney, P. E., Chan, F. A., & Cole, C. (1981). The impact of sex therapy on sexual behaviors and marital communication. *Journal of Sex and Marital Therapy, 7,* 70–79.

Chesney, A. P., Blakeney, P. E., Cole, C., & Chan, F. A. (1981). A comparison of couples who have sought sex therapy with couples who have not. *Journal of Sex and Marital Therapy, 7,* 131–140.

Christopher, F. S. (1988). An initial investigation into a continuum of premarital sexual pressure. *Journal of Sex Research, 25,* 255–266.

Christopher, F. S., & Frandsen, M. M. (1990). Strategies of influence in sex and dating. *Journal of Social and Personal Relationships, 7,* 89–105.

Cornog, M. (1986). Naming sexual body parts: Preliminary patterns and implications. *Journal of Sex Research, 22,* 393–398.

Craig, M. E., Kalichman, S. C., & Follingstad, D. R. (1989). Verbal coercive sexual behavior among college students. *Archives of Sexual Behavior, 18,* 421–434.

Cupach, W. R., & Comstock, J. (1990). Satisfaction with sexual communication in marriage: Links to sexual satisfaction and dyadic adjustment. *Journal of Social and Personal Relationships, 7,* 179–186.

Cupach, W. R., & Metts, S. (1986). Accounts of relational dissolution: A comparison of marital and non-marital relationships. *Communication Monographs, 53,* 311–334.

D'Augelli, A., & D'Augelli, J. F. (1985). The enhancement of sexual skills and competence: Promoting lifelong sexual unfolding. In L. L'Abate & M. A. Milan (Eds.), *Handbook of social skills training and research* (pp. 170–191). New York: Wiley.

Edgar, T., & Fitzpatrick, M. A. (1988). Compliance-gaining in relational interaction: When your life depends on it. *Southern Speech Communication Journal, 53,* 385–405.

Falbo, T., & Peplau, L. A. (1980). Power strategies in intimate relationships. *Journal of Personality and Social Psychology, 38,* 618–628.

Fay, A. (1977). Sexual problems related to poor communication. *Medical Aspects of Human Sexuality, 11,* 48–63.

Fowers, B. J., & Olson, D. H. (1989). ENRICH marital inventory: A discriminant validity and cross-validation assessment. *Journal of Marital and Family Therapy, 15,* 65–79.

Ginsburg, G. P. (1988). Rules, scripts and prototypes in personal relationships. In S. Duck (Ed.), *Handbook of personal relationships* (pp. 23–39). New York: Wiley.

Glass, S. P., & Wright, T. L. (1977). The relationship of extramarital sex, length of marriage, and sex differences on marital satisfaction and romanticism: Athanasiou's data reanalyzed. *Journal of Marriage and the Family, 39*, 691–703.

Hatfield, E., Sprecher, S., Pillemer, J. T., Greenberger, D., & Wexler, P. (1988). Gender differences in what is desired in the sexual relationship. *Journal of Psychology and Human Sexuality, 1*, 39–52.

Hays, R. B. (1988). Friendship. In S. W. Duck (Ed.), *Handbook of personal relationships* (pp. 391–408). London: Wiley.

Hecht, M. L. (1978). The conceptualization and measurement of interpersonal communication satisfaction. *Human Communication Research, 4*, 253–264.

Hinde, R. A. (1984). Why do the sexes behave differently in close relationships? *Journal of Social and Personal Relationships, 1*, 471–501.

Hudson, W. W., Harrison, D. F., & Crosscup, P. C. (1981). Short-form scale to measure sexual discord in dyadic relationships. *Journal of Sex Research, 17*, 157–174.

Jesser, C. J. (1978). Male responses to direct verbal sexual initiatives of females. *Journal of Sex Research, 14*, 118–128.

Knapp, M. L. (1984). *Interpersonal communication and human relationships*. Boston: Allyn & Bacon.

Koss, M., & Oros, C. (1982). Sexual experiences survey: A research instrument investigating sexual aggression and victimization. *Journal of Consulting and Clinical Psychology, 50*, 455–457.

LaPlante, M. N., McCormick, N., & Brannigan, G. G. (1980). Living the sexual script: College students' views of influence in sexual encounters. *Journal of Sex Research, 16*, 338–355.

Lewin, M. (1985). Unwanted intercourse: The difficulty of saying no. *Psychology of Women Quarterly, 9*, 184–192.

LoPiccolo, J., & Miller, V. H. (1975). A program for enhancing the sexual relationship of normal couples. *Counseling Psychologist, 5*, 41–45.

Maddock, J. W. (1977). Sexual health: An enrichment and treatment program. In D. H. Olson (Ed.), *Treating relationships* (pp. 355–381). Lake Mills, IA: Graphic.

Masters, W. H., Johnson, V. E., & Kolodny, R. (1986). *Sex and human loving*. Boston: Little, Brown.

McCormick, N. B. (1979). Come-ons and put-offs: Unmarried students' strategies for having and avoiding sexual intercourse. *Psychology of Women Quarterly, 4*, 194–211.

Metts, S., & Cupach, W. R. (1987, July). *Sexual themes and marital adjustment*. Paper presented at the Third International Conference on Social Psychology and Language, Bristol, England.

Metts, S., & Cupach, W. R. (1989). The role of communication in human sexuality. In K. McKinney & S. Sprecher (Eds.), *Human sexuality: The societal and interpersonal context* (pp. 139–161). Norwood, NJ: Ablex.

Metts, S., Cupach, W. R., & Imahori, T. (1989, November). *Perceptions of sexual compliance-resisting messages in three types of cross-sex relationships*. Paper presented at the Speech Communication Association convention, San Francisco.

Montgomery, B. M. (1987, May). *Sociable vs. sensual flirting: The influence of gender*. Paper presented at the International Communication Association convention, Montreal, Canada.

Moore, M. M. (1985). Nonverbal courtship patterns in women: Context and consequences. *Ethology and Sociobiology, 6*, 237–247.

Muehlenhard, C. L. (1988). "Nice women" don't say yes and "real men" don't say no: How miscommunication and the double standard can cause sexual problems. *Women and Therapy, 7*, 95–108.

Muehlenhard, C. L., & Hollabaugh, L. C. (1988). Do women sometimes say no when they mean yes? The prevalence and correlates of women's token resistance to sex. *Journal of Personality and Social Psychology, 54,* 872–879.

Muehlenhard, C. L., & Linton, M. (1987). Date rape and sexual aggression in dating situations: Incidence and risk factors. *Journal of Counseling Psychology, 34,* 186–196.

Murnen, S. K., Perot, A., & Byrne, D. (1989). Coping with unwanted sexual activity: Normative responses, situational determinants, and individual differences. *Journal of Sex Research, 26,* 85–106.

O'Brien, C. P. (1981). Commentary. *Medical Aspects of Human Sexuality, 15,* 117.

O'Meara, J. D. (1989). Cross-sex friendship: Four basic challenges of an ignored relationship. *Sex Roles, 21,* 525–543.

Patton, D., & Waring, E. M. (1985). Sex and marital intimacy. *Journal of Sex and Marital Therapy, 11,* 176–184.

Peplau, L. A., Rubin, Z., & Hill, C. T. (1977). Sexual intimacy in dating relationships. *Journal of Social Issues, 33,* 86–109.

Perlman, S. D., & Abramson, P. R. (1982). Sexual satisfaction among married and cohabiting individuals. *Journal of Consulting and Clinical Psychology, 50,* 458–460.

Perper, T., & Weis, D. L. (1987). Proceptive and rejective strategies of U.S. and Canadian college women. *Journal of Sex Research, 23,* 455–480.

Pillard, R. C., & Weinrich, J. D. (1987). The periodic table model of the gender transpositions: Part I. A theory based on masculinization and defeminization of the brain. *Journal of Sex Research, 23,* 425–454.

Planalp, S., Rutherford, D. K., & Honeycutt, J. M. (1988). Events that increase uncertainty in personal relationships II: Replication and extension. *Human Communication Research, 14,* 516–547.

Rawlins, W. K. (1982). Cross-sex friendship and the communicative management of sex-role expectations. *Communication Quarterly, 30,* 343–352.

Roche, J. P. (1986). Premarital sex: Attitudes and behavior by dating state. *Adolescence, 21,* 107–121.

Sanders, J. S. (1978). Male and female vocabularies for communicating with a sexual partner. *Journal of Sex Education and Therapy, 4,* 15–18.

Sanders, J. S., & Robinson, W. L. (1979). Talking and not talking about sex: Male and female vocabularies. *Journal of Communication, 29,* 22–30.

Sapadin, L. A. (1988). Friendship and gender: Perspectives of professional men and women. *Journal of Social and Personal Relationships, 5,* 387–404.

Sarver, J. M., & Murry, M. D. (1981). Knowledge of human sexuality among happily and unhappily married couples. *Journal of Sex Education and Therapy, 7,* 23–25.

Schenk, J., Pfrang, H., & Rausche, A. (1983). Personality traits versus the quality of the marital relationship as the determinant of marital sexuality. *Archives of Sexual Behavior, 12,* 31–42.

Shotland, R. L., & Craig, J. M. (1988). Can men and women differentiate between friendly and sexually interested behavior? *Social Psychology Quarterly, 51,* 66–73.

Simkins, L., & Rinck, C. (1982). Male and female sexual vocabulary in different interpersonal contexts. *Journal of Sex Research, 18,* 160–172.

Simon, W., & Gagnon, J. H. (1986). Sexual scripts: Permanence and change. *Archives of Sexual Behavior, 15,* 97–120.

Simon, W., & Gagnon, J. H. (1987). A sexual scripts approach. In J. H. Geer & W. O'Donohue (Eds.), *Theories of human sexuality* (pp. 363–383). New York: Plenum Press.

Snyder, D. K. (1979). Multidimensional assessment of marital satisfaction. *Journal of Marriage and the Family, 41,* 813–823.

Spitzberg, B. H., & Cupach, W. R. (1984). *Interpersonal communication competence.* Beverly Hills, CA: Sage.

Sprague, J., & Quadagno, D. (1989). Gender and sexual motivation: An exploration of two assumptions. *Journal of Psychology and Human Sexuality, 2,* 57–76.

Tullman, G. M., Gilner, F. H., Kolodny, R. C., Dornbush, R. L., & Tullman, G. D. (1981). The pre- and post-therapy measurement of communication skills of couples undergoing sex therapy at the Masters and Johnson Institute. *Archives of Sexual Behavior, 10,* 95–109.

Wells, J. W. (1989). Sexual language usage in different interpersonal contexts: A comparison of gender and sexual orientation. *Archives of Sexual Behavior, 18,* 127–143.

Wheeless, L. R., Wheeless, V. E., & Baus, R. (1984). Sexual communication, communication satisfaction, and solidarity in the developmental stages of intimate relationships. *Western Journal of Speech Communication, 48,* 217–230.

Wood, J. T. (1982). Communication and relational culture: Bases for the study of human relationships. *Communication Quarterly, 30,* 75–83.

Zilbergeld, B., & Ellison, C. R. (1979). Social skills training as an adjunct to sex therapy. *Journal of Sex and Marital Therapy, 5,* 340–350.

Zimmer, D. (1983). Interaction patterns and communication skills in sexually distressed, maritally distressed, and normal couples: Two experimental studies. *Journal of Sex and Marital Therapy, 9,* 251–265.

6 Factors Affecting Sexual Decisions in the Premarital Relationships of Adolescents and Young Adults[1]

F. Scott Christopher
Mark W. Roosa
Arizona State University

PREMARITAL SEXUAL DECISION MAKING

Premarital sexual activity has become a normative behavior for today's youth. Rates of sexual intercourse among young teens have increased dramatically, and high numbers of individuals are engaging in first coitus at early ages (Hofferth, Kahn, & Baldwin, 1987). For example, by the age of 14, 22.7% of female adolescents and 37.3% of male adolescents report that they have engaged in their first act of intercourse (Zelnik & Shah, 1983). Such early initiation into sexual involvement has correspondingly increased the number of coital partners sexually active youths have been involved with. One study of college-aged individuals found that males had averaged six partners and females averaged five partners over their dating history (DeLamater & MacCorquodale, 1979). These figures demonstrate that premarital sexual activity has become the norm for most adolescents and single young adults today.

Research into this activity has often focused on long-term negative outcomes such as teenage pregnancies, births, and abortions (Henshaw, 1987; Trussell, 1988). However, positive outcomes can also occur. Premarital sexual interaction is likely to take place in a close dating relationship where partners experience intimacy and commitment (DeLamater & MacCorquodale, 1979; Zelnik & Shah, 1983). Many of these close relationships make the transition to marriage, and theoreticians have speculated that interaction patterns established while dating

[1]The authors would like to thank Laura Owens and Mary Beardsley for their valued effort in helping with the library research for this project.

influence early marital interaction patterns (e.g. Levinger, 1983). Thus, premarital sexual activity has the potential of impacting a number of important life outcomes, and the importance of examining premarital sexual decision making is underscored.

Our review of the sexual decision-making (whether or not to become sexually active and variables influencing this decision) literature is made with two caveats. First, although theories of this phenomenon exist (cf. Libby & Carlson, 1973), these early models focused on decision making as a cognitive process and failed to acknowledge, other important influences. Recent research has revealed that not only cognitions but close relationships (DeLamater & MacCorquodale, 1979), affect (Christopher & Frandsen, 1990), peer sexual activity, and family relationships (Fisher, 1986a, 1986b) are related to premarital sexual decision making. Thus, we take a broad view of this construct throughout the review.

Second, past reviews have often failed to separate the findings of studies of early adolescents and young adults. We believe that the social contexts for the sexual activity of these two groups, as well as their developmental differences, are so divergent that it is important to treat research on these two populations as different, but related, literatures.

This review is organized along lines proposed by the Close Relationships Model (Kelley et al., 1983). This model posits that dyadic interactions, such as premarital sexual involvement, are influenced by different causal conditions. These conditions include the influences of relationship, social environment, physical environment, and individual factors. Causality within the model is bidirectional: Causal conditions influence dyadic interaction, and dyadic interaction influences causal conditions.

The match between the model and research in this area of study is imperfect. Research on premarital sexual decision making has focused only on how causal conditions have influenced premarital sexual activity. Furthermore, little work has been done on physical environment factors. Therefore, this chapter examines the variables that fit into the remaining three categories. The match is also imperfect in that, with only a few exceptions (cf. Peplau, Rubin, & Hill, 1977), the research has been cross sectional and correlational, which rules out tests of causal relations. We consequently use the model primarily as a way of organizing the variables that have been researched.

EARLY AND MIDDLE ADOLESCENT
SEXUAL DECISION MAKING

Most aspects of early adolescent sexual behavior are covert and, therefore, beyond the view of the general public. However, the most visible aspects of this behavior—such as the over 1 million pregnancies, almost .5 million births, and over 400,000 abortions to U.S. adolescents each year (Moore, 1989)—have increased the interest of researchers in teenage sexual behavior. Although much about this behavior remains to be explained, progress has been made in many areas.

It is quite clear that throughout most of this century there have been a continuing increase in the proportion of adolescents who are sexually active and a decline in the age at which adolescents initiate coital behavior (Hofferth et al., 1987; Moore, 1989; Zelnik & Shah, 1983). In general, coital rates are higher for males than females, and rates for blacks are higher than those for whites (Furstenberg, Morgan, Moore, & Peterson, 1987; Moore, 1989; Zelnik & Shah, 1983). In the sections that follow we review the literature on relational, social, and individual factors that seem to be involved in adolescents' decisions to become sexually active.

Relationship Factors in Sexual Decision Making

Interestingly, very few studies have examined the nature of dyadic relationships among early teenage dating couples as they relate to premarital sexual decision making. This deficiency is even more intriguing when we realize that most adolescent sexual behavior takes place within dating relationships, and that the age at which dating begins (Leigh, Weddle, & Loewen, 1988; Lewis, 1973; Miller, McCoy, & Olson, 1986) and the stage of dating (Miller, McCoy, & Olson, 1986; Zelnik & Shah, 1983) are related to the onset of premarital sexual behavior. Jorgensen, King, and Torrey (1980) provided the only insights into the nature of teens' decision making within ongoing dating relationships. In their study the quality of the interpersonal relationship was more consistently and strongly related to sexual behavior than other peer or family variables. They reported that relationship satisfaction was positively related to the frequency of sexual behavior and that female power in the relationship was negatively related to the frequency of intercourse. A study based on college students' recall found that those who initiated intercourse at age 16 or before had less committed relationships with their first sexual partner than did those who deferred intercourse (Faulkenberry, Vincent, James, & Johnson, 1987). It is unfortunate that these are the only studies to examine the nature of teenage dating relationships and their influence on sexual behavior.

Social Environment Influences on Sexual Decision Making

As the primary socialization agents of children, parents and families have received much attention for their impact on adolescent sexual decision making. A number of the family factors that have been studied are, at best, indirect influences on teenage sexual behavior. For instance, high parental education (Forste & Heaton, 1988; Leigh et al., 1988; Thornton & Camburn, 1987; Udry & Billy,

1987), high parental income (Leigh et al., 1988; Miller & Bingham, 1989), two-parent families (Forste & Heaton, 1988; Leigh et al., 1988; Miller & Bingham, 1989; Newcomer & Udry, 1987; Ostrov, Offer, Howard, Kaufman, & Meyer, 1985; Rawlins, 1984; Udry & Billy, 1987), and conservative parental attitudes toward premarital or extramarital sex (Baker, Thalberg, & Morrison, 1988; Jessor & Jessor, 1974; Moore, Peterson, & Furstenberg, 1986; Shelley, 1981) have been reported to be related to either more conservative teenage premarital sex attitudes and/or later onset of coitus. However, the use of such general variables without the benefit of a theory to explain why they have an influence may be troublesome.

For instance, although it is argued that two-parent families can better monitor a teens' behavior and provide more conservative models of sexual behavior than one-parent families (Miller & Olson, 1988; Newcomer & Udry, 1987; Thornton & Camburn, 1987), these arguments have not been adequately tested. In fact, daughters of nondating single mothers are no more likely to be sexually active at an early age than daughters in two-parent families, whereas daughters of dating single mothers are at high risk of becoming sexually active (Peterson, Moore, Furstenberg, & Morgan, 1985, as cited in Strouse & Fabes, 1987). Thus, parental modeling may be more important than parental monitoring. The finding of a curvilinear relationship between parental control and adolescent sexual behavior lends support to this argument (Miller, McCoy, Olson, & Wallace, 1986).

Similarly, conservative parental sexual attitudes may be indicative of the socialization children receive (Thornton & Camburn, 1987) as well as of the type of sexual behavior parents model for their children. However, these relationships are probably moderated by the quality of both parent-child communication (Fisher, 1986a) and the parent–child relationship; these more complex causal paths have received little attention. Similarly, high maternal education is related to more permissive parental sexual attitudes but reduced teenage sexual activity (Thornton & Camburn, 1987), a finding that contradicts studies that have looked at only bivariate relationships. Studies using longitudinal data show no relationship between maternal sex attitudes and daughters' sexual behavior (Newcomer & Udry, 1985, 1987). Apparently, more theory-driven research and the use of multivariate, longitudinal models are needed.

Although several studies have examined the effect of parent–child communication on teenage sexual behavior, there is little consensus on the nature of this relationship. Fox (1980) reported that early discussions of sexual behavior, higher quality mother–daughter discussions, and higher frequency of discussions were related to a reduced frequency of premarital sex. In contrast, parental discussion with males may lead to higher levels of sexual activity, especially if the parents hold very traditional values (Moore et al., 1986). Fisher (1986a) reported that high levels of parent–child communication are related to greater similarity of sex attitudes, especially in late adolescence and for females. However, the direction of these relationships may be confused; the frequency of parent–child discussions may increase after the suspected loss of virginity (Fox, 1980). Furthermore, Inazu and Fox (1980) reported that indirect forms of sexual socialization, such as socioemotional support or modeling nonmarital sexual behavior, are more influential than more direct forms, such as sexually oriented communication. However, longitudinal data do not support a relationship between parent–child communication and teenage sexual behavior (Newcomer & Udry, 1985). Perhaps the biggest problems these studies faced were measurement issues, such as who to use as a reporter—because there is little agreement between parents and adolescents (Fisher, 1986b; Miller, McCoy, Olson & Wallace, 1986; Newcomer & Udry, 1985)—and what aspects of communication to assess.

As children approach and enter adolescence, they tend to spend more time with peers and less time with parents. Given this normative shift in interpersonal relationships, peer group influences on sexual behaviors should increase relative to parental influence, which may be expected to remain fairly constant or to decline modestly. Unfortunately, research on adolescent sexual decision making has not adequately addressed this issue. In fact, most studies include either peer or family influences, not both. Among the few studies that have examined peer influences, most have looked at peer sexual attitudes or behavior as a source of influence. Apparently white, but not black, adolescents have friends with similar premarital sexual attitudes (Brown, 1985) and behaviors (Billy & Udry, 1985). Also, females, especially white females, whose sex attitudes are similar to those of their friends, or whose friends of both sexes are sexually active, are at high risk of becoming sexually active (Shah & Zelnik, 1981; Udry & Billy, 1987). However, when females' sex attitudes are similar to those of their mothers, they are less likely to become sexually active. Popularity with members of the opposite sex seems to be the only peer influence that increases the risk for males' becoming sexually active (Udry & Billy, 1987). Furthermore, longitudinal research by Billy, Landale, Grady, and Zimmerle (1988) suggests caution is needed when interpreting the causal direction of peer influences. They found that white teens chose sexually active friends *after* they had become sexually active themselves.

In addition to the lack of information on the relative influence of parents and peers on adolescents' sexual decision making, a serious measurement issue makes interpretation of most studies on peer influence troublesome at best. Only Udry and his colleagues (Billy & Udry, 1985; Udry & Billy, 1987) have obtained data from the peers themselves. Although this approach is more complex and costly, the degree of accuracy in adolescents' perceptions of their peers' attitudes and behaviors, and the potential self-serving biases in the reporting of these perceptions, raises questions about relying solely on the target adolescent for data.

Individual Factors in Sexual Decision Making

Biological factors.   The beginning of adolescence is marked by puberty, a time of internal and external physiological changes that prepare young humans for eventual reproduction. Many changes are readily apparent and signal that a person is approaching, or has reached, sexual maturity. Given the complex hormonal and physical changes that accompany puberty, it is surprising that little research exists on how these changes are related to the emerging sexuality of adolescents. Recent studies, primarily by Udry and his colleagues (Smith, Udry, & Morris, 1985; Udry, 1979; Udry & Billy, 1987; Udry, Billy, Morris, Grof, & Raj, 1985; Udry, Talbert, & Morris, 1986), have begun to show the potential for research in this area.

Using data from a panel study of white adolescent females and their mothers, Newcomer and Udry (1984) showed that the earlier menarche occurs, the longer the female is exposed to the risk of becoming sexually active, the more sexual opportunities she has, and the earlier she makes the transition to first intercourse. Furthermore, the timing of menarche is probably strongly influenced by genetics, so that positive correlations between mothers' and daughters' sexual histories may be due to the similarity in their timing of menarche. Similar findings regarding the onset of puberty and first intercourse have been reported in two other studies: a panel study of black and white females (Udry, 1979) and a study of black males and females (Zabin, Smith, Hirsch, & Hardy, 1986). Interestingly, in the second study over 10% of the females and over 40% of the males reported that first intercourse preceded the onset of puberty. In contrast, Leigh et al. (1988) failed to find a relationship between age of menarche and onset of coital behavior in a national cross-sectional study of black adolescents. The reason for this contradiction is not readily apparent.

Udry and his colleagues (Smith, Udry, & Morris, 1985; Udry & Billy, 1987; Udry, Billy, Morris, Groff, & Raj, 1985; Udry, Talbert, & Morris, 1986) argued that all sexual motivation in adolescents is determined by hormones, specifically androgens. Furthermore, according to these researchers hormones seem to be the prime determinant of adolescent male sexual behavior, and the mechanisms that drive female sexual behavior are more complex and include social factors. Given that most studies ignore biological influences, these results question the validity of most purely psychological or sociological models of teenage sexual behavior. At best, other studies use age as a proxy for adolescent development. However, it should be noted that purely biological models explain only 11%–24% of the variance in adolescent sexual behavior (Udry et al., 1986).

Biological factors have recently been suggested as a possible explanation of the differences in sexual activity between black and white adolescents. Social and economic factors are often used to explain differences in the age of coital initiation and rates of sexual activity between black and white adolescents. However, Furstenberg et al. (1987) reported that contextual factors, such as whether or not blacks attend integrated or segregated schools, may explain differences better than social class. Alternatively, Rushton and Bogaert (1988) suggested that genetic differences, not educational or social class differences, between whites and blacks may explain differences in sexual behaviors. They reported that, in behaviors such as speed of occurrence of premarital sex, the number of sex partners, and the rapidity of the menstrual cycle, college-educated whites showed more sexual restraint than non-college-educated whites and that both of these groups showed more restraint than college-educated blacks. Because Rushton and Bogaert's data were not free of social influences, additional research is needed to determine the reasons for differences in sexual behavior of black and white adolescents.

Personality factors.   Although a number of personality factors have been used in studies of adolescent premarital sexual behavior, few have received systematic attention, and few of the findings are stable or clearly interpretable. Two factors that have received considerable attention are religiosity and attitudes toward premarital sex. Several researchers reported that religious beliefs may influence the risk of premarital sexual behavior or the age of transition to sexual activity. High rates of church attendance or high religiosity (Brown, 1985; Fisher, 1986b; Forste & Heaton, 1988; Jessor, Costa, Jessor, & Donovan, 1983; Leigh et al., 1988; Miller & Bingham, 1989; Miller & Olson, 1988), being Catholic (Forste & Heaton, 1988), being Mormon (Miller & Bingham, 1989; Miller & Olson, 1988), or being a member of a conservative church (Leigh et al., 1988) have been related to more conservative attitudes toward sex, to lower rates of premarital coitus, and to later coital transition. Interestingly, the effects of religiosity as a social control mechanism seem to be greater for males than for females (Thornton & Camburn, 1987), perhaps because of the greater number of other social controls influencing females. Fisher (1986b) reported that the influence of religion on sexual permissiveness increases with age, suggesting that early coital transitions may need to be explained by other factors. Similarly, adhering to a strict moral code and having an intolerance of deviance, both of which are likely to be related to religiosity, have been shown to be related to later onset of sexual behavior (Jessor et al., 1983). The exact mechanisms by which religion influences sexual behavior are not known. Perhaps religious involvement or belief provides adolescents with clear sets of rules to follow, conservative models of sexual behavior, a rationale for saying no, or a way of avoiding opportunities for sexual behavior.

There also is evidence that attitudes toward premarital sex are related to sexual behavior (Miller & Olson, 1988; Thornton & Camburn, 1987). Miller and Olson (1988) have reported that attitudes toward premarital sex were the best predictors of premarital sexual behavior for teens and explained 25% of the variance in virginity status. However, the direction of causality is questionable. Billy et al. (1988) have found that becoming sexually active leads to the acquisition of more positive premarital sexual attitudes for black and white teens. Thus, attitudes may change to conform to current behavior (Thornton & Camburn, 1987). In fact, startling inconsistencies exist between adolescent sexual attitudes and behaviors. As many as 25% of premaritally sexually active teens reported that they believe premarital sex is wrong (Zabin, Hirsch, Smith, & Hardy, 1984). Further-more, 83% of sexually active teens in the same study reported that the best age for first intercourse was older than their personal experience. The relationship of sexual attitudes to sexual behavior for this developmental period is probably quite complex and requires further research.

Other factors such as locus of control and self-esteem also have been associ-ated with adolescent premarital sexual behavior (cf. Strouse & Fabes, 1987). However, research to date has produced inconsistent findings for both of these variables. The influence of such personality variables is likely complex and may interact with other variables such as gender, age, and attitudes. Certainly more research is needed before the role of personality variables in teenage premarital sexual decision making is understood.

Theories of Early Adolescent Sexual Behavior

Although there have been scores of studies about various aspects of early adoles-cent premarital sexual behavior, the vast majority have been theoretically barren (Miller & Fox, 1987; Strouse & Fabes, 1987). However, some researchers have attempted to synthesize this literature around theoretical perspectives (Miller & Fox, 1987) or to develop theories to explain adolescents' decisions to become premaritally sexually active (Smith, 1989; Smith & Udry 1985; Strouse & Fabes, 1987). Because of the need for theory to organize and inform this research, two theoretical models are described briefly.

Strouse and Fabes (1987) used social exchange theory to organize factors that increase or decrease the likelihood that an adolescent female will make the "transition to nonvirginity." These authors argued that becoming premaritally sexually active is not a rational, conscious, or deliberate decision-making pro-cess for most adolescents; rather, it is more spontaneous. However, research has identified several factors that push or pull adolescents toward or away from a condition of "transition proneness," the degree of risk that an adolescent will become a nonvirgin. Strouse and Fabes organized the variables in their model into five spheres of influence: (a) attractions within the family (the more attrac-tive the family situation, the less likely the child will become sexually active); (b) social control barriers (socialization factors such as religiosity, conservative sex-ual values); (c) alternative attractions (factors that increase the likelihood of the onset of coitus); (d) personal readiness (factors that may influence the degree of susceptibility to other push–pull factors); and (e) social milieu (cultural and ethnic factors). Unfortunately, it is not clear how these influences interact or combine to predict the state of "transition proneness." Strouse and Fabes (1987) offered a general proposition for the dynamic interaction of these factors:

> Given a particular social milieu, the degree of transitional proneness is determined by one's level of attractions within the family, relative to the level of perceived alternative attractions, mediated by endogenous propensities and personal read-iness, and inversely related to the level of social control barriers. (p. 345)

This model can be criticized for focusing exclusively on females and continuing a major bias in this field of research; equal attention should be given to developing models that explain the sexual behavior of males. Furthermore, there have been no empirical tests of this model to date.

More recently, Smith (1989) has espoused a biosocial model of adolescent sexual behavior that attempts to integrate biological, social, and cultural influences within a single model. According to this model, hormonal changes associated with puberty account for changes in both sexual drive and appearance that, in turn, influence the way others see the adolescent as a sexual being. Social influences, such as peers and media, shape adolescents' sexual attitudes. Cultural influences, such as parents, role models, partners, and religion, provide the adolescent with both behavioral norms and opportunities for sexual behavior. Cultural factors provide the milieu within which social factors operate and may determine which social factors are most influential. Thus, biological and social factors are useful for predicting the progression of both black and white adolescents along a continuum of sexual behavior, and cultural factors help explain why the continua of sexual behaviors are different for blacks and whites.

A study by Smith et al. (1985) illustrates the value of combining biological and social influences. Biological influences were assessed by asking questions about androgen development (e.g., body hair) of both males and females and questions about estrogen development (e.g., breast size) of females. Social influences were assessed using best friends' reports of sexual behavior. For males, these biological and social indicators accounted for less than 13% and 19%, respectively, of the variance in sexual activity, but in combination they accounted for almost 25%. For females, biological factors alone accounted for less than 14% of the variance in sexual behavior. However, a model that combined biological factors, friends' sexual behavior, and an interaction between androgen development and best friends' sexual behavior explained over 34% of the variance. Most importantly, best friends' sexual behavior had little relationship to an adolescent female's sexual behavior unless she was at a high level of androgen (pubertal) development. Thus, the effect of using both biological and social factors was not just additive, as it was in the case of males, but there was a significant interaction between these factors. This illustrates the level of complexity that must be included in our models in order to increase our understanding of adolescent sexual behavior and the benefit of including both biological and social factors in our models.

OLDER ADOLESCENTS AND YOUNG ADULTS

Two literatures have evolved that examine the correlates of the premarital sexual decision making of older adolescents and young adults. The first has focused on individuals who have chosen to be either sexually active or restrictive while dating. The second has concentrated on individuals who have experienced, or chose to use, sexual pressure and aggression while dating. We only address the first literature, as Muehlenhard, Goggins, Jones, and Sutterfield (this volume) cover the second.

Relationship Factors in Sexual Decision Making

One of the most consistent findings in this literature highlights the positive correlation between premarital relationship development and sexual involvement (Burgess & Wallin, 1953; Christopher & Cate, 1985; Ehrman, 1959; Kirkendall, 1961; Peplau, et al., 1977). Males and females, however, approach this dyadic involvement differently, and these differences set the context for later relationship development. It is therefore important to examine gender differences to more fully understand how relationship factors impact sexual decision making.

Gender differences.   Males and females hold different beliefs about how sexual involvement and dating should interact with each other. Males expect greater levels of sexual involvement with fewer dates when compared to females (Knox & Wilson, 1981). Women are more concerned with the emotional climate of the relationship and consider this climate in their sexual decision making (Roche, 1986). Understandably, males and females are aware of these gender differences (Knox & Wilson, 1981).

It is not surprising, then, that males feel more positive about engaging in coitus in casual dating relationships devoid of love and are more likely to seek coitus for pleasure. Women, on the other hand, more often require emotional involvement and commitment as prerequisites for engaging in intercourse (Carroll, Volk, & Hyde, 1985; Christopher & Cate, 1984). Yet relationship quality does enter into the decision making of males. They are more likely, however, to use an opportunity for sexual intercourse when love is not present; fewer women would be likely to engage in coitus under similar circumstances (Carroll et al., 1985).

Gender differences also exist in how a male and a female interpret nonverbal cues while interacting with each other. Laboratory studies have shown that males see a greater number of sexual cues in both friendly and sexually interested interactions than females, and they see more sexual cues than are actually presented (Abbey & Melby, 1986; Shotland & Craig, 1988). This suggests that males and females have different thresholds for interpreting sexual-intent cues from a member of the opposite sex (Shotland & Craig, 1988). Such differences can lay the groundwork for misperceptions about a dating partner's sexual desire. At least one study has shown that such misperceptions occur. However, contrary to the findings of laboratory studies, this investigation of monogamous dating couples failed to find gender differences; females were just as likely as males to misperceive their partners' sexual wishes (Frandsen, 1989).

Relationship properties.   Research has identified different dimensions of dating relationships that play a role in premarital sexual decision making. One characteristic that has demonstrated qualitative changes in its role over the past three decades is relationship commitment. Studies in the 1950s revealed that *if* a couple decided to engage in premarital intercourse, then it was most likely to happen after the couple became engaged (e.g., Burgess & Wallin, 1953). Later investigators made comparisons of data sets from the 1950s and 1960s, and from the 1960s and 1970s. They found that the incidence of premarital coitus at the going steady stage of dating had increased dramatically and that there were also smaller increases in those who engaged in coitus while casually dating (Bell & Chaskes, 1970; Sherwin & Corbett, 1985).

More recent work has been able to show that commitment plays a different role for different couples. Two research teams developed similar typologies that demonstrate how commitment is used differentially by dating couples (Christopher & Cate, 1985; Peplau et al., 1977). Both typologies acknowledge that some couples choose to engage in coitus with minimal levels of commitment. Peplau et al. (1977) labeled these couples *sexually liberated couples.* These individuals saw coitus with love as desirable, but sex without love as acceptable. Christopher and Cate (1985) described a similar type called *rapid involvement couples.* These individuals engaged in coitus on their first date and were influenced to engage in coitus by feelings of physical arousal. Similarly, Peplau et al. reported that their type focused more on eroticism than on emotional intimacy in their sexual decision making.

Both typologies also identified couples who chose to limit their sexual involvement by not engaging in sexual intercourse. Peplau et al. called these couples *sexually traditional couples,* and Christopher and Cate labeled them *low involvement couples.* These individuals saw love as an insufficient reason to justify engaging in premarital intercourse; the act of coitus was to be saved for marriage. Further, they held sexually conservative attitudes and had limited lifetime sexual experience. Peplau et al. reported that it was often the women who controlled the level of sexual involvement with this particular couple type.

The typologies diverged for the remaining couple types. Peplau et al. (1977) found that there was one additional type, *sexually moderate couples.* These individuals saw intercourse as permissible if the dyad was in love even if they did not have a long-term commitment. Christopher and Cate (1985), however, utilized an empirical approach to show that there were two additional types. *Gradual involvement couples* engaged in intercourse when they were considering becoming a couple. Although positive emotions affected their decision to engage in coitus, it appeared that they used their sexual interaction as part of their decision to move toward becoming a monogamous couple. Christopher and Cate's (1985) final type, *delayed involvement couples,* were very different from gradual involvement couples. These individuals experienced low levels of sexual activity during early dating stages. However, the advent of a monogamous dating commitment was a sexual watershed for these couples. Their sexual involvement became much more extensive and varied with this commitment. Thus, relationship commitment played an important role in their sexual decision making.

An additional relationship property that has been shown to have a major impact on sexual decision making is relationship intimacy. Early work by Ehrman (1959b) showed that love played a role in the sexual decisions of both males and females, a finding that was replicated almost two decades later (Peplau et al., 1977). More recently, Christopher and Cate (1984, 1988) found that loving, liking, and stating what a relationship means play a large role in individuals' decisions to engage in their first act of intercourse in a dating relationship, and that love is predictive of sexual involvement when couples are considering becoming a couple. Finally, DeLamater and MacCorquodale (1979) showed that the emotional intimacy of the relationship is the strongest predictor of how sexually intimate an individual is likely to be.

Relationship intimacy is not the only relationship dimension that influences sexual interaction. Equity between dating partners has been shown to be important. Couples who have equitable relationships experience higher levels of sexual involvement than couples whose inequitable relationships are characterized as either underbenefiting or overbenefiting. In addition, equitable couples engaged in intercourse because *both* dyadic partners wanted it, whereas inequitable couples indicated that the coital decision rested primarily in one dating partner (Walster, Walster, & Traupmann, 1978).

Relationship conflict is also related to sexual decision making. Christopher and Cate (1985) found that each of their couple types experienced high levels of conflict when they experienced or approached premarital intercourse. Also, conflict was a better predictor of sexual activity than love for first dates and casual dating (Christopher & Cate, 1988). The relationship between conflict and sexual activity was positive for both of these studies. However, these findings leave the question of causal direction in this relationship unanswered. Further, the scale used to measure conflict was a general measure of relationship conflict. The specific themes of such conflict are thus unknown.

Finally, relationship maintenance behaviors and ambivalence are related to sexual involvement during the early stages of dating (Christopher & Cate, 1988). Maintenance behaviors include self-disclosure and attending to one's partner's needs. It is easy to see why these behaviors are predictive of sexual involvement. Such actions foster emotional intimacy, which in itself aids in the development of sexual intimacy. The positive relationship between sexual intimacy and ambivalence is more surprising and suggests that questions about one's relationship future may be tested by engaging in precoital behaviors. It may also be that precoital behaviors may be used to extend the length of a relationship while ambivalence about future involvement is resolved (Christopher & Cate, 1988). The specifics of the causal relationship for both variables need to be investigated in future research.

Premarital sexual influence.   Individuals in dating relationships attempt to influence their dating partners' sexual decision making. Studies of these attempts began by identifying individual influence techniques and uncovered techniques that were used to increase coital chances, including physical persistence (Christopher, 1988), reward, coercion, and seduction (La Plante, McCormick, & Brannigan, 1980; McCormick, 1979), or to reject a partner's advances, including avoiding and ignoring cues (Perper & Weis, 1987).

An alternative approach focused not on individual sexual influence techniques, but on identifying a typology of strategies composed of related influence techniques. This approach has yielded four strategies (Christopher & Frandsen, 1990), two of which were dyadically oriented. The first focused on the use of emotional and physical closeness and was positively related to sexual involvement. The second highlighted the use of logic and reason and was used to limit sexual interaction. Further, it revealed ways in which sexual involvement is negotiated.

The two remaining strategies were positively related to each other and involved imposing one's sexual wishes on a partner. The first, antisocial acts, included both overt acts, such as the use of force, insults, and ridicule, and covert acts that attempted to make a partner feel guilty. The second, pressure and manipulation, involved planned pressure, persuasion, persistence, and dishonesty.

Social Environment Factors in Sexual Decision Making

Many early researchers examined the effects of social networks on young adults' sexual interactions. Often these investigators used reference group theory to guide their efforts. This theory posits that young adults' sexual interactions are influenced by the individuals they use as referents for identifying proper behavior. Researchers who used this approach established whether individuals perceived their primary reference group to be parents or peers (Lewis, 1973; Teevan, 1972; Walsh, Ferrell, & Tolone, 1976). When parents were used as a reference group, individuals were less sexually involved. However, if individuals were more peer oriented, and they perceived peers to be sexually active, they were also likely to be sexually active.

More recent research has reinforced and expanded these earlier findings. Studies have continued to show that perceived peer sexual activity has an impact on sexual involvement (Daugherty & Burger, 1984; DeLamater & MacCorquodale, 1979; Reed & Weinberg, 1984). However, gender differences may exist as to how peer networks affect sexual expression. Males, more than females, report that feelings of obligation and pressure play a salient role in their decision to first engage in sexual intercourse in a new relationship. Furthermore, this sense of pressure appears to originate, in part, because friends are seen as engaging in coitus (Christopher & Cate, 1984). Males have reported that they feel that their friends pressure them to engage in coitus and that they gain in social status by experiencing coitus and telling their friends about it (Carns, 1973; Muehlenhard & Cook, 1988). Females, however, are more restrictive in informing friends of their sexual activity (Carns, 1973). Thus, it appears that a modeling effect occurs when males and females perceive their friends' sexual expression. However, males are additionally motivated to engage in coitus by social network status gains.

More recent work on the impact of parents on sexual decision making has focused on the role of parent–child communication. Darling and Hicks (1982) found that male and female college students received different sexual messages from their parents, and these messages affected their offspring differently. Although parental messages about sex failed to affect the incidence of sexual intercourse for daughters, it had a direct and positive influence on sons. Other investigators have shown that engaging in intercourse for sons was negatively related to general *nonsexual* communication with both parents. In contrast, this same relationship held, but was weaker, for mothers and daughters, but not for fathers and daughters (Fisher, 1987).

Individual Factors in Sexual Decision Making

A major research effort has examined the role of individual factors in premarital sexual decision making for young adults. It has concentrated on personality factors and the influence of one's dating and sexual history.

Personality.   Several personality constructs have been linked to sexual expression. For instance, religiosity has consistently been shown to be negatively related to sexual activity (Mahoney, 1980; Reed & Weinberg, 1984). Those who frequently attend church are less likely to engage in premarital intercourse than those who rarely attend church. (DeLamater & MacCorquodale, 1979; Herold & Goodwin, 1981). Frequent churchgoers appear to hold moral or ethical objections to engaging in coitus outside of marriage.

Sexual guilt also has an inhibitive impact on sexual responsiveness and behavior (Mosher, 1966, 1973). Individuals who possess high levels of sex guilt have low sexual desire, responsiveness, and passion (Kutner, 1971) and are likely to think that engaging in premarital intercourse is morally wrong (Mosher & Cross, 1971). In addition, sex guilt is more likely to be experienced by virgins than nonvirgins (D'Augelli & Cross, 1975) and by individuals whose moral reasoning is bound by convention (Propper & Brown, 1986).

Not all individuals who experience sexual guilt restrict their sexual involvement (Lewis, Gibbons, & Gerrard, 1986). Some women have high levels of sex guilt but are also sexually active (Gerrard & Gibbons, 1982). These women seem to engage in sexual behaviors contrary to their personal standards, which creates cognitive dissonance. Furthermore, women who experience such dissonance may actively seek reasons for these inconsistencies in their lives. Such inconsistencies may result in their being more easily influenced by dating partners who offer convincing reasons for engaging in coitus, and becoming erratic in their use of contraceptives because they believe that coitus is unlikely to occur (Lewis et al., 1986).

Self-monitoring is another personality construct that has been linked to premarital sexual expression (Snyder, Simpson, & Gangestad, 1986). The construct of self-monitoring was developed to differentiate between people who base their behavior on social and interpersonal cues of situational appropriateness (high self-monitors) and people who act upon their own attitudes and dispositions (low self-monitors). High self-monitors have unrestricted orientations toward sexual relationships. Thus, high self-monitors, when compared to low self-monitors, endorse casual sex, have higher numbers of sexual partners, and experience more one-night stands (Snyder et al., 1986). Low self-monitors are more likely to adopt a committed dating style (Snyder & Simpson, 1984) and have a more limited sexual history (Snyder et al., 1986). (For more detail on personality factors, see Chapter 4).

Personal standards of premarital sexual conduct are also related to premarital sexual involvement (Carrol, 1988). However, different approaches have been used to examine this relationship. In his seminal work, Reiss (1960) suggested that four sexual standards are used to guide the decision to becoming sexually active: the double standard, permissiveness without affection, permissiveness with affection, and abstinence. Reiss (1967) demonstrated that these attitudes are reflective of premarital sexual expression.

Later work by D'Augelli and D'Augelli (1977) proposed an alternative typology that linked sexual behavior to sexual standards based on the moral and relationship reasoning behind different types of sexual decisions. Virgins were either inexperienced in sexual matters, adamant about retaining their virginal status, or potentially a nonvirgin given the correct characteristics in a dating partner who was yet to be found. Nonvirgins either engaged in coitus because of relationship commitment, were not as concerned with commitment as with reaching a mutual understanding with a coital partner, or were confused about the role of sexual involvement in their lives.

More recent work by Gfellner (1988) has offered yet a third typology, which focuses on an individual's understanding of sexual encounters. Individuals are classified as hedonistic, conventional, interpersonal, or interdependent based on how integrated and complex their conceptualizations of sexual interactions are. This typology, however, has received support by examining its relationship only to sexual attitudes rather than to sexual behavior.

These three personal standard typologies appear to share common qualities. Each hypothesizes that standards vary from being individually oriented to dyadically oriented, and that being dyadically oriented represents a higher level of moral reasoning than does being individually oriented. They further posit that personal standards have direct causal connections to sexual behavior. However, these authors have failed to test this hypothesis adequately. It is noteworthy that few multivariate tests exist of how personal standards are related to sexual expression relative to other salient variables. DeLamater and MacCorquodale (1979) are one exception. Their path analysis revealed that personal standards operated indirectly on sexual behavior through relationship intimacy and lifetime sexual behaviors, and that lifetime sexual behavior affected personal standards directly. Thus, although personal standards affect sexual decisions made in a relationship indirectly, past sexual experiences are likely to shape personal standards.

The influence of two sources of personal fear on coital decisions has also been investigated. The first of these is the fear of contracting a sexually transmitted disease (STD). It has often been hypothesized by practitioners that fear of STDs, and especially fear of Acquired Immune Deficiency Syndrome (AIDS), negatively impacts sexual expression. In fact, research findings do not support this hypothesis. Single dating individuals rank fear of STDs low in influencing their sexual decision making (Jedlicka & Robinson, 1987), and although there is concern about AIDS among dating individuals, fear of AIDS is unrelated to coital frequency. Furthermore, those who cite fear of AIDS as entering into their sexual decisions are infrequent daters who are not involved in a relationship and would normally have little opportunity to become sexually involved (Carrol, 1988).

The second source of fear, pregnancy, appears to play a larger role. It has been ranked as a salient restraint on intercourse by both single men and women (Jedlicka & Robinson, 1987). However, this finding must be viewed with caution. Other research has shown that availability and use of birth control do not enter into the decision to engage in first coitus in a new relationship (Christopher & Cate, 1984). Therefore, although this may constrain some individuals from engaging in coitus, more salient influences may outweigh this particular constraint.

Dating and sexual history. There are a number of life experiences that are positively related to premarital sexual expression for this age group. Early dating, dating often, having a large number of dating partners, and experiencing a large number of monogamous dating relationships in one's life have all been positively related to sexual involvement (Bell & Chaskes, 1970; Caroll, 1988; Herold & Goodwin, 1981; Lewis, 1973; Reed & Weinberg, 1984; Schulz, Bohrnstedt, Borgatta, & Evans, 1977). These variables are likely interrelated and triggered by early dating. Individuals who begin dating at a young age have greater opportunities to date frequently and to experience more monogamous relationships, and thus they have greater opportunities to engage in precoital and coital behaviors. It is therefore not surprising that these variables are positively related to being sexually involved.

Lifetime sexual behavior has also been shown to be an important predictor of current sexual involvement. Not surprisingly, being sexually active in the past has a substantial influence on the current sexual behavior of an individual (Caroll, 1988; DeLamater & MacCorquodale, 1979). Sexual experience may interact with gender in close relationships in which only one member is a virgin; these couples are more likely to experience intercourse when the nonvirgin is female as opposed to when the nonvirgin is male (Peplau et al., 1977).

Theories of Older Adolescent/Young Adult Sexual Involvement

Several theoreticians during the 1960s and 1970s developed premarital sexual involvement theories for single individuals. These theories have had different foci, including moral reasoning and personal sexual standards (D'Augelli & D'Augelli, 1977), sexual motivations based on affective change and hedonism (Hardy, 1964), social exchange (Libby & Carlson, 1973), and premarital sexual attitudes (Clayton, 1972; Reiss, 1960). With the exception of Reiss' work (1960, 1967), few researchers have attended to any of these theories in their investigations of premarital sexual interaction and decision making. Therefore, the validity of the theories is difficult to judge.

The investigations of Reiss' theory of sexual permissiveness also have limited value when considering sexual involvement. Although a number of Reiss' theoretical propositions and assumptions have been tested (cf. Heltsley & Broderick, 1969; Middendorp, Brinkman, & Koomen, 1970; Sprecher, McKinney, & Orbuch, 1987), Reiss' theory centers on attitudes rather than behaviors. This limits the theory's utility, as multivariate tests of the contribution of sexual attitudes to behavioral expression have revealed attitudes to be distal rather than proximal influences (cf. DeLamater & MacCorquodale, 1979). Further, this theory shares a weakness with the other theories in that it fails to acknowledge an array of important variables that have been shown to contribute to sexual involvement. Thus, there is a demonstrated need for a multivariate theory of premarital sexual decision making that will inspire investigators to test its propositions.

Future Directions

Theory and research focus. Despite the wealth of research on premarital sexuality, much remains to be done. The beginnings of theory development in the area of early adolescent sexuality should help to build stronger studies in the future. There is a corresponding need to develop more sophisticated and viable theories for the study of older adolescent and young adult sexual involvement. In addition, theoreticians in both areas need to recognize that researchers have uncovered a number of salient variables that demonstrate the contributions of relational, social, and individual influences. Past theoretical works in each area of study have failed to include critical variables from these causal domains.

For instance,' Udry and colleagues have illustrated the value of including biological factors in our studies of coital onset. One must also wonder if biological influences play a parallel role in the sexual lives of young adults. Unfortunately, early adolescent studies that have used biological factors (other than age) have generally used few of the social variables that have been identified as potentially influential factors in their models. Further, biological factors in older adolescent sexuality have not only been ignored, but have often been actively discounted (Hardy, 1964).

Other gaps in research and theory are equally apparent. Only a few studies of the onset of coital behavior have focused on what may be some of the most critical factors in this behavior: relationship factors. Although there seems to be agreement that early and middle adolescent sexual behavior generally occur within a dating relationship, only Jorgensen et al. (1980) have actually attempted to study these factors. It is interesting that so much attention has been given to other close relationships (e.g., parents, peers, best friends) that may influence early sexual decision making, and that the impact of the relationship most directly related to sexual activity has been ignored. Further, length of dating and dating stage do not provide suitable proxies for the dynamics of the dyadic relationship in which the negotiation of sexual activity takes place. Such variables do not recognize or represent the complexity of the process whereby the values, motivations, and family and peer influences of two individuals are combined into a single decision or act. It is arguable that only by understanding these relationships better can we ever hope to develop theoretical models with high levels of predictability. Certainly it is a major oversight that so little attention has been paid to these most critical of close interpersonal relationships in the lives of early adolescents.

Finally, it is also necessary to investigate the interrelationship of premarital sexual involvement with additional close relationship properties besides intimacy and commitment. Dating relationships involve a number of dyadic experiences, and as our understanding of premarital relationship dimensions increases, there is a corresponding need to investigate how these properties are related to premarital sexuality at both early and later stages of individual development. Perhaps this question is especially relevant when one considers that sexual involvement follows a patterned progression of behaviors (cf. DeLamater & MacCorquodale, 1979). Is this pattern linked to concurrent patterns of verbal and nonverbal dyadic communication, affect changes, and interpersonal attributions? And are these not additionally linked to decisions made before and/or during actual sexual interaction?

In any event, this literature review has established that the state of both research and theory development should preclude further studies with simplistic models that try to explain premarital sexual behavior with one or two variables. Multivariate models are needed to tease apart the complex additive and interactive influences that have been shown to play a role during both early and later sexual expression. Such models need to attend carefully to the role and interplay of relational, social, and individual factors.

Methodological issues. Methodological improvements are needed in a number of areas before research on premarital sexuality can make major advancements. These include the development, acceptance, and use of standard measurements of such variables as sexual attitudes, behaviors, pressure, and aggression. Because of the current plethora of measurement instruments, it is difficult, and perhaps risky, to compare studies. Research on premarital sexual behavior and decision making would also benefit greatly from more longitudinal studies. The transition to sexual activity is clearly a developmental event. However, the overwhelming majority of studies on this topic are cross sectional. The use of a developmental perspective in this area would increase our confidence in the variables identified as related to events such as the onset of coital behavior. It would also help our understanding of how early sexual and relational experiences are related to later sexual expression and dating-relationship development.

Finally, with a limited number of exceptions, our knowledge of older adolescents' and young adults' sexuality is severely biased by the overuse of college samples. Such samples tend to be composed of white, educated, and middle- and upper-class youths. When sexual expression occurs in a college milieu, it is relatively easy to make romantic contacts. This environment may effect such important influences on sexual expression as perceived peer behavior and social pressures felt by males. Although some work has suggested that students and nonstudents are more similar than dissimilar (DeLamater & MacCorquodale, 1979), additional investigations are necessary to ensure that the conclusions of past research are applicable to the broader population.

REFERENCES

Abbey, A., & Melby, C. (1986). The effects of nonverbal cues on gender differences in perceptions of sexual intent. *Sex Roles, 15,* 283–298.

Baker, S. A., Thalberg, S. P., & Morrison, D. M. (1988). Parents' behavioral norms as predictors of adolescent sexual activity and contraceptive use. *Adolescence, 23,* 265–282.

Bell, R. R., & Chaskes, J. B. (1970). Premarital sexual experience among coeds, 1958 and 1968. *Journal of Marriage and the Family, 32,* 81–84.

Billy, J. O. G., Landale, N. S., Grady, W. R., & Zimmerle, D. M., (1988). Effects of sexual activity on adolescent social and psychological development. *Social Psychology Quarterly, 51,* 190–212.

Billy, J. O. G., & Udry, J. R. (1985). Patterns of adolescent friendship and effects on sexual behavior. *Social Psychology Quarterly, 48,* 27–41.

Brown, S. V. (1985). Premarital sexual permissiveness among black adolescent females. *Social Psychology Quarterly, 48,* 381–387.

Burgess, E. W., & Wallin, P. (1953). *Engagement and marriage.* Philadelphia: Lippincott.

Carns, D. (1973). Talking about sex: Notes on first coitus and the double standard. *Journal of Marriage and the Family, 35,* 677–687.

Carroll, J. L., Volk, D. K., & Hyde, S. J. (1985). Differences between males and females in motives for engaging in sexual intercourse. *Archives of Sexual Behavior, 14,* 131–139.

Carroll, L. (1988). Concern with AIDS and the sexual behavior of college students. *Journal of Marriage and the Family, 50,* 405–411.

Christopher, F. S. (1988). An initial investigation into a continuum of premarital sexual pressure. *Journal of Sex Research, 25,* 255–266.

Christopher, F. S., & Cate, R. M. (1984). Factors involved in premarital sexual decision-making. *Journal of Sex Research, 20,* 363–376.

Christopher, F. S., & Cate, R. M. (1985). Premarital sexual pathways and relationship development. *Journal of Social and Personal Relationships, 2,* 271–288.

Christopher, F. S., & Cate, R. M. (1988). Premarital sexual involvement: A developmental investigation of relational correlates. *Adolescence, 23,* 793–803.

Christopher, F. S., & Frandsen, M. M. (1990). Strategies of influence in sex and dating. *Journal of Social and Personal Relationships, 7,* 89–106.

Clayton, R. (1972). Premarital sexual intercourse: A substantive test of the contingent consistency model. *Journal of Marriage and the Family, 34,* 273–279.

Darling, C. A., & Hicks, M. W. (1982). Parental influences on adolescent sexuality: Implications for parents as educators. *Journal of Youth and Adolescence, 11,* 231–245.

D'Augelli, J. F., & Cross, H. L. (1975). Relationship of sex guilt and moral reasoning to premarital sex in college women and in couples. *Journal of Consulting and Clinical Psychology, 43,* 40–47.

D'Augelli, J. F., & D'Augelli, A. R. (1977). Moral reasoning and premarital sexual behavior: Toward reasoning about relationships. *Journal of Social Issues,* 46–66.

Daugherty, L. R., & Burger, J. M. (1984). The influence of parents, church, and peers on the sexual attitudes and behaviors of college students. *Archives of Sexual Behavior, 13,* 351–359.

DeLamater, J. D., & MacCorquodale, P. (1979). *Premarital sexuality: Attitudes, relationships, behavior.* Madison: University of Wisconsin Press.

Ehrman, W. (1959a). *Premarital dating behavior.* New York: Henry Holt & Company.

Ehrman, W. (1959b). Premarital sexual behavior and sex codes of conduct with acquaintances, friends, and lovers. *Social Forces, 38,* 158–164.

Faulkenberry, J. R., Vincent, M., James, A., & Johnson, W. (1987). Coital behaviors, attitudes, and knowledge of students who experience early coitus. *Adolescence, 22,* 321–332.

Fisher, T. D. (1986a). An exploratory study of parent-child communication about sex and the sexual attitudes of early, middle, and late adolescents. *Journal of Genetic Psychology, 147,* 543–557.

Fisher, T. D. (1986b). Parent–child communication about sex and young adolescents' sexual knowledge and attitudes. *Adolescence, 21,* 517–527.

Fisher, T. D. (1987). Family communication and the sexual behavior and attitudes of college students. *Journal of Youth and Adolescence, 16,* 481–495.

Forste, R. T., & Heaton, T. B. (1988). Initiation of sexual activity among female adolescents. *Youth and Society, 19,* 250–268.

Fox, G. L. (1980). The mother–adolescent daughter relationship as a sexual socialization structure: A research review. *Family Relations, 29,* 21–28.

Frandsen, M. M. (1989). *Attributional processes in premarital sexual interaction.* Unpublished master's thesis, Arizona State University, Tempe.

Furstenberg, F. F., Jr., Morgan, S. P., Moore, K. A., & Peterson, J. L. (1987). Race differences in the timing of adolescent intercourse. *American Sociological Review, 52,* 511–518.

Gerrard, M., & Gibbons, F. X. (1982). Sexual experience, sex guilt, and sexual moral reasoning. *Journal of Personality, 50,* 345–359.

Gfellner, B. M. (1988). Relations between sexual attitudes, gender, and sexual behavior concepts of older adolescents. *Journal of Adolescent Research, 3,* 305–316.

Hardy, K. R. (1964). An appetitional theory of sexual motivation. *Psychological Review, 71,* 1–18.

Heltsley, M. E., & Broderick, C. B. (1969). Religiosity and premarital sexual permissiveness: Reexamination of Reiss's traditionalism proposition. *Journal of Marriage and the Family, 31,* 441–443.

Henshaw, S. K. (1987). Characteristics of U.S. women having abortions, 1982–1983. *Family Planning Perspectives, 19,* 5–8.

Herold, E. S., & Goodwin, M. S. (1981). Adamant virgins, potential nonvirgins, and nonvirgins. *Journal of Sex Research, 17,* 97–113.

Hofferth, S. L., Kahn, J. R., & Baldwin, W. (1987). Premarital sexual activity among U.S. teenage women over the past three decades. *Family Planning Perspectives, 19,* 46–53.

Inazu, J. K., & Fox, F. L. (1980). Maternal influence on the sexual behavior of teenage daughters. *Journal of Family Issues, 1,* 81–102.

Jedlicka, D., & Robinson, I. E. (1987). Fear of venereal disease and other perceived restraints on the occurrence of premarital coitus. *Journal of Sex Research, 23,* 391–396.

Jessor, R., Costa, F., Jessor, L., & Donovan, J. E. (1983). Time of first intercourse: A prospective study. *Journal of Personality and Social Psychology, 44,* 608–626.

Jessor, S. L., & Jessor, R. (1974). Maternal ideology and adolescent problem behavior. *Developmental Psychology, 10,* 246–254.

Jorgensen, S. R., King, S. L., & Torrey, B. A. (1980). Dyadic and social network influences on adolescent exposure to pregnancy risk. *Journal of Marriage and the Family, 42*(1), 141–155.

Kelley, H., Berscheid, E., Christensen, A., Harvey, J., Huston, T., Levinger, G., McClintock, E., Peplau, L., & Peterson, D. (1983). Analyzing close relationships. In H. Kelley, E. Berscheid, A. Christensen, J. Harvey, T. Huston, G. Levinger, E. McClintock, L. Peplau, & D. Peterson (Eds.), *Close relationships* (pp. 20–67). New York: Freeman Press.

Kirkendall, L. A. (1961). *Premarital intercourse and interpersonal relationships.* New York: Gramercy Publishing Company.

Knox, D., & Wilson, K. (1981). Dating behaviors of university students. *Family Relations, 30,* 255–258.

Kutner, S. J. (1971). Sex guilt and sex behavior sequence. *Journal of Sex Research, 7,*107–115.

La Plante, M. N., McCormick, N., & Brannigan, G. (1980). Living the sexual script: College students' views of influence in sexual encounters. *Journal of Sex Research, 16,* 338–355.

Leigh, G. K., Weddle, K. D., & Loewen, I. R. (1988). Analysis of the timing of transition to sexual intercourse for black adolescent females. *Journal of Adolescent Research, 3,* 333–344.

Levinger, G. (1983). Development and change. In H. Kelley, E. Berscheid, A. Christensen, J. Harvey, T. Huston, G. Levinger, E. McClintock, L. Peplau, & D. Peterson (Eds.), *Close relationships* (pp. 315–359) New York: Freeman Press.

Lewis, R. A. (1973). Parents and peers: Socialization agents in the coital behavior of young adults. *Journal of Sex Research, 9,* 156–170.

Lewis, R. J., Gibbons, F. X., & Gerrard, M. (1986). Sexual experience and recall of sexual vs. nonsexual information. *Journal of Personality, 54,* 676–693.

Libby, R. W., & Carlson, J. E. (1973). A theoretical framework for premarital sexual decisions in the dyad. *Archives of Sexual Behavior, 2,* 365–378.

Mahoney, E. R. (1980). Religiosity and sexual behavior among heterosexual college students. *Journal of Marriage and the Family, 16,* 97–113.

McCormick, N. B. (1979). Come-ons and put-offs: Unmarried students' strategies for having and avoiding sexual intercourse. *Psychology of Women Quarterly, 42,* 194–211.

Middendorp, C. P., Brinkman, W., & Koomen, W. (1970). Determinants of premarital sexual permissiveness: A secondary analysis. *Journal of Marriage and the Family, 32,* 369–378.

Miller, B. C., & Bingham, C. R. (1989). Family configuration in relation to the sexual behavior of female adolescents. *Journal of Marriage and the Family, 51,* 499–506.

Miller, B. C., & Fox, G. L. (1987). Theories of adolescent heterosexual behavior. *Journal of Adolescent Research, 2,* 269–282.

Miller, B. C., McCoy, J. K., & Olson, T. D. (1986). Dating age and stage as correlates of adolescent sexual attitudes and behavior. *Journal of Adolescent Research, 1,* 361–371.

Miller, B. C., McCoy, J. K., Olson, T. D., & Wallace, C. M. (1986). Parental discipline and control attempts in relation to adolescent sexual attitudes and behavior. *Journal of Marriage and the Family, 48,* 503–512.

Miller, B. C., & Olson, T. D. (1988). Sexual attitudes and behavior of high school students in relation to background and contextual factors. *Journal of Sex Research, 24,* 194–200.

Moore, K. A. (1989). *Facts at a glance 1989.* Annual fact sheet, Child Trends, Inc., Washington, DC.

Moore, K. A., Peterson, J. L., & Furstenberg, F. F. (1986). Parental attitudes and the occurrence of early sexual activity. *Journal of Marriage and the Family, 48,* 777–782.

Mosher, D. L. (1966). The development and multitrait-multimethod matrix analysis of three measures of three aspects of guilt. *Journal of Consulting and Clinical Psychology, 30,* 25–29.

Mosher, D. L. (1973). Sex differences, sex experiences, sex guilt, and explicitly sexual films. *Journal of Social Issues, 29,* 95–112.

Mosher, D. L., & Cross, H. J. (1971). Sex guilt and premarital sexual experiences of college students. *Journal of Consulting and Clinical Psychology, 36,* 27–32.

Muehlenhard, C. L., & Cook, S. W. (1988). Men's self-report of unwanted sexual activity. *Journal of Sex Research, 24,* 58–72.

Newcomer, J. F., & Udry, J. R. (1984). Mothers' influence on the sexual behavior of their teenage children. *Journal of Marriage and the Family, 46,* 477–485.

Newcomer, S. F., & Udry, J. R. (1985). Parent-child communication and adolescent sexual behavior. *Family Planning Perspectives, 17*(4), 169–174

Newcomer, S. F., & Udry, J. R. (1987). Parental marital status effects on adolescent sexual behavior. *Journal of Marriage and the Family, 49,* 235–240.

Ostrov, E., Offer, D., Howard, K. I., Kaufman, B., & Meyer, H. (1985). Adolescent sexual behavior. *Medical Aspects of Human Sexuality, 19,* 28–36.

Peplau, L., A., Rubin, Z., & Hill, C. T. (1977). Sexual intimacy in dating relationships. *Journal of Social Issues, 33,* 86–109.

Perper, T., & Weis, D. L. (1987). Proceptive and rejective strategies of U.S. and Canadian college women. *Journal of Sex Research, 23,* 455–480.

Propper, S., & Brown, R. A. (1986). Moral reasoning, parental sex attitudes, & sex guilt in female college students. *Archives of Sexual Behavior, 15,* 331–340.

Rawlins, J. M. (1984). Parent-daughter interaction and teenage pregnancy in Jamaica. *Journal of Comparative Family Studies, 15,* 131–138.

Reed, D., & Weinberg. M.S. (1984). Premarital coitus: Developing and establishing sexual scripts. *Social Psychology Quarterly, 47,* 129–138.

Reiss, I. L. (1960). *Premarital sexual standards in America.* Glencoe, Free Press.

Reiss, I. L. (1967). *The social context of premarital sexual permissiveness.* New York: Holt, Rinehart & Winston.

Roche, J. P. (1986). Premarital sex: Attitudes and behavior by dating stage. *Adolescence, 21,* 107–121.

Rushton, J. P., & Bogaert, A. F. (1980). Race vs. social class differences in sexual behavior: A follow-up test of the r/k dimension. *Journal of Research in Personality, 22,* 259–272.

Schulz, B., Bohrnstedt, G. W., Borgatta, E. F., & Evans, R. R. (1977). Explaining premarital sexual intercourse among college students: A casual model. *Social Forces, 56,* 148–165.

Shah, F. & Zelnik, M. (1981). Parent and peer influence on sexual behavior, contraceptive use, and pregnancy experiences of young women. *Journal of Marriage and the Family, 43,* 339–348.

Shelley, S. I. (1981). Adolescent attitudes as related to perception of parents and sex education. *Journal of Sex Research, 17,* 350–367.

Sherwin, R., & Corbett, S. (1985). Campus sexual norms and dating relationships: A trend analysis. *Journal of Sex Research, 21,* 258–274.

Shotland, R. L., & Craig, J. M. (1988). Can men and women differentiate between friendly and sexually interested behavior? *Social Psychology Quarterly, 51,* 66–73.

Smith, E. A. (1989). A biosocial model of adolescent sexuality behavior. In G. R. Adams, R. Montemayor & T. P. Gullotta (Eds). *Biology of adolescent behavior and development* (pp. 143–167). Newbury Park, CA: Sage.

Smith, E. A., & Udry, J. R. (1985). Coital and non-coital sexual behavior of white and black adolescents. *American Journal of Public Health, 75,* 1200–1203.

Smith, E. A., Udry, J. R., & Morris, N. M. (1985). Pubertal development and friends: A biosocial explanation of adolescent sexual behavior. *Journal of Health and Social Behavior, 26,* 183–192.

Snyder, M., & Simpson, J. A. (1984). Self-monitoring and dating relationships. *Journal of Personality and Social Psychology, 47,* 1281–1291.

Snyder, M. Simpson, J. A., & Gangestad, S. (1986). Personality and sexual relations. *Journal of Personality and Social Psychology, 51,* 181–190.

Sprecher, S., McKinney, K., & Orbuch, T. (1987). Has the double standard disappeared? An experimental test. *Social Psychology Quarterly, 50,* 24–31.

Strouse, J. S., & Fabes, R. A. (1987). A conceptualization of transition to nonvirginity in adolescent females. *Journal of Adolescent Research, 2,* 331–348.

Teevan, J. (1972). Reference groups and premarital sexual behavior. *Journal of Marriage and the Family, 34,* 283–291.

Thornton, A., & Camburn, D. (1987). The influences of the family on premarital sexual attitudes and behavior. *Demography, 24,* 323–340.

Trussell, J. (1988). Teenage pregnancy in the United States. *Family Planning Perspectives, 20,* 262–272.

Udry, J. R. (1979). Age at menarche, at first intercourse, and at first pregnancy. *Journal of Biosocial Science, 11,* 433–441.

Udry, J. R., & Billy, J. O. G. (1987). Initiation of coitus in early adolescence. *American Sociological Review, 52,* 841–855.

Udry, J. R., Billy, J. O. G., Morris, N. M., Groff, T. R., & Raj, M. H. (1985). Serum androgenic hormones motivate sexual behavior in adolescent boys. *Fertility and Sterility, 43,* 90–94.

Udry, J. R., Talbert, L. M., & Morris, N. M. (1986). Biosocial foundations for adolescent female sexuality. *Demography, 23,* 217–227.

Walsh, R. H., Ferrell, M. Z., & Tolone, W. L. (1976). Selection of reference group, perceived reference group permissiveness, and personal permissiveness attitudes and behavior: A study of two consecutive panels (1967–1971; 1970–1974). *Journal of Marriage and the Family, 38,* 495–508.

Walster, E., Walster, G. W., & Traupmann, J. (1978). Equity and premarital sex. *Journal of Personality and Social Psychology, 36,* 82–92.

Zabin, L. S., Hirsch, M. B., Smith, E. A., & Hardy, J. B. (1984). Adolescent sexual attitudes and behavior: Are they consistent? *Family Planning Perspectives, 16*(4), 181–185.

Zabin, L. S., Smith, E. A., Hirsch, M. B., & Hardy, J. B. (1986). Ages of physical maturation and first intercourse in black teenage males and females. *Demography, 23,* 595–605.

Zelnik, M., & Shah, F. K. (1983). First intercourse among young Americans. *Family Planning Perspectives, 15,* 64–72.

7 Extradyadic Relationships and Sexual Jealousy

Robert G. Bringle
Purdue University

Bram P. Buunk
University of Groninjen

Each human relationship encompasses some degree of specialness, exclusivity, and a definition of boundaries. This is particularly true for sexual relationships. Although there is no necessary association between sexual intimacy and sexual exclusivity, most individuals expect and prefer their concurrence. In general, there can be little doubt that extradyadic sexual relationships constitute a serious violation of one of the basic assumptions of a committed intimate relationship. Terms such as *cheating, infidelity,* and *unfaithfulness* reflect the normative transgression that a sexual relationship with a third person usually implies. Such a transgression by one's partner, or even the thought that such a transgression *might* occur, may evoke jealousy in varying degrees. Jealousy, then, is any aversive emotional reaction that occurs as the result of a partner's extradyadic relationship that is real, imagined, or considered likely to occur (Bringle & Buunk, 1985, p. 242).

For centuries, jealousy has been acknowledged as one of the most prevalent and potentially destructive experiences in love relationships. Despite the risk of evoking jealousy, there is a substantial number of people who, for various reasons and under a wide variety of circumstances, become involved in jealousy-evoking extradyadic relationships. These may include relationships that arise out of a desire to test one's market value while dating, temporary secretive affairs and flings, extramarital relationships that are mutually agreed upon, and mate swapping. All such relationships will be referred to here as *extradyadic relationships*. *Affairs* are a subset of extradyadic relationships and refer to sexual relationships that occur outside a committed intimate relationship without the consent of the partner.

In this chapter we first discuss the nature of various forms of jealousy. This is a major issue with respect to all forms of extradyadic sexual behavior, and the different types of jealousy are relevant to problems facing many intimate relationships in general. We then discuss the attitudes toward extradyadic sexual relationships, the process of becoming involved in such relationships, various forms of extradyadic involvement, and the consequences of extradyadic sexual involvement. Last, two nontraditional arrangements for allowing extradyadic relationships, sexually open marriages and swinging, are discussed.

JEALOUSY AND EXTRADYADIC RELATIONSHIPS

There are numerous relationships that exist in addition to the primary romantic relationship: There are collateral relationships with friends, co-workers, neighbors, and family members. However, only a few of these extradyadic relationships will evoke jealousy in the partners of the primary romantic relationship. What is it that causes most of these extradyadic relationships to be viewed as benign, but some of them as jealousy evoking? First, jealousy will be evoked particularly when the collateral relationship touches upon areas of the primary relationship that are considered unique and special. As Bryson (1977) pointed out, one would not be jealous of a lover's friend, nor of a friend's lover, but one would be jealous of a lover's lover. Nevertheless, a lover's involvement with friends, hobbies, work, or family can be a cause of jealousy, albeit such circumstances typically produce much less intense reactions than a lover's lover (e.g., see Hansen, 1982).

However, jealousy is particularly likely to arise when the extradyadic relationship has an actual or potential *sexual* content, as the sexual realm is very sensitive to insecurity and competition. Even in the absence of actual extradyadic sexual behavior by the partner, its conceivability haunts each person to some degree. Even an imaginary sexual attraction (e.g., sexual fantasies) may evoke more jealousy than an actual close, but nonsexual, relationship with a third person. Nevertheless, extradyadic sexual behavior will generate the most jealousy when it is perceived to threaten the very *existence* of the primary relationship. The prototypic case occurs when the partner falls in love with someone else and establishes a covert, long-term, emotionally involving extradyadic sexual relationship. In such a case, the threat that the partner will end the primary relationship becomes very real. In general, the common thread among events that precipitate intense jealousy is that they have some sexual connotations and that they are appraised as potentially reducing unique relationship outcomes. When the loss affects numerous areas encompassed by the relationship, when the areas are viewed as being special or irreplaceable, and when the effects are both immediate and have long-term implications, then the emotional reactions will be proportionately more extreme.

Suspicious Jealousy

As relationships develop, persons become sensitive to the potential for loss. Ironically, this may be more salient in relationships when stability is not firmly established than it is later in relationships when passion is blunted and commitment is well entrenched (see Berscheid, 1983). Nonetheless, many individuals realize that, in general, relationships are unstable. Most premarital relationships are terminated prior to marriage, and divorce rates are reported to be high. Furthermore, persons are told in the popular media that extradyadic relationships are common. Accordingly, even when there is no clear evidence of jealousy-evoking extradyadic relationships, some persons will display, to varying degrees, the following qualities: worrying, vigilance, suspiciousness, mistrust, snooping, testing the relationship, and attempting to control the partner's behavior. Also termed "preventive jealousy" (Buunk, 1989) or "behavioral jealousy" (Pfeiffer & Wong, 1989), *suspicious jealousy* is a rather consistent pattern of behaviors and feelings, and it is most prevalent among individuals with low self-esteem who are relatively dependent upon and insecure about their relationships (Buunk, 1989).

Although suspicious jealousy usually occurs in the absence of clear, unequivocal signs of threatening extradyadic involvement, there may be circumstantial evidence to support such jealousy. Minor events, such as watching the partner engage in an animated discussion with someone of the opposite sex, the partner being late, and telephone calls that are wrong numbers can result in worrying, agitation, and apprehension. Suspicious jealousy is not necessarily unhealthy jealousy. When there is a pattern of minor incidents suggesting that the partner might be involved with someone else, vigilance to determine what is happening may be a prudent response that reflects reasonable concern and good strategies to cope with the situation. Furthermore, emotional reactions to these events may forewarn the partner of what will happen if there are serious transgressions and thereby serve the role of *preventing* extradyadic involvements.

On the other hand, suspicious jealousy may be self-defeating and may negatively affect the person's self-esteem. In its most extreme forms, suspicious jealousy may be associated with paranoid personality disorder or elaborate paranoid delusional systems. Furthermore, chronic suspiciousness and mistrust that fails to abate in the absence of actual major jealousy-evoking events can disrupt the relationship. Attempts to control the partner's behavior and deter that which the person had no intention of doing anyway may create a cycle of reactance, resentment, counteraccusation, counterthreat, and provocation. Finally, continually protesting minor transgressions in an attempt to warn the partner of one's resolve may seriously attenuate relationship outcomes.

Reactive Jealousy

Reactive jealousy is the upset that accompanies the revelation of anticipated, current, or past extradyadic sexual behavior by the partner. "Anticipated" includes the case in which the partner's intentions are threatening (e.g., the partner announces the intention to start other romantic and sexual relationships). Also, relationships that ended prior to the current relationship may result in jealousy. If there is no immediate threat posed by the previous relationship, then the negative feelings are suspicious jealousy and envy resulting from social comparison (Salovey & Rodin, 1986, 1989). However, if a past partner reemerges, then reactive jealousy is evoked because of the new threat.

As noted before, the most extreme case of reactive jealousy occurs when a partner actually engages in proscriptive extradyadic sexual relationships. For most individuals in all societies, extradyadic sexual behavior is an indisputable and unambiguous cause for jealousy. For instance, in a seven-nation study (Hungary, Ireland, Mexico, the Netherlands, the Soviet Union, the United States, and Yugoslavia), Hupka et al. (1985) found widespread upset over extradyadic sexual involvement, although there were cross-cultural variations concerning other events (see also Buunk & Hupka, 1987). Reactive jealousy has rather reliably evoked anger or hostility, fear or anxiety, and sadness (Bryson, 1976; Buunk & Bringle, 1989; Hupka, 1984; Hupka & Eshett, 1988; Mathes, Adams, & Davies, 1985; Radecki Bush, Bush, & Jennings, 1988; Salovey & Rodin, 1986).

JEALOUSY AND EXTRADYADIC RELATIONSHIPS
IN TRADITIONAL RELATIONSHIPS

Premarital Relationships

The scripts for traditional relationships include a search and selection phase followed by courtship and commitment to exclusivity. At least, that is the ultimate hope for virtually all young adults. Results of random samples of high school seniors indicate that over 90% do not expect to remain single (Bachman, Johnston, & O'Malley, 1986). However, many relationships are terminated before marriage vows are exchanged. This section explores the relationship between jealousy and extradyadic sexual relations in traditional premarital relationships.

Attitudes toward premarital extradyadic relationships.   As people date, they move toward recognition as a couple by themselves and others around them. This transition is typically associated with the couple becoming more committed and more exclusive. The movement toward exclusivity may be implicit, but is usually discussed and is associated with greater relationship satisfaction (Baxter & Bullis, 1986). Lieberman (1988) studied attitudes toward premarital extradyadic sexual intercourse among college undergraduates. Respondents were presented with a target relationship, in which two persons spent a great deal of time together and considered themselves a pair with some expectations of exclusivity. About two thirds of the student sample thought that extradyadic sexual intercourse by one of these persons with a third person was wrong. When queried about attitudes toward extramarital sexual relations, a greater percentage (above 80%) expressed disapproval. These findings not only reflect the tacit understanding in long-term dating relationships against extradyadic sexual behavior, but also illustrate that the proscriptions are not as strong for dating as for marriage. Margolin (1989) found a more restrictive view of marital extradyadic behavior only for males.

Violation of the exclusivity of dating relationships is not limited to sexual intercourse with others. Roscoe, Cavanaugh, and Kennedy (1988) asked about hypothetical instances of behaviors and found that dating, spending time with another, and sexual behavior short of intercourse (e.g., kissing, petting) also were perceived as constituting unfaithfulness while dating. Female respondents were more likely than males to mention spending time with another, whereas males were more likely than females to mention extradyadic sexual behavior. The most frequently mentioned justifications for premarital extradyadic behavior were, in descending frequency: dissatisfaction with the relationship, boredom, revenge, anger or jealousy, being unsure of the relationship, and variety. Females were more likely than males to mention relationship dissatisfaction as a reason, whereas males were more likely than females to mention lack of communication and sexual incompatibility.

Roscoe et al. (1988) also provided insight into the ways dating persons would cope with learning that their dating partner was unfaithful. The most frequently mentioned behaviors and consequences were, in descending order: terminate the relationship, confront and find out the reason, talk it over, consider terminating the relationship, and work to improve the relationship. Females were more likely than males to indicate that they would discuss the problem with the partner.

Jealousy and premarital extradyadic relationships. Exchange theories analyze interdependency between persons in terms of their respective abilities to influence and control the outcomes of the other (Kelley, 1979, 1983; Thibaut & Kelley, 1959, 1986). Evaluation of relationship outcomes includes comparing outcomes to Comparison Level (CL), which is the minimum level of outcomes they believe they deserve from any relationship. During the course of relationship development, outcomes shift from only being evaluated from one person's perspective to being evaluated in terms of their joint outcomes. A second concept from social exchange theory that is relevant to understanding jealousy is *degree of dependency,* which is the degree to which the partners have the ability to control and influence each other's outcomes. Dependency is a function of the degree to which current outcomes exceed Comparison Level for Alternative

(CLalt), outcomes available from alternative relationships. Finally, *relative dependency* refers to the degree to which one is more or less dependent upon the relationship, compared to the partner. The less dependent person in a couple is assumed to have more rewarding activities outside the present relationship, more attractive alternative relationships, and therefore has more power in the relationship.

Across all of the differences in sexual attitudes and behaviors evident in premarital relationships, the following propositions from exchange theory have been found to hold in samples that were composed of either totally or predominantly nonmarried couples: The frequency and intensity of jealousy were found to be greater to the degree that a person was attracted to the other person (Mathes & Severa, 1981, men only), to the degree that a person was dependent upon the relationship (Mathes & Severa, 1981; Radecki Bush et al., 1988; White, 1984), and to the degree that a person was more involved than the partner (Bringle, Renner, Terry, & Davis, 1983; Radecki Bush et al., 1988; White, 1980, 1981).

A dependent individual in a premarital relationship will not only be relatively more jealous: Occasionally, it seems, such a person will intentionally induce jealousy in the partner. White (1980) found that the most frequent reasons for doing so were to test the relationship (e.g., "to see if he still cared") and to increase specific rewards (e.g., "wanting more attention"). White's study also showed that females were more likely than males to induce jealousy, particularly females who thought they were relatively more involved in the relationship than their partners. Induction of jealousy took the form of exaggerating or discussing an attraction to someone else, flirting, and actually dating others.

Marriage

Traditional marriage is a legal, social, economic, and emotional contract. It is also a contract for sexual fidelity. However, history indicates that the sanctity of this bonding has always been tenuous, even prior to the religious prohibitions most clearly seen in the Judeo-Christian creed. Romantic love, which serves as the partial basis for marriage in our Western culture, was the feeling reserved for one's mistress in medieval Europe during the period of arranged marriages (Stone, 1977). These liaisons were not adultery, but gallantry among the aristocratic court. Nor was extramarital behavior the province of males only. For example, wealthy women in Rome considered liaisons a way of expressing their individuality. However, the double standard of greater acceptability of and access to extramarital behavior has been more common for men than for women (Murstein, 1974). Furthermore, most cultures have punished women more severely than men for extramarital transgressions. For example, husbands could protect their honor and kill wandering wives in traditional Greek culture (Safilios-Rothschild, 1969). Until quite recently in France, the *crime passionel* was acceptable for men, and in Belgium only the wife's infidelity constituted legal grounds for divorce.

Yet, in spite of the presumption of fidelity, extramarital affairs have occurred with remarkable consistency throughout history. What attitudes prevail concerning extramarital sexual relations? What influences the decision to engage in extramarital sex? And what are the consequences of affairs?

Attitudes toward extramarital relationships.   The permissiveness of feelings toward the acceptability, morality, and intentions for extramarital sexual relations will vary within any population. Numerous studies have found that males, in contrast to females, have more permissive attitudes toward extramarital sexual relations in general. In addition, attitudes toward extramarital relations are more permissive among younger individuals, among the better educated and those from the upper-middle class, among persons who were less religious, among those living in urban areas, and among those holding liberal political orientations and liberal views on sexual matters, such as premarital sex, masturbation, and pornography (for reviews, see Buunk & van Driel, 1989; Reiss, Anderson, & Sponaugle, 1980; Sponaugle, 1989).

Nevertheless, although identifying these correlates increases our understanding of the variability in attitudes, a consistent finding is that a majority of respondents in Western society disapprove of extramarital relationships under all circumstances (e.g., Glenn & Weaver, 1979; Lawson & Samson, 1988; Singh, Walton, & Williams, 1976). This negative attitude is more prominent in American samples than those from Sweden, Denmark, Belgium, and the Netherlands (Buunk & van Driel, 1989; Christensen, 1973). Furthermore, the degree of disapproval has been found to be a function of the nature of the extramarital involvement. For instance, Thompson (1984) found that the combination of emotional and sexual extramarital involvement was viewed as more unacceptable than just sexual involvement; extramarital emotional involvement without sexual involvement was perceived as less unacceptable than either of the other types of extramarital involvement. In addition, Weis and Felton (1987) showed that the types of specific activities that were rated as acceptable in the spouse's absence were spending an evening at an opposite-sex married friend's home (in the absence of that person's spouse) and going to a movie with that person. Having dinner in a secluded place, dancing, spending a few days in a secluded cabin, petting, and sexual involvement were all perceived as unacceptable by the majority of respondents, with increasing percentages indicating unacceptability to each choice, respectively.

Involvement in extramarital relationships.   Estimates are that, during marriages in contemporary American culture, at least one half of the individuals have extramarital sexual relations (e.g., Blumstein & Schwartz, 1983; Pietropinto & Simenauer, 1977; Thompson, 1983). There seems a clear discrepancy, then, between the overwhelming negative attitude that is found in research and the actual behavior of married persons (e.g., Weis & Felton, 1987). Apparently, factors other than attitudes must affect extramarital sexual involvement, and various studies have shown that this is indeed the case. For example, Buunk (1980a) demonstrated the clear importance of contextual factors including the norms of one's reference group, the invitation to have extramarital sex, and the incidence of extramarital relationships in one's reference group. In general, opportunity plays an important role in fostering extramarital involvement. Buunk (1984) found that this was mentioned by 81% of those involved in extramarital relations. However, perceived opportunity may be confounded with other factors, including attitudes toward sexuality and life-styles. A study by Gerstel (1969) of commuter marriages (couples who lived apart for professional reasons at least three days a week) showed that 60% had *not* had extramarital relations and that most of those who did had also had extramarital relations prior to the commuting circumstances. Nevertheless, persons indisposed to affairs may behave in remarkably uncharacteristic ways and end up in extramarital relationships when external circumstances push them past their moral barriers.

Opposite-sex friendships may constitute a particularly powerful opportunity for sexual affairs. Atwater (1979) found that, for many women, extramarital sex developed within the context of friendship. Such entanglements may not start with the intent of beginning an extramarital affair out of dissatisfaction with the marital relationship, but may evolve to that point in the process of developing an intimate friendship. This is consistent with the finding by Wiggins and Lederer (1984) that those who had affairs with co-workers had happier marriages than those who had affairs with others (neighbors, strangers).

Usually, becoming involved in extramarital relationships implies a decision process that identifies the costs and benefits and compares them with the expected values of alternative decisions. Meyering and Epling-McWerther (1986) found that men's decisions to become involved in extramarital affairs were most affected by the perceived payoffs, such as variety. In contrast, women's decisions were most affected by the perceived costs (e.g., guilt, destroying the marriage).

In various cases, dissatisfaction with the marital relationship may push individuals into affairs. Although Meyering and Epling-McWerther (1986) reported that men used marital problems more often as an excuse for adultery than women did, in general it seems that dissatisfaction with the marital relationship is a more important motive for women to become entangled in extramarital relationships, especially when it comes to emotional involvement (Glass & Wright, 1985). For example, Atwater (1979) found that about half of the women who had been involved in extramarital relationships mentioned an unsatisfactory marriage as part of their motivation. In general, the occurrence of extramarital sexual relations has been found to be related to marital dissatisfaction (Buunk, 1987a; Edwards & Booth, 1976; Spanier & Margolies, 1983; Wiggins & Lederer, 1984) and dissatisfaction with marital sex (e.g., Buunk, 1980a; Swieczkowski & Walker, 1978). However, there are some qualifications on this conclusion. For instance, Glass and Wright (1977) found that those who had affairs reported lower marital satisfaction, except for women in younger marriages and men in older marriages. Furthermore, it is not always clear if marital dissatisfaction is a cause or a consequence of the extramarital involvement. Extramarital relations may result not only from general marital processes that influence satisfaction but also from specific behaviors by the partner. Buunk (1982) found a strong correlation between inclinations toward extramarital relations and the readiness to tolerate the behavior in the spouse. Such reciprocity may take the form of revenge ("You did it so I'll do it") or inducement ("I'll let you do it so that I can do it").

A last, but rather important factor that can influence the involvement process is the desire for novelty, variety, and excitement, which contrasts to the blunting of positive emotions in marriages (Berscheid, 1983; Knapp & Whitehurst, 1977; Neubeck, 1969; Ramey, 1975). Sensation seeking can be augmented by the secretive nature of many affairs. In addition to the desire for a new experience, curiosity, personal growth toward freedom, and independence may also contribute to the attractiveness of an extramarital affair (Atwater, 1979; Knapp & Whitehurst, 1977).

Consequences of extramarital relationships.   The consequences that are anticipated in an affair are not necessarily the outcomes that are encountered. Furthermore, the factors that draw a person into an affair are not always the same ones that maintain the relationship. Nevertheless, research does indicate that extramarital affairs usually produce positive consequences such as good and stimulating sex, intensive communication, and personal growth. For instance, Atwater (1982) found that about 60% of the women enjoyed sex more with their extramarital partners than with their husbands. Many reported a sense of learning, self-recognition, and self-discovery as consequences of extramarital sexual experiences.

On the other hand, there are usually a number of aversive consequences that occur, not instead of, but in addition to the positive consequences. Many of the feelings (e.g., guilt, fear, anxiety, conflict, fear of pregnancy and sexually transmitted disease) that dissuade individuals from engaging in affairs were often experienced by those who entered them (Atwater, 1979). Spanier and Margolies (1983) found guilt experienced more by females (59%) than by males (34%). They also found that those experiencing guilt reported less satisfaction with the affair. According to Hunt (1974), nearly everyone involved in extramarital relationships experiences fear, anxiety, and guilt, although most overcome such feelings as time passes.

In addition to these *intra*personal consequences, there may occur serious consequences for the marital relationship when the affair is disclosed to, or discovered by, the spouse. While minor jealousy-evoking events may provide the occasion for relationship growth, extramarital affairs that have involved deception of the partner are often more traumatic in their effect. Research by Spanier and Margolies (1983) indicated that there was strong disapproval by respondents of the spouse having an extramarital affair, and respondents also believed that the spouse would disapprove, although the latter point was somewhat less true of males than females. Bringle (1989) also found that persons were more accurate in their knowledge of their spouses' attitudes on sexual jealousy than on social, work, or family jealousy. Therefore, most persons who enter into extramarital affairs know their partners will disapprove. Disclosure at some later time, then, will trigger feelings of not only betrayal but also indignation over the deceit. These feelings along with anger, sadness, and fear constitute reactive jealousy, which may seriously disrupt the relationship (Buunk, 1989).

Jealousy and extramarital relationships. Jealousy-evoking events in general, and extramarital affairs in particular, cause immediate problems for the couple. The offended persons are emotionally upset; this anger generates strained interactions, arguments, threats, and, not infrequently, violence (Buunk, 1986; Daly, Wilson, & Weghorst, 1982). The partner's extradyadic sexual behavior *in and of itself,* however, is not the only problem. If this were the case, then a person would not be upset if it were discovered that a spouse had had an affair at some point during the marriage. Nevertheless, in most individuals, it would create a negative emotional reaction. *It is the meaning of the behavior, both to the person and the relationship,* that is the basis for such a reaction. One's satisfaction with a relationship is dependent not only on the outcomes provided, but also on contextual features. A covert affair may not noticeably reduce outcomes within the marital relationship. However, satisfaction is also a function of the *meaning* attached to the outcomes (Thibaut & Kelley, 1986), which is accentuated by knowing they are provided exclusively to the spouse. When a partner discovers that some of these rewards have been provided to a rival, then their specialness is violated and their value is attenuated. An additional reason why any extradyadic sexual behavior is viewed as an offense worthy of one of the most extreme reactions displayed in the relationship's history is that it represents a *regressive transformation* from the person considering the *couple's joint outcomes* to decisions being made on appraisals that are based on *individualistic outcomes.*

Disclosure of an affair creates the need for the offending person to explain the extradyadic relationship to the spouse. Atwater (1979) has suggested that both justifications and excuses are used to explain affairs. Justifications are aimed at protecting one's self-image through accepting responsibility but attenuating the negative consequences (e.g., "there is nothing wrong with an occasional affair when the loyalty to the marriage remains intact"). Excuses acknowledge the negative consequences but deny personal responsibility for the event (e.g., "I was just drunk and depressed"). Atwater found that, for women, justifications were more frequent than excuses. The most common justification was self-fulfillment. This is consistent with Glass and Wright's (1985) conclusion that women's extramarital affairs were more oriented toward emotional issues, whereas for men, affairs were more sexually oriented. Hupka, Jung, and Silverthorn (1987) showed that, in addition to justifications and excuses, apologies (e.g., "I don't know what got into me") were also used to explain affairs, and were viewed as particularly appropriate when the intent was to maintain the relationship.

The meaning of extramarital behavior and its impact on the marriage vary as a result of marital history. Lawson and Samson (1988) found that individuals least worried about sexual fidelity were those who were more than 10 years into their only marriage and who themselves had at least one affair. Among those in their original marriages, respondents who had not had an extramarital affair strongly adhered to exclusivity (over 90%); however, of those who had had an extramarital affair, only about one half clung to the belief of exclusivity. Those most fearful of adultery were women who had remarried following a divorce caused by either their own or their husbands' adultery. In a sample of individuals whose partners had had or were having affairs, Buunk (1981) examined a subgroup who reported a decrease in jealousy. Perceived causes of their reduced jealousy were (a) finding ways to increase independence, (b) learning to accept jealousy, (c) increasing trust, and (d) communication with the spouse.

Although extramarital affairs play a role in one third of divorces (Burns, 1984), research has not shown how many affairs fail to result in divorce. Buunk (1987a) studied a group of married and cohabiting men and women who had had extradyadic sexual involvement and who had broken up; they were compared to a matched group who had extradyadic sexual involvement and remained together. He found that the group that had terminated the relationship reported greater relationship dissatisfaction, were more likely to attribute the extradyadic relationship to a motive of aggression and deprivation, and, interestingly, held a stronger disapproval of long-term extramarital relationships. The two groups did not differ in the number of extradyadic relationships or the degree of involvement in those relationships.

It is often rather complicated to determine both the reasons for and the consequences of extramarital relationships and the accompanying jealousy because virtually all of the research is retrospective and correlational in nature. For example, Bringle (1989) found that jealousy and marital outcomes were negatively related. However, it is not clear if jealous persons have less satisfactory relationships because of the jealousy, or if unsatisfactory marriages spawn jealousy-evoking events and subsequent jealousy. In any event, one needs to be extremely cautious in taking at face value the causes that individuals attribute to their own and their partners' extramarital behavior. For instance, Spanier and Margolies (1983) reported that, although most persons described their affairs as being a consequence of marital problems, *spouses' affairs* were characterized as a *cause* of marital problems. Buunk (1987a) found that these effects interacted with gender. Males were three times more likely to blame the breakup of the relationship on their wives' affairs than on their own affairs. Females were significantly more likely to identify relationship problems as the cause for the breakup.

These findings illustrate that recounts run the risk of reflecting a self-serving bias and cannot be taken as valid observations of what actually happened. Nevertheless, recounts, distorted or not, take on an identity of their own and are of phenomenological significance to the partners in their current and future interactions (Duck & Sants, 1983).

JEALOUSY AND EXTRADYADIC RELATIONSHIPS IN NONTRADITIONAL RELATIONSHIPS

Although most marriages start with the presumption of fidelity, the negative attitude toward affairs may be eroded by time, particularly when affairs have actually occurred (Lawson & Samson, 1988). Looking only at individuals who were still in their first marriage, there is some evidence of a divergence in that a core remained faithful and professed fidelity, whereas another group seemed to "have made 'adjustments' to one another, altering the rules of conduct and/or stressing other aspects of their relationship" (Lawson & Samson, 1988, p. 420). One adjustment made is an explicit decision between the marriage partners to have other sexual partners. Lawson and Samson (1988) found that the number of liaisons a married person had was strongly related to agreements between partners concerning fidelity or nonexclusivity. An allied decision by the couple is *under what conditions* should extramarital sexual activities occur. Two nontraditional arrangements occur with sufficient regularity to warrant further examination; these are open marriages and swinging.

Sexually Open Marriages

The concept of the open marriage gained wide visibility through the book *Open Marriage* by George and Nena O'Neill (1972). Instead of advocating extramarital sex, as is often mistakenly assumed, the O'Neills had a neutral attitude toward this behavior. They did consider it possible for some couples to integrate such relationships into marriage. This last type of arrangement has been designated as *sexually open marriage*. Buunk and van Driel (1989) identified such marriages as "all those marriages in which both spouses have a positive attitude toward extramarital relationships and give each other the freedom to pursue such relationships" (p. 99), and in which both spouses do actually pursue such relationships. However, there is variability concerning the ground rules couples agree upon to allow these extradyadic relations. Buunk (1980b) found the following guidelines being employed:

1. *Marriage primacy.* Most participants in his sample of open marriages stressed the importance of honesty, putting the marriage first, showing respect for the feelings of all involved, and devoting sufficient time and energy to the spouse.

2. *Restricted intensity*. About one third of Buunk's respondents advocated restricting the intensity and degree of involvement of the extradyadic contacts; some also held that the extradyadic relationships be brief; and one third of the couples had agreed that the extradyadic relationship would be terminated upon the request of the partner.

3. *Visibility*. This encompasses several tactics to keep the partner informed about the extradyadic relationship, including, in Buunk's sample, restricting such relationships to those persons the partner knew, no more than one such relationship, and prior consultation with the spouse (Watson, 1981, found in her sample that excluding close friends and business associates was a preferred ground rule).

4. *Invisibility*. A small group of Buunk's sample decided to manage the extradyadic involvements in a more covert fashion by limiting the partner's awareness.

In contrast to covert extramarital affairs, sexually open marriages typically evolve after a period of 5 to 10 years of marriage (Ramey, 1975). Participants in open marriages ascribe to a philosophy that such relationships will benefit the person and the marriage (Knapp & Whitehurst, 1977). Furthermore, open marriages reflect rather stable and happy marriages (Buunk, 1980a; Rubin, 1982; Rubin & Adams, 1986), although some marital deprivation may be a motivating factor (Buunk, 1984). Buunk (1980b) also found that nearly all subjects emphasized the good quality of communications with the outside partner, and a large majority reported that new aspects of their personality emerged in the collateral relationship. However, the picture of who participates in open marriages and its consequences is not untarnished. Watson (1981) found that, although participants in such marriages were self-assured, flexible, independent, and tolerant, almost three quarters of the sample had been in marital therapy. A study by Wheeler and Kilmann (1983) showed that, although participants reported more liberal attitudes on sexual behavior and greater sexual satisfaction, they were also higher in need for social approval, interrupted and disagreed more often, and resolved conflicts less satisfactorily.

One might presume that persons in sexually open marriages, because of their personal characteristics and the arrangements that are established, are able to maintain this life-style, in part, because of the absence of jealousy. In fact, this is *not* consistent with research findings. Although most partners in an open marriage felt that the collateral relationships did not constitute a major threat to the marriage, at least 80% reported feelings of jealousy (Buunk, 1981; Ramey, 1975). Furthermore, about a quarter of the respondents reported that, at certain moments, their marriages had been threatened by the extramarital involvements. Buunk (1987b) conducted a 5-year follow-up on his sample of open marriages and found, somewhat surprisingly, that there was a trend for an increase in the experience of jealousy across that time period. Thus, even for persons who consciously make an atypical effort to attenuate jealousy, the presence of a collateral sexual relationship elicits rather typical reactions. Buunk's (1987b) study also showed that over the 5-year period, the quality of the marital relationship had deteriorated, sexual satisfaction in the marriage had declined, and emotional dependency on the spouse was lessened. Whether these findings were part of trends typical in all marriages or the result of the collateral relationship cannot be determined; however, they are in contrast to the expectations that open marriages foster growth for both the persons and the marriage (Knapp, 1976; Knapp & Whitehurst, 1977; O'Neill & O'Neill, 1972).

These conflicting effects may help explain why research provides divergent views of the stability of open marriages. On the one hand, Rubin and Adams (1986) found that the overwhelming majority of couples (21 of 23) had maintained an open relationship during a 5-year period. In contrast, Watson (1981) reported that only 1 of 19 couples in a 2-year follow-up had maintained an open relationship. Interestingly, Buunk (1987b) described a more intricate pattern over a 5-year period: While the sample as a whole was less inclined to engage in extramarital sexual relationships, particularly long-term affairs, the majority of persons still favored incidental extramarital contacts.

Swinging

Swinging has some similarities to open marriages. It is a mutual agreement between the marital partners for extramarital sexual relationships. However, swinging is a more couple-oriented activity to the extent that the extramarital sexual relationships occur with both persons present and only within specified times and settings. The actual sexual contact may be open (occurs in the presence of others) or closed (occurs in separate rooms); in either case, the participants most typically arrive as a couple and depart as a couple. Furthermore, the sexual activity is, to a greater extent than with open marriages, engaged in for its own sake. The philosophy is one of recreational, body-oriented sexuality rather than emotional involvement and personal growth (Denfield & Gordon, 1970; Gilmartin, 1977; Walshok, 1971).

Various portraits of swingers emerge from research comparing them to nonswinger samples. They are described as less religious than nonswingers (Gilmartin, 1974; Jenks, 1985c). In his study on group sex, Bartell (1971) reported swingers to be politically conservative and ethnocentric, but Gilmartin (1974) found them to be quite liberal. Possibly clarifying these findings, Jenks (1985a) found that swingers were more liberal than nonswingers concerning their own sexual behavior (e.g., abortion, pornography, divorce), but more conservative on issues less relevant to their sexual life-styles (e.g., capital punishment, social welfare). Swingers, though, in many ways were not different from nonswingers (Jenks, 1985b, 1985c).

Jealousy seems to be less prominent among swingers than among nonswingers (Jenks, 1985c). However, swingers reported jealous feelings as well as feelings of envy and exclusion (Gilmartin, 1977), guilt, problems in the marriage, and boredom (Denfield, 1974). Liaisons outside the swinging context, expressions of love and commitment, and feelings of emotional intimacy are considered inappropriate and unacceptable by swingers. Interestingly, the most significant reason for dropping out of swinging was the wives' inability to tolerate this form of extramarital sex (Murstein, Case, & Gunn, 1985). This finding is consistent with the presumption that, although swinging is a couple-oriented activity, it is probably instigated by the male's desire for sexual variety, for the benefit of the male, and the wife serves the functional role of creating the opportunity (why else would it be known as "wife swapping"?) Interestingly, one of the more ironic scenarios in swinging is the husband's upset (jealousy and envy) over the wife enjoying the swinging too much (Gilmartin, 1977).

CONCLUSION

The potential or actual occurrence of extradyadic relationships and the suspicious and reactive jealousy that is generated by them are interrelated phenomena. Jealousy over minor events may be construed as a sign of love, and it forewarns of the certitude of reactive jealousy occurring if an extradyadic sexual relationship were perpetrated. These reactions, as well as mild suspicious jealousy, may serve a preventive role that deters liaisons. Ironically, the potential fury of reactive jealousy also causes most affairs to be covert, which accentuates the aversive consequences following disclosure. The intensity of reactive jealousy also serves as a protest and a punishment to the transgressing partner. Such a response might prevent subsequent incidents and preserve the relationship. However, fervent and vicious reactions can antagonize the partner and destroy the relationship. The social-psychological research on jealousy demonstrates that jealousy is a phenomenologically valid and inevitable construct for virtually everyone who forms relationships involving sexual intimacy. It is noteworthy that jealousy is a persistent phenomenon, even in couples who are open to extramarital relationships.

Jealousy seems, in part, to serve as the glue that helps maintain the couple as a couple. On the other hand, it can be the explosive force that destroys the couple and alienates the persons from each other. Whatever the consequences, jealousy will reliably surface whenever sexual extradyadic involvements that violate norms of exclusivity occur in intimate relationships.

REFERENCES

Atwater, L. (1979). Getting involved: Women's transition to first extramarital sex. *Alternative Lifestyles, 2*, 33–68.

Atwater, L. (1982). *The extramarital connection*. New York: Irvington.

Bachman, J. G., Johnston, L. D., & O'Malley, P. M. (1986). *Monitoring the future*. Ann Arbor: Survey Research Center, Institute for Social Research, University of Michigan.

Bartell, G. D. (1971). *Group sex: A scientist's eyewitness report on the American way of swinging*. New York: Wyden.

Baxter, L. A., & Bullis, C. (1986). Turning points in developing romantic relationships. *Human Communication Research, 12,* 469–493.

Berscheid, E. (1983). Emotion. In H. H. Kelley, E. Berscheid, A. Christensen, J. H. Harvey, T. L. Huston, G. Levinger, E. McClintock, L. A. Peplau, & D. R. Peterson (Eds.), *Close Relationships* (pp. 110–168) New York: Freeman.

Blumstein, P., & Schwartz, P. (1983). *American couples*. New York: Morrow.

Bringle, R. G. (1989). *Dispositional jealousy, homogamy, and marital quality*. Manuscript submitted for publication.

Bringle, R. G., & Buunk, B. (1985). Jealousy and social behavior: A review of person, relationship, and situational determinants. In P. Shaver (Ed.), *Review of personality and social psychology, Vol. 6: Self, situation and social behavior* (pp. 241–264). Beverly Hills, CA: Sage.

Bringle, R. G., Renner, P., Terry, R., & Davis, S. (1983). An analysis of situational and person components of jealousy. *Journal of Research in Personality, 17,* 354–368.

Bryson J. B. (1976, August). *The nature of sexual jealousy: An exploratory study*. Paper presented at the meeting of the American Psychological Association, Washington, DC.

Bryson, J. B. (1977, August). *Situational determinants of the expression of jealousy*. Paper presented at the meeting of the American Psychological Association, San Francisco.

Burns, A. (1984). Perceived causes of marriage breakdown and conditions of life. *Journal of Marriage and the Family, 46,* 551–562.

Buunk, B. (1980a). Extramarital sex in the Netherlands: Motivations in social and marital context. *Alternative Lifestyles, 3,* 11–39.

Buunk, B. (1980b). Sexually open marriages. Ground rules for countering potential threats to marriage. *Alternative Lifestyles, 3,* 312–328.

Buunk, B. (1981). Jealousy in sexually open marriages. *Alternative Lifestyles, 4,* 357–372.

Buunk, B. (1982). Anticipated sexual jealousy: Its relationship to self-esteem, dependency and reciprocity. *Personality and Social Psychology Bulletin, 8,* 310–316.

Buunk, B. (1984). Jealousy as related to attributions for the partner's behavior. *Social Psychology Quarterly, 47,* 107–112.

Buunk, B. (1986). Husband's jealousy. In R. A. Lewis & R. Salt (Eds.), *Men in families* (pp. 97–114). Beverly Hills, CA: Sage.

Buunk, B. (1987a). Conditions that promote break-ups as a consequence of extradyadic involvements. *Journal of Social and Clinical Psychology, 5,* 237–250.

Buunk, B. (1987b). Long-term stability and change in sexually open marriages. In L. Shamgar-Handelman & R. Polomba (Eds.), *Alternative patterns of family life in modern societies* (pp. 61–72). Rome: Istituto di Ricerche sulla Popolazione (Collana Monografie 1).

Buunk, B. (1989, May). Types and manifestations of jealousy: An exchange-theoretical perspective. In G. L. White (Chair), *Themes for progress in jealousy research*. Symposium conducted at the meeting of the 2nd Iowa Conference on Personal Relationships, Iowa City, IA.

Buunk, B., & Bringle, R. G. (1989). *The emotional nature of jealousy*. Manuscript under review.

Buunk, B., & Hupka, R. (1987). Cross-cultural differences in the elicitation of sexual jealousy. *Journal of Sex Research, 23,* 12–22.

Buunk, B., & van Driel, B. (1989). *Variant lifestyles and relationships*. Newbury Park, CA: Sage.

Christensen, H. T. (1973). Attitudes toward marital infidelity: A nine-culture sampling of university student opinion. *Journal of Comparative Family Studies, 4,* 197–214.

Daly, M., Wilson, M., & Weghorst, S. J. (1982). Male sexual jealousy. *Ethology and Sociobiology, 3,* 11–27.

Denfield, D. (1974). Dropouts from swinging: The marriage counselor as informant. In J. R. Smith & L. G. Smith (Eds.), *Beyond monogamy. Recent studies of sexual alternatives in marriage* (pp. 260–267). Baltimore: Johns Hopkins University Press.

Denfield, D., & Gordon, M. (1970). The sociology of mate swapping: Or the family that swings together clings together. *Journal of Sex Research, 6,* 85–100.

Duck, S., & Sants, H. (1983). On the origin of the specious: Are personal relationships really interpersonal states? *Journal of Social and Clinical Psychology, 1,* 27–41.

Edwards, J. N., & Booth, A. (1976). Sexual behavior in and out of marriage: An assessment of correlates. *Journal of Marriage and the Family, 38,* 73–81.

Gerstel, N. R. (1969). Marital alternative and the regulation of sex: Commuter couples as a test case. *Alternative Lifestyles, 2,* 145–176.

Gilmartin, B. (1974). Sexual deviance and social networks. A study of social, family and marital interaction patterns among co-marital sex participants. In J. R. Smith & L. G. Smith (Eds.), *Beyond monogamy. Recent studies of sexual alternatives in marriage* (pp. 291–323). Baltimore, MD: Johns Hopkins University Press.

Gilmartin, B. (1977). Jealousy among the swingers. In G. Clanton & L. G. Smith (Eds.), *Jealousy* (pp. 152–158). Englewood Cliffs, NJ: Prentice-Hall.

Glass, S. P., & Wright, T. L. (1977). The relationship of extramarital sex, length of marriage, and sex differences on marital satisfaction and romanticism: Athanasiou's data reanalyzed. *Journal of Marriage and the Family, 39,* 691–703.

Glass, S. P., & Wright, T. L. (1985) Sex differences in type of extramarital involvement and marital dissatisfaction. *Sex Roles, 12,* 1101–1120.

Glenn, N. D., & Weaver, C.N. (1979). Attitudes toward premarital, extramarital, and homosexual relations in the U.S. in the 1970s. *Journal of Sex Research, 15,* 108–118.

Hansen, G. L. (1982). Reactions to hypothetical jealousy producing events. *Family Relations, 31,* 513–518.

Hunt, N. (1974). *Sexual behavior in the 1970s.* Chicago: Dell.

Hupka, R. (1984). Jealousy: Compound emotion or label for a particular situation? *Motivation and Emotion, 8,* 141–155.

Hupka, R. B., Buunk, B., Falus, G., Fulgosi, A., Ortega, E., Swain, R., & Tarabrina, N. V. (1985). Romantic jealousy and romantic envy: A seven-nation study. *Journal of Cross-Cultural Psychology, 16,* 423–446.

Hupka, R. B., & Eshett, C. (1988). Cognitive organization of emotion. Differences between labels and descriptors of emotion in jealousy situations. *Perceptual and Motor Skills, 66,* 935–949.

Hupka, R. B., Jung, J., & Silverthorn, K. (1987). Perceived acceptability of apologies, excuses, and justifications in jealousy predicaments. *Journal of Social Behavior and Personality, 2,* 303–313.

Jenks, R. J. (1985a). A comparative study of swingers and non-swingers: Attitudes and beliefs. *Lifestyles: A Journal of Changing Patterns, 8,* 5–20.

Jenks, R. J. (1985b). Swinging: A replication and test of a theory. *Journal of Sex Research, 21,* 199–205.

Jenks, R. J. (1985c). Swinging: A test of two theories and a proposed new model. *Archives of Sexual Behavior, 14,* 517–527.

Kelley, H. H. (1979). *Personal relationships: Their structure and process.* Hillsdale, NJ: Erlbaum.

Kelley, H. H. (1983). The situational origins of human tendencies: A further reason for the formal analysis of human structure. *Personality and Social Psychology Bulletin, 9,* 8–30.

Knapp, J. (1976). An exploratory study of seventeen sexually open marriages. *Journal of Sex Research, 12,* 206–219.

Knapp, J., & Whitehurst, R. N. (1977). Sexually open marriage and relationships: Issues and prospects. In R. W. Libby & R. N. Whitehurst (Eds.), *Marriage and alternatives: Exploring intimate relationships* (pp. 147–160). Glenview, IL: Scott, Foresman.

Lawson, A., & Samson, C. (1988). Age, gender and adultery. *British Journal of Sociology, 39,* 409–440.

Lieberman, B. (1988). Extrapremarital intercourse: Attitudes toward a neglected sexual behavior. *Journal of Sex Research, 24,* 291–299.

Margolin, L. (1989). Gender and the prerogatives of dating and marriage: An experimental assessment of a sample of college students. *Sex Roles, 20,* 91–102.

Mathes, E. W., Adams, H. E., & Davies, R. M. (1985). Jealousy: Loss of relationship rewards, loss of self-esteem, depression, anxiety, and anger. *Journal of Personality and Social Psychology, 48,* 1552–1561.

Mathes, E. W., & Severa, N. (1981). Jealousy, romantic love and liking: Theoretical considerations and preliminary scale development. *Psychological Reports, 49,* 23–31.

Meyering, R. A., & Epling-McWerther, E. A. (1986). Decision-making in extramarital relationships. *Lifestyles, A Journal of Changing Patterns, 8,* 115–129.

Murstein, B. I. (1974). *Love, sex and marriage through the ages.* New York: Springer.

Murstein, B. I., Case, D., & Gunn, S. P. (1985). Personality correlates of ex-swingers. *Lifestyles, 8,* 21–34.

Neubeck, G. (1969). *Extramarital relations.* Englewood Cliffs, NJ: Prentice-Hall.

O'Neill, N., & O'Neill, G. (1972). *Open marriage: A new lifestyle for couples.* New York: M. Evans.

Pfeiffer, S. M., & Wong, P. T. P. (1989). Multidimensional jealousy. *Journal of Personal and Social Relationships, 6,* 181–196.

Pietropinto, A. & Simenauer, J. (1977). *Beyond the male myth: What women want to know about men's sexuality. A nationwide survey.* New York: Times Books.

Radecki Bush, C. R., Bush, J. P., & Jennings, J. (1988). Effects of jealousy threats on relationship perceptions and emotions. *Journal of Social and Personal Relationships, 5,* 285–303.

Ramey, J. W. (1975). Intimate groups and networks: Frequent consequences of sexually open marriage. *Family Coordinator, 24,* 515–530.

Reiss, I., Anderson, G. E., & Sponaugle, G. C. (1980). A multivariate model of the determinants of extramarital sexual permissiveness. *Journal of Marriage and the Family, 52,* 395–411.

Roscoe, B., Cavanaugh, L. E., & Kennedy, D. R. (1988). Dating infidelity: Behaviors, reasons and consequences. *Adolescence, 13,* 35–43.

Rubin, A. M. (1982). Sexually open versus sexually exclusive marriage: A comparison of dyadic adjustment. *Alternative Lifestyles, 5,* 101–108.

Rubin, A. M., & Adams, J. R. (1986). Outcomes of sexually open marriages. *Journal of Sex Research, 22,* 311–319.

Safilios–Rothschild, C. (1969). Attitudes of Greek spouses toward marital infidelity. In G. Neubeck (Ed.), *Extramarital relations* (pp. 77–93). Englewood Cliffs, NJ: Prentice-Hall.

Salovey, P., & Rodin, J. (1986). The differentiation of social-comparison jealousy and romantic jealousy. *Journal of Personality and Social Psychology, 50,* 1100–1112.

Salovey, P., & Rodin, J. (1989). Envy and jealousy in close relationships. In C. Hendrick (Ed.), *Review of personality and social psychology* (vol. 10, pp. 221–246). Newbury Park, CA: Sage.

Singh, B. K., Walton, B. L., & Williams, J. S. (1976). Extramarital sexual permissiveness: Conditions and contingencies. *Journal of Marriage and the Family, 38,* 701–712.

Spanier, G. B., & Margolies, R. L. (1983). Marital separation and extramarital sexual behavior. *Journal of Sex Research, 19,* 23–48.

Sponaugle, G. C. (1989). Attitudes toward extramarital relations. In K. McKinney & S. Sprecher (Eds.), *Human sexuality: The societal and interpersonal context.* Norwood, NJ: Ablex Publishing.

Stone, L. (1977). *The family, sex and marriage in England, 1500–1800.* Harmondsworth, UK: Penguin.

Swieczkowski, J. B., & Walker, C. E. (1978). Sexual behavior correlates of female orgasm and marital happiness. *Journal of Nervous and Mental Disease, 166,* 335–342.

Thibaut, J. W., & Kelley, H. H. (1959). *The social psychology of groups.* New York: Wiley.

Thibaut, J. W., & Kelley, H. H. (1986). *The social psychology of groups.* New Brunswick, NJ: Transaction Books.

Thompson, A. P. (1983). Extramarital sex: A review of the research literature. *Journal of Sex Research, 19,* 1–22.

Thompson, A. P. (1984). Emotional and sexual components of extramarital relations. *Journal of Marriage and the Family, 46,* 35–42.

Walshok, J. L. (1971). The emergence of middle class deviant subcultures: The case of swingers. *Social Problems, 18,* 488–495.

Watson, M. A. (1981). Sexually open marriage: Three perspectives. *Alternative Lifestyles, 4,* 3–12.

Weis, D. L., & Felton, J. R. (1987). Marital exclusivity and the potential for future marital conflict. *Social Work, 32,* 45–49.

Wheeler, J., & Kilmann, J. (1983). Comarital sexual behavior: Individual and relationship variables. *Archives of Sexual Behavior, 12,* 295–306.

White, G. L. (1980). Inducing jealousy: A power perspective. *Personality and Social Psychology Bulletin, 6,* 222–227.

White, G. L. (1981). Relative involvement, inadequacy and jealousy: A test of a causal model. *Alternative Lifestyles, 4,* 291–309.

White, G. L. (1984). Comparison of four jealousy scales. *Journal of Research in Personality, 18,* 115–130.

Wiggins, J. D., & Lederer, D. A. (1984). Differential antecedents of infidelity in marriage. *American Mental Health Counselors Association Journal, 6,* 152–161.

8 Sexual Violence and Coercion in Close Relationships

Charlene L. Muehlenhard
Mary F. Goggins
Jayme M. Jones
Arthur T. Satterfield
University of Kansas

Popular culture perpetuates the myth that coercive sex is something that occurs between strangers in dark alleys. For example, sexual assault prevention programs often advise women not to go out alone at night, not to trust strangers, and so forth. This message, that women risk being sexually assaulted by strangers, carries with it the implication that women are safe from sexual violence in close relationships.

Social scientists have only recently challenged these myths by studying sexual assault that occurs in marital and dating relationships. They have found a high prevalence of sexual assault in marriage (Finkelhor & Yllo, 1985; Russell, 1982) and in dating relationships (Koss, Dinero, Seibel, & Cox, 1988; Koss, Gidycz, & Wisniewski, 1987).

This chapter covers sexual violence and coercion in close relationships. The discussion includes sexual coercion of both females and males in both heterosexual and homosexual relationships. The discussion will be limited to adult relationships; thus, sexual coercion in parent–child relationships is beyond the scope of this chapter. Sexual harassment, which occurs in business or academic relationships, is also beyond the scope of this chapter.

Sexual coercion will be construed broadly, including nonviolent, as well as violent, sexual coercion. Nonviolent sexual coercion includes verbal sexual coercion—that is, coercing a partner to have sex using verbal means (other than verbal threats of physical force); examples include threatening to end a relationship or making one's partner feel guilty for refusing. Nonviolent sexual coercion also includes sexual coercion that results not from one individual's coercing another, but from social norms, gender roles, and the relative power of women and men in society. This chapter includes the prevalence, causes, and consequences of sexual violence and coercion in close relationships.

THE PREVALENCE OF SEXUAL COERCION
IN CLOSE RELATIONSHIPS

Sexual Assault

Sexual assault is commonly defined as sexual penetration obtained through force, threats of force, or while the victim was unable to consent (e.g., due to being intoxicated, drugged, or unconscious).[1] Some researchers (e.g., Russell, 1982, 1984) have limited their definitions to penile–vaginal intercourse; others (e.g., Koss et al., 1987) also have included oral and anal intercourse. Most studies of sexual assault in close relationships have focused on female victims of male partners, although some studies have focused on male victims of female partners and sexual assault in lesbian and gay relationships.

Women sexually assaulted by men. The sexual assault of women by men is the most prevalent form of violent sexual coercion. Early studies of sexual assault were based on incidents reported to the police; because sexual assault by strangers is much more likely to be reported than sexual assault by acquaintances (Koss et al., 1988; Russell, 1984), most of the early research focused primarily on sexual assault by strangers. Recently, however, researchers have investigated sexual assault in close relationships, including heterosexual dating, marital, and homosexual relationships.

Sexual assault in heterosexual dating relationships. A survey of over 3,000 female college students in the United States revealed that 15% had been sexually assaulted. Over half of all these sexual assaults—53%—occurred between women and men who were dating. In spite of the myth that sexual assaults on dates are most likely to occur on first dates, Koss et al. (1988) found that more sexual assaults occurred between steady dating partners than between casual dating partners. Fewer than 1% of the sexual assaults between dating partners had been reported to the police.

Russell (1984), in her study of 930 randomly selected women in San Francisco, found that 3% had been sexually assaulted by dates; 2%, by boyfriends; and 5%, by lovers and ex-lovers[2] (all these categories would have been subsumed under the category *dating partner* in Koss's study). By comparison, Russell found that 3% of the women had been sexually assaulted by strangers. Similarly, Finkelhor and Yllo (1985), in their survey of 323 Boston area women, found that 10% had been sexually assaulted by dates, compared with 3% who had been sexually assaulted by strangers.

---

[1]Although most researchers have used the term *rape* (e.g., Koss et al., 1987; Russell, 1982, 1984), the term *sexual assault* is being used here because it connotes a wider range of behaviors and victims (e.g., forced oral and anal as well as vaginal intercourse, male as well as female victims).

[2]Russell defined *lover* as "a friend, date, or boyfriend with whom voluntary sexual intercourse had occurred prior to the first rape experience" (p. 61). *Date* and *boyfriend* were not defined.

Sexual assault in marriage. Russell (1982, 1984) found that 8% of the women in her sample had been sexually assaulted by their husbands or ex-husbands. This figure represents 12% of the women who had ever been married. This figure becomes 14% if attempted sexual assaults are included. As high as these figures are, they are probably underestimates. Russell surveyed women from randomly selected households. This sampling procedure excluded women in mental hospitals, prisons, shelters, nursing homes, and halfway houses, as well as women murdered by violent partners. As Russell (1982) pointed out, these women have a high likelihood of having been sexually abused by their partners; thus, the actual prevalence of sexual assault in marriage is probably even higher than these figures suggest.

Most of the women sexually assaulted by their husbands had experienced repeated attacks: A third reported 2 to 20 incidents, and another third reported over 20 incidents (Russell, 1982). Many of these women did not label their experience as rape. Russell found that none of these incidents had been reported to the police (in part due to the fact that, at the time of the study, it was not a crime for a husband to sexually assault his wife in California).

Finkelhor and Yllo (1985) reported that 10% of the married or previously married women they surveyed reported that their husbands had used force or threat of force to try to have sex with them. They found that 50% of these women had been sexually assaulted by their husbands 20 or more times.

Men sexually assaulted by women. Male victims of sexual assault have received much less attention than female victims. The most obvious reason is that the overwhelming majority of sexual assault victims are female (Koss et al., 1987; Sarrel & Masters, 1982). Studies have found that between 0% and 10% of sexual assault victims treated at medical centers were male (Forman, 1982; Kaufman, DiVasto, Jackson, Voorhees, & Christy, 1980). Most of these male victims had been sexually assaulted by other men.

Some studies have identified instances of men's being sexually coerced by women. Sarrel and Masters (1982) searched files of 4,200 men who had sought help at the Yale Human Sexuality Program and the Masters and Johnson Institute. They identified four men who had been physically forced to engage in sex with women and three men who had had sex with women when "traditional sex roles were completely reversed by an act of overt female aggression" (Sarrel & Masters, 1982, p. 125). One of these incidents had occurred in a close relationship. The sexual victimization of men might be more common than these numbers suggest because men seem reluctant to disclose such incidents and are sometimes not believed when they do (Sarrel & Masters, 1982).

Struckman-Johnson (1988) found that 16% of the 268 college men surveyed reported being forced to engage in sexual intercourse with a woman during a date. Of the men who reported being forced to have sexual intercourse, most (52%) reported that the pressure had been psychological; 28% reported that the pressure had been both physical and psychological; 10% reported that the pressure had been physical; and 10% reported a lack of consent due to intoxication. There are several controversial issues related to situations in which men are sexually coerced by women. One such issue relates to the meaning of physical and psychological coercion to women and men (Harney & Muehlenhard, 1991). For example, a recent study found that similar percentages of men and women (6.5% vs. 5.8%) reported having unwanted sexual intercourse because a partner used physical force against them (Muehlenhard & Cook, 1988). On the surface, this finding seems to suggest that men and women face similar problems with forced sex. It is likely, however, that these experiences have different meanings for women than for men. Men are generally larger and stronger than women (Archer & Lloyd, 1985). Women fear male violence more than men fear female violence (Gordon & Riger, 1989). It is considered appropriate for women but not men to resist sexual advances (Zilbergeld, 1978). Therefore, being grabbed or held down by a partner—although overtly physical in nature—would probably have more of a psychological component for men (e.g., not wanting to look unmasculine for refusing sex) but more of a physical component for women (e.g., not being able to resist his weight or fearing that resistance will lead to physical injury).

In addition, the issue of men's being sexually assaulted by women has political implications. Some feminists fear that it will deflect attention from the problem of women's being assaulted by men. Focusing on men as victims could make the problem appear gender neutral, when in fact women are sexually assaulted much more frequently than men, and fear of sexual assault has a much greater impact on women's lives than on men's lives (Gordon & Riger, 1989; Stanko, 1988).

Sexual assault in lesbian and gay relationships.   The prevalence of sexual violence in lesbian and gay relationships is difficult to estimate because there has been little research on this problem. There could be several reasons for this: Men are often regarded as always wanting sex (Zilbergeld, 1978); thus, the idea that men could be forced into unwanted sex seems implausible to many people. Conversely, women are often regarded as being less sexual than men (Finkelhor & Yllo, 1985); thus, the idea that women would be sexually coercive seems implausible to many people. Ideas about what behaviors constitute sex come into play: If only penile–vaginal intercourse counts as sex (Rubin, 1984; Zilbergeld, 1978), then coercive sex requires both a man and a woman. Finally, because society often regards homosexual relationships as abnormal or immoral, there has been little concern about the rights of individuals involved in such relationships.

Some lesbian and gay relationships do involve sexual violence and coercion (Hart, 1986; Lobel, 1986; Waterman, Dawson, & Bologna 1989). Waterman et al. (1989) surveyed 36 female and 34 male college students who were involved in homosexual relationships. They found that 31% of the lesbians and 12% of the gay men reported being forced by their partners to have sex. Although this sample is too small to allow definitive conclusions about the prevalence of sexual violence in lesbian and gay relationships, these results suggest that this is a prevalent problem.

Among the issues involved in comparing the relative frequency of coercive sex in homosexual and heterosexual relationships is the issue of what sexual behaviors count as sex. In her landmark study of rape, Russell (1982, 1984) included only incidents of forced penile–vaginal intercourse. If she had regarded other kinds of forced sexual behaviors as rape, the percentage of women raped by their husbands would have been even higher. In lesbian and gay relationships, what counts as sex would be more diverse than just penile–vaginal intercourse; thus, prevalence rates found in a study of heterosexual relationships might not be comparable to prevalence rates found in a study of homosexual relationships.

Nonviolent Sexual Coercion

Nonviolent sexual coercion takes several forms. It includes verbal sexual coercion, in which one partner uses verbal means to coerce the other to engage in unwanted sexual activity. Available data suggest that verbal sexual coercion is even more prevalent than violent sexual coercion. In Koss's (Koss et al., 1987) nationwide study of college students, 44% of the women reported engaging in unwanted sexual intercourse because they felt overwhelmed by men's continual arguments and pressure; 10% of the men reported obtaining sexual intercourse with unwilling women using this strategy. In a study comparing women's and men's experiences with unwanted sexual intercourse, 9.1% of the women and 7.3% of the men reported engaging in unwanted sexual intercourse because their partners threatened to end the relationships or find new partners or because they feared that the partner would no longer be interested in them (Muehlenhard & Cook, 1988). Furthermore, 11.5% of the women and 13.4% of the men reported engaging in unwanted sexual intercourse because their partners made them feel guilty or inadequate or questioned their sexuality. Occasionally a partner used a threat of bodily self-harm to coerce a partner to engage in unwanted sexual intercourse (reported by 0.2% of the women and 1.4% of the men).

In addition, sexual coercion occurs as a consequence of social norms, gender role stereotypes, and the relative power of women and men in society. Societal norms about appropriate sexuality often make people feel as if they have to engage in sex in order to avoid being deviant. The economic oppression of women often pressures them to participate in sexual relationships with men in order to obtain financial support. Because such pressure is often so subtle and insidious as to be rendered almost invisible, the prevalence of unwanted sex due to such pressure is difficult to estimate (see Muehlenhard & Schrag, 1991). These forms of subtle coercion are discussed further later in this chapter.

CAUSES OF SEXUAL COERCION
IN CLOSE RELATIONSHIPS

Beliefs About Close Relationships

Several beliefs about close relationships contribute to sexual violence and coercion in these relationships. Some of these beliefs are discussed below.

"Close relationships should be private." Many people believe that what happens between two individuals in an intimate relationship is the concern of only those individuals, and no one has the right to interfere (Gelles & Straus, 1988; Shotland & Straw, 1976). Consistent with this belief, women who are sexually assaulted by their husbands or dating partners are less likely than women who are sexually assaulted by strangers to discuss the attack with anyone or to report it to the police (Koss et al., 1988; Russell, 1984).

"Close relationships should be sexual." Also contributing to sexual coercion in close relationships is the belief that intimate relationships should be sexual. Husbands who sexually assault their wives often believe that it is their wives' duty to submit to their sexual demands (Finkelhor & Yllo, 1985; Russell, 1982). In addition, many wives submit to sex because they, too, believe that it is their duty (Finkelhor & Yllo, 1985; Russell, 1982). Russell (1982) found that many of the wives in her study regarded sex as a marital duty and had always complied with their husbands' demands, regardless of their own desire to have sex. Russell speculated that compliance is the only reason that many of these wives had never been sexually assaulted. These women were "unrapeable" because they had never refused.

Shotland (1989) viewed this belief as a causal factor when sexual assault occurs after a couple has been dating regularly (termed *relational date rape*). According to Shotland's model, the male might expect that, at some point, the relationship should become sexual. If it did not, he might interpret this as a sign of lack of love on the woman's part, and he might feel that the relationship is inequitable. He might also engage in a social comparison process, in which he compares the relationship with other men's relationships or his partner's prior relationships; he might decide that the relationship is inadequate. He might then force sex to rectify the situation.

The belief that close relationships should be sexual can also be a source of pressure for men to engage in unwanted sexual behavior (Muehlenhard & Cook, 1988). Even without the threat of force, the norm that relationships should be sexual can have a powerful impact.

"The man should be the 'head of the household.'" Believing that the man should be the head of the household or the person in control of the relationship

can lead a husband to feel entitled to sex or whatever else he wants in the relationship. Sexual assault can result from a husband's desire to dominate his wife, to have her fulfill his wishes, or to have her as his exclusive possession (Finkelhor & Yllo, 1985; Russell, 1982). Frieze (1983) found that 78% of the women she interviewed who had been sexually assaulted by their husbands reported that the cause of the assault was their husbands' belief that such an action would prove his manhood. This ideology of male control could also perpetuate sexual assault in dating relationships (Muehlenhard, Linton, Felts, & Andrews, 1985).

Stereotypes About Masculinity and Femininity

Sexual coercion by males.   Being masculine involves being dominant and aggressive; being feminine involves being submissive and passive. Sexual assault is a logical extension of a system in which men are taught to fight for what they want, whereas women are taught to be passive and yielding and to put men's needs above their own (Brownmiller, 1975; Reynolds, 1984; Russell, 1984).

There is greater empirical support for linking masculinity and committing sexual assault than for linking femininity and being a victim of sexual assault. Several studies have found that sexually aggressive men are more traditional in their gender role attitudes than are other men (Koss & Dinero, 1988; Koss, Leonard, Beezley, & Oros, 1985; Muehlenhard & Falcon, 1990). There is little evidence, however, that women who experience sexual coercion are more traditional than other women (Koss & Dinero, 1989; Muehlenhard & Calvin, 1989; Muehlenhard & Linton, 1987). This is understandable because men decide whether to be sexually aggressive, whereas women do not decide whether they will be victimized.

Peer pressure, combined with stereotypes about masculinity, contributes to men's sexual aggression against women. Sexually aggressive men report more peer pressure to have sex than nonaggressive men (Kanin, 1967). Men in groups may have a common sense of masculinity, power, and sexual conquest that reduces inhibitions against sexual violence; this can lead to gang rape (Ehrhart & Sandler, 1985). In addition, men in groups often protect one another from being accused of sexual aggression. These peer groups support and sustain earlier learned values regarding the appropriateness of sexual aggression (Kanin, 1967).

Shotland (1989) hypothesized that a man who engages in sexual assault during the first few dates with a woman (termed *beginning date rape*) may be dating her with the intent to sexually assault her, knowing that sexual assault is less likely to be labeled as rape if it involves a dating partner rather than a stranger. Shotland speculated that such men are misogynistic and antisocial and that they have a need for more frequent, and more varied, sexual experiences than other men. In some ways, these men seem to have carried the negative aspects of the masculine stereotype to an extreme.

Sexual coercion of males.   Men are vulnerable to pressure resulting from myths about male sexuality. Stereotypes portray males as sexually experienced and always ready for sex (Zilbergeld, 1978). Thus, many men feel that they must engage in sex in order to become sexually experienced. Furthermore, if a woman makes a sexual advance, many men feel that they cannot refuse, lest they appear inadequate. A study of college students found that more men (63%) than women (46%) had engaged in unwanted sexual intercourse (Muehlenhard & Cook, 1988). Men cited gender role stereotypes more often than did women as reasons for unwanted sexual intercourse. More men than women had engaged in unwanted sexual intercourse because their partners enticed them and they were unable to refuse, because they wanted to become more sexually experienced, because they wanted to be accepted by a popular group, because of peer pressure, and because they were afraid to appear homosexual, shy, afraid, unmasculine, or inexperienced.

The Sexual Double Standard

The sexual double standard allows men more sexual freedom than women (Di-Iorio, 1989; Muehlenhard & McCoy, in press; Muehlenhard & Quackenbush, 1988; Sprecher, McKinney, & Orbuch, 1987). Men are allowed—in fact, expected—to be sexually active, but women are disparaged if they engage in sex outside of a narrow set of guidelines (e.g., if they engage in sex outside of a committed relationship).

The sexual double standard contributes to sexual coercion in close relationships in several ways. Men are expected to be sexually active. Thus, they might ignore women's protests in order to obtain sex and comply with cultural expectations about male sexuality.

Women, on the other hand, are not expected to be too eager to engage in sex with a new dating partner. Instead, women are expected to offer token resistance, saying no even when they mean yes. This message is found in television, movies, pornography, and jokes (Cowan, Lee, Levy, & Snyder, 1988; Malamuth & Check, 1981; Smith, 1976; Waggett, 1989; Zilbergeld, 1978). These media depict scenarios in which a woman refuses sex, the man forces her, and the outcome is positive: The woman either becomes sexually aroused or falls in love with the man. Men who take no for an answer are depicted as unmasculine. Data show that some women do indeed engage in token resistance to sex, especially when they think that their partners accept the sexual double standard (Muehlenhard & Hollabaugh, 1988; Muehlenhard & McCoy, in press). Many men believe that women's refusals are insincere (Muehlenhard et al., 1985; Shotland & Goodstein, 1983), perhaps because of their exposure to the media or because of their own experiences with women who appeared to offer token resistance to sex. These men may proceed to have sex with women in spite of their protests, in some cases apparently not recognizing that their behavior constitutes sexual assault (Bart & O'Brien, 1985; Warshaw, 1988).

Gender Differences in Perceptions of Sexual Interest

Men interpret behavior more sexually than women do. That is, men are more likely than women to interpret a variety of behaviors and situations to mean that the other person is interested in sex (Abbey, 1982; Goodchilds & Zellman, 1984; Muehlenhard, 1988). This may occur because men are socialized to attend more carefully to potentially sexual cues (Abbey, 1982).

Because men frequently perceive situations more sexually than women do, men are likely to feel that sexual advances are justified when women feel that they are unsolicited and unjustified. This may lead to sexual assault in an intimate relationship in one of two ways. When such a misunderstanding occurs between a man and a woman, he might ignore her clarification because he is sure that her intentions are sexual (i.e., he is sure that her resistance is merely token, as described above). Alternatively, he might ignore her clarification because he feels that she "led him on" by behaving "suggestively" (Muehlenhard, 1988). Many people believe that "leading a man on" justifies sexual assault (Goodchilds & Zellman, 1984; Muehlenhard & MacNaughton, 1988).

Shotland (1989) hypothesized that, when sexual assault occurs after several dates, but before the two people have established the rules of their relationship (termed *early date rape*), gender differences in perceptions of sexual interest are likely to be implicated. According to Shotland's model, misperception of sexual intent, along with belief systems that support sexual assault (e.g., adversarial sexual beliefs and the acceptance of interpersonal violence) and excitation-transfer (misinterpreting sexual excitation as anger about having been rejected and vice versa), is likely to lead to sexual assault in this stage of the relationship.

Legal and Religious Influences

In many states, husbands can legally sexually assault their wives whenever they wish. Legislation often includes a marital exemption by defining *sexual assault* or *rape* as sexual penetration or intercourse "with a woman *not his wife;* by force or threat of force; against her will and without her consent" (Estrich, 1987, p. 8, italics added). The laws in many states still imply that a wife is the property of her husband by giving the husband the permanent right to sexual relations once the wife says, "I do." Laura X[3] (personal communication, February 16, 1990), founder of the National Clearinghouse on Marital Rape, supplied the following statistics: In 7 states, sexual assault in marriage cannot be prosecuted under any circumstances; in 26 states, it can be prosecuted only under certain circumstances, such as if the assault is extraordinarily violent; in just 17 states, married women have full legal protection against being sexually assaulted by their husbands.

The marital exemption came out of a traditional patriarchal ideology leading

---

[3]According to Laura X, "X stands for women's history being anonymous, and replaces women's legal owner's names."

to the subjugation of women (Brownmiller, 1975). The Hale Doctrine, which originally legalized sexual assault in marriage, was written when women were treated as the property of first their fathers and then their husbands (Bidwell & White, 1986; Brownmiller, 1975; Jeffords, 1984; Russell, 1982). From this perspective, a wife is not given the right to say no, and if she does refuse sex, her husband can force her because it is his prerogative to do so (Hanneke & Shields, 1985; Weingourt, 1985).

Although many states have modified their laws to limit the marital exemption in sexual assault law, 12 states have modified their laws to expand this exemption (Finkelhor & Yllo, 1985). These states granted the right of sexually assaulting one's partner to cohabiting boyfriends as well as husbands. In addition, several other states gave men the right to sexually assault their "voluntary sexual companions." In these states, a man who has previously had consensual sexual intercourse with a woman can no longer be charged with first degree sexual assault if he subsequently forces her to have sex (Finkelhor & Yllo, 1985). These laws codify society's attitudes about the rights of men and women in close relationships.

Judeo-Christian thought has promoted the idea that husbands are entitled to have sex with their wives (Jeffords, 1984). "For centuries, the Catholic church has taught that it is a sin for women to refuse their husbands' sexual intimacy. Wives were actually obliged to report such refusals in confession" (Finkelhor & Yllo, 1985, p. 86). Research has shown that highly religious people are less likely than less religious people to support criminalizing sexual assault in marriage (Finkelhor & Yllo, 1985).

Economic Coercion

Economic coercion in marriage.   Because women, as a group, are economically oppressed and dependent on men for support (Hewlett, 1986), women are much more vulnerable than men to both explicit and implicit economic coercion (Muehlenhard & Schrag, 1991). If a woman needs the economic support of her partner to support herself or her children, and if she knows that her partner expects her to engage in sex with him, then she may feel that she has no option other than to comply with his sexual expectations. In some cases, her partner might make explicit threats; for example, he might threaten to leave her or to withhold money from her unless she has sex with him (Finkelhor & Yllo, 1985). In other cases, the demands might be implicit; a woman might know that her partner expects the relationship to be sexual and that refusing to have sex with him would put the relationship at risk. In either case, she is pressured to engage in unwanted sexual activity. She might even technically consent—that is, she might passively acquiesce or perhaps even initiate sex—but the situation is nevertheless coercive. Some feminist writers have questioned whether women can ever truly consent to sex in a male-dominated culture that affords women little economic or political power (Dworkin, 1987).

Evidence suggests that economic dependence puts some women more at risk of being sexually assaulted by their husbands than others. Finkelhor and Yllo (1985) found that women who did not finish high school reported being sexually assaulted by their husbands four times more than women who graduated. Frieze (1983) found that women who had several children, who had never been employed before marriage, or who had less formal education were more likely than other women to have been sexually assaulted by their husbands. Russell (1982) found no relationship between a wife's financial dependence on her husband and the likelihood of his sexually assaulting her; she did, however, find a strong relationship between a wife's financial dependence on her husband and the likelihood of her remaining in the marriage. Women who were least likely to leave a husband who had sexually assaulted them were those women who had several children, who had been employed less than half of their adult lives, and whose husbands were their sole providers.

Economic coercion in dating. Economics also is a source of sexual coercion in dating situations. The man often pays all the dating expenses (Muehlenhard & Linton, 1987), and he might feel entitled to a return on his investment. College students—especially males with traditional gender role attitudes—regard sexual assault as more justified if the man pays all the dating expenses than if the woman pays her own expenses (Muehlenhard, 1988). Dates that involve sexual aggression are especially likely to have involved the man's paying all the dating expenses (Muehlenhard & Linton, 1987).

Alcohol and Drug Intoxication

Both women and men implicate the use of alcohol in many accounts of sexual aggression. Both the perpetrators and victims of sexual assault in close relationships often attribute the assault to the perpetrator's being intoxicated (Bowker, 1983; Frieze, 1983).

Alcohol and drug intoxication can be viewed as both causes of and excuses for sexual violence. Those who view alcohol as a cause of sexual violence posit that alcohol serves as a facilitator of aggressive behavior by weakening self-control (Levine & Kanin, 1987).

Alternatively, alcohol can be viewed as a socially acceptable excuse for socially unacceptable behavior (Reynolds, 1984). Studies using a balanced placebo design, in which subjects' levels of intoxication and their beliefs about their levels of intoxication are manipulated independently, show that actually being intoxicated results in changes such as interference with information processing and motor coordination. Believing that one is intoxicated results in a greater likelihood of engaging in behavior that is socially inappropriate (Hull & Bond, 1986). Thus, it might be the belief that one's behavior is excused by intoxication, rather than intoxication per se, that increases the risk of sexual assault. Consistent with this hypothesis, high school students (Goodchilds & Zellman, 1984), college students

(Richardson & Campbell, 1982), incarcerated rapists (Wolfe & Baker, 1980), and criminal statutes (Amir, 1971) regard rapists as less responsible for the sexual assault if they were intoxicated, whereas victims are regarded as more responsible for the assault if they were intoxicated (Richardson & Campbell, 1982).

Violent Family of Origin

The victim's family of origin.   Women who were sexually abused as children are more likely than other women to be sexually victimized by their husbands (Finkelhor & Yllo, 1985; Frieze, 1983; Russell, 1982). Why would a woman's background relate to the likelihood of her being sexually assaulted by her husband? Perhaps young women from abusive families are desperate to leave home and thus are less discriminating in their choice of partners (Finkelhor & Yllo, 1985). Women who were sexually abused as children may not like sex and may refuse their husbands more often, and some of these husbands may respond by raping their wives (Russell, 1982). Perhaps women who were abused as children tolerate more abuse from their husbands because they view it as the norm. Alternatively, the relationship between child sexual abuse and sexual assault in marriage may merely be a result of reporting bias: Perhaps women who are willing to discuss child sexual abuse are also willing to discuss sexual assault (Russell, 1982).

The perpetrator's family of origin.   Husbands who sexually assault their wives often come from families in which their fathers had abused their mothers (Bidwell & White, 1986; Bowker, 1983). Furthermore, there is evidence that being sexually abused as a child is linked to becoming sexually abusive (Davis & Leitenberg, 1987). In Lobel's (1986) book on lesbian battering, several of the women who had been sexually assaulted by their partners mentioned that their partners had themselves been abused as girls. As Russell (1982) pointed out, however, a history of sexual abuse cannot fully account for becoming an abusive adult; if it could, women would sexually abuse children more than men would, but this is not the case.

Compulsory Heterosexuality

Although it is not typically thought of as a form of sexual coercion, compulsory heterosexuality is a phenomenon that pressures both women and men to participate in heterosexual relationships. This phenomenon has been discussed by feminist authors such as Rich (1980). Heterosexuality is made compulsory in many ways. Homosexual role models are absent in children's books and television shows, which depict marriage as the ultimate goal for a woman (Weitzman, 1979). Laws promote heterosexuality both indirectly, such as by making the legal benefits of marriage available only to heterosexual couples, and directly, such as by making homosexual acts illegal (Weitz, 1989). Thus, women and men who might prefer same-sex relationships are often coerced into unwanted heterosexual behavior.

Negative attitudes toward homosexuality may also lead to violent sexual assault in homosexual relationships. In some cases, sexual assault in lesbian and gay relationships may result from internalized homophobia (Joyce Grover, Lawrence Women's Transitional Care Services personal communication, April 26, 1990).[4]

CONSEQUENCES OF SEXUAL COERCION
IN CLOSE RELATIONSHIPS

Evaluating the consequences of sexual coercion in close relationships is constrained by a limited amount of data. Early studies on the consequences of sexual assault used female subjects who had reported these incidents to police departments or emergency rooms. Researchers now know, however, that only a very small percentage of sexual assaults are ever reported and that, whereas sexual assault by strangers is overrepresented, sexual assault by acquaintances is underrepresented (Koss et al., 1988; Russell, 1984). The small percentage of sexual assaults by acquaintances that are reported may be unrepresentative in various ways. For example, assaults by acquaintances that are reported to the police may be more violent than those that are not reported. Only recently have studies of randomly selected samples allowed social scientists to investigate the consequences of both reported and unreported sexual assault (e.g., Burnam et al., 1988; Koss et al., 1988).

Although it is likely that the emotional, physical, and sexual consequences discussed below apply to both heterosexual and homosexual relationships, sexual assault in lesbian and gay relationships presents some additional problems. According to Joyce Grover (personal communication, April 26, 1990), lesbian and gay communities may not want to acknowledge that violence can occur within the community, leading to the further isolation of the victim. Support services— police, court personnel, medical service providers, and domestic violence programs—may be homophobic. Legal remedies (e.g., restraining orders) may not be available to protect an individual from a same-sex partner. Furthermore, attempting to use these support services might necessitate coming out (publicly revealing one's homosexuality), which could result in loss of one's job and other forms of discrimination (also see National Coalition Against Domestic Violence, 1990).

Little is known about the consequences of nonviolent sexual coercion. The little that is known suggests that the consequences of nonviolent coercion are not

---

[4]Similarly, sexual assault in some lesbian relationships may result from internalized misogyny.

always less serious than the consequences of violent sexual coercion. Murnen, Byrne, and Perot (1989) found that women who had been verbally coerced into engaging in unwanted sexual intercourse felt more guilty than women who had been physically coerced.

Because of these limitations of the available data, the following discussion is based primarily on studies of women who have been sexually assaulted by men.

The Relative Seriousness of Sexual Assault by Acquaintances and Strangers

Many people believe that sexual assault in dating, cohabiting, and marital relationships is far less traumatic than sexual assault by a stranger (Russell, 1982). Although persons living in a society that treats women as the sexual possessions of their partners might draw such conclusions, research indicates that these assertions are unfounded.

Koss et al. (1988) examined differences in the experiences of women sexually assaulted by strangers and women sexually assaulted by acquaintances (i.e., nonromantic acquaintances, casual dates, steady dates, spouses, or family members). Sexual assaults by acquaintances were more likely than sexual assaults by strangers to involve a single offender and multiple episodes, and they were less likely to be reported to the police or discussed with another person. In addition, sexual assaults by acquaintances were rated as less violent than sexual assaults by strangers, except that sexual assaults by husbands or family members were rated as being just as violent as sexual assaults by strangers. No differences were found between the groups with regard to their reported level of depression, anxiety, relationship satisfaction, and sexual satisfaction. Thus, sexual assault by both strangers and acquaintances is highly traumatic for victims.

Some researchers have found that sexual assault in marriage often results in more significant long-term effects than any other type of sexual assault (Russell, 1982). Finkelhor and Yllo (1985) proposed that women sexually assaulted by their husbands suffer additional trauma because of their close relationships with the perpetrators. These victims often experience betrayal, entrapment, and ongoing abuse. They frequently have no one with whom they can discuss these experiences, and they continue to live with their attackers, rather than with a memory (Russell, 1982).

Emotional Consequences

Betrayal and humiliation. Feeling betrayed and humiliated is common among persons who experience sexual violence in close relationships (Finkelhor & Yllo, 1985). Victims often feel shocked and betrayed when they realize that a person they know and love could commit such acts of violence against them. Because their perpetrators know them, victims may feel that the sexual assault is a personal attack rather than a more indiscriminant act of violence. In many cases, the victim's sense of betrayal leads to a deterioration, or termination, of the relationship.

Along with the sense of betrayal often goes a feeling of humiliation. Victims of sexual assault frequently feel dirty, denigrated, and used (Burgess & Holmstrom, 1974; Finkelhor & Yllo, 1985). In close relationships, the sense of humiliation is perhaps heightened by the fact that the perpetrator has violated the victim both sexually and emotionally. Also, the victim may be faced with continually reliving the humiliation if the relationship is sustained.

Problems with trust and intimacy. One of the more long-term effects of sexual assault experienced by victims is distrust of others (Finkelhor & Yllo, 1985; King & Webb, 1981; Koss et al., 1988). In cases of sexual assault by strangers, victims typically become afraid of, and unable to trust, persons unknown to them and persons who resemble the perpetrator in some way (Burgess & Holmstrom, 1974; Kilpatrick, Resick, & Veronen, 1981). For victims of sexual assault in close relationships, the distrust becomes more pronounced. It has been suggested that the closer the relationship between the victim and the perpetrator, the greater the loss of trust will be (Finkelhor & Yllo, 1985; King & Webb, 1981; Koss et al., 1988). These victims may generalize their distrust to include both acquaintances and strangers. Women who are sexually victimized by men in close relationships may experience an inability to trust or develop intimate relationships with any men (Finkelhor & Yllo, 1985). Some women may feel so violated by the men who abused them that they may withdraw from contact with men, and they may even express outright hatred for men in general (Finkelhor & Yllo, 1985).

Guilt. Self-blame or guilt is another common response to sexual assault (Becker, Skinner, Abel, Howell, & Bruce, 1982; Burgess & Holmstrom, 1974; Finkelhor & Yllo, 1985; King & Webb, 1981; Sutherland & Scherl, 1970). Some victims believe that they caused the assault by not being good partners; others feel guilty for not resisting strongly enough or not communicating effectively with their partners (Finkelhor & Yllo, 1985; King & Webb, 1981). These types of guilty feelings are particularly common when sexual assault occurs in dating or marital relationships (King & Webb, 1981). In addition, some women appear to be more likely than others to blame themselves. Finkelhor and Yllo (1985) found that women who held the most traditional ideas about being a wife tended to blame themselves more for being sexually assaulted by their husbands than women who held less traditional ideas.

Fear. Due to the traumatic nature of sexual assault, fearfulness is also a common response (Becker et al., 1982; Burgess & Holmstrom, 1974; Finkelhor & Yllo, 1985; Kilpatrick et al., 1981; King & Webb, 1981). Victims sexually assaulted by strangers often experience phobias related to the particular circumstances of their assault, such as fear of being alone, fear of being outdoors, or fear of people walking behind them (Burgess & Holmstrom, 1974; Kilpatrick et al., 1981; King & Webb, 1981). In contrast, victims of sexual assault in close relationships often experience paralyzing fear of their partners (Finkelhor & Yllo, 1985). These victims may live in terror for many years, never knowing when their partners might lash out and assault them again. Often, even after these victims have ended their abusive relationship, they remain plagued by fears that their ex-partners might return and sexually assault or kill them (Finkelhor & Yllo, 1985). Even after victims gain conscious control over their fearfulness, they may continue to experience fear in the form of nightmares related to their assault experiences (Burgess & Holmstrom, 1974; Finkelhor & Yllo, 1985).

Anger. Feeling anger toward the perpetrator is a common reaction to being sexually assaulted (Becker et al., 1982; Burgess & Holmstrom, 1974; Finkelhor & Yllo, 1985; Russell, 1982). In close relationships, victims are often forced to choose between hiding the anger they feel in order to continue the relationship and expressing their anger to the perpetrator, which may terminate the relationship. For victims who choose to stay in such relationships, denial and control of angry feelings are often attempts to prevent further victimization in the relationship (Finkelhor & Yllo, 1985).

Depression. Victims of sexual assault often exhibit symptoms of depression, including loss of appetite, changes in sleep patterns, fatigue, irritability, and suicidal ideation (Atkeson, Calhoun, Resick, & Ellis, 1982; Ellis, Atkeson, & Calhoun, 1981; King & Webb, 1981; Koss et al., 1988; Sutherland & Scherl, 1970). These feelings last an average of 4 months in victims of sexual assault by strangers (Atkeson et al., 1982). In close relationships, the victims may suffer long-term depression if they choose to remain in the relationship due to their continued contact with the perpetrators. Koss et al. (1988) found that 28% of the sexual assault victims were depressed to the point of considering specific methods for committing suicide; there was no significant difference between women victimized by strangers and those victimized by acquaintances, dating partners, or husbands.

Physical Consequences

Many sexual assault victims experience physical injuries. Some experience physical reactions like nausea and vomiting immediately following the assault (Finkelhor & Yllo, 1985). Forced vaginal or anal intercourse often results in damage to the genitals or the rectum. In addition, many victims of sexual assault in marriage experience physical injuries due to physical battering by the perpetrator (Finkelhor & Yllo, 1985; Koss et al., 1988), including black eyes, bruises, cuts, abrasions, and broken bones.

Sexual Consequences

Changes in sexual behavior and satisfaction are common in victims of sexual assault (Becker et al., 1982; Burgess & Holmstrom, 1974; Feldman-Summers, Gordon, & Meagher, 1979; Finkelhor & Yllo, 1985; King & Webb, 1981; Koss et al., 1988). Because many victims associate particular sexual behaviors with the painful memories of the assault, they may be dissatisfied with, afraid of, or repulsed by engaging in these specific behaviors (Feldman-Summers et al., 1979). The behaviors that cause difficulty for victims are typically the sexual behaviors that were involved in the assault. In contrast, sexual assault victims are less likely to report a decrease in satisfaction with affectionate behaviors like hugging and holding hands (Feldman-Summers et al., 1979). In victims sexually assaulted by strangers, levels of satisfaction with sexual behaviors generally improve after 2 months; however, these levels of satisfaction are still not as high as the reported levels of pre-assault satisfaction (Feldman-Summers et al., 1979). In close relationships, victims of sexual assault may experience more long-term decreases in sexual satisfaction due to both the violation of trust they have experienced and the fact that they have often been assaulted repeatedly (Finkelhor & Yllo, 1985; Koss et al., 1988). Some victims may grow to hate sex and may continue to experience sexual problems and aversions even after terminating their abusing relationships (Finkelhor & Yllo, 1985).

CONCLUSIONS

Contrary to the myths that sexual violence occurs only between strangers in dark alleys or that sexual coercion in close relationships is not serious, research shows that sexual violence and coercion in close relationships are both prevalent and serious. There are many areas, however, in which more research is desperately needed. More research is needed on the causes of sexual coercion in close relationships in order to provide better programs for prevention. More research is needed on consequences of sexual coercion in close relationships, as well as ways of helping victims overcome these consequences. More research is needed on the sexual assault of men by their female partners and sexual assault within lesbian and gay relationships. Finally, more research is needed on nonviolent sexual coercion—unwanted sex that results from the subtle but powerful effects of economic forces and social norms.

REFERENCES

Abbey, A. (1982). Sex differences in attributions for friendly behavior: Do males misperceive females' friendliness? *Journal of Personality and Social Psychology, 42,* 830–838.

Amir, M. (1971). *Patterns in forcible rape.* Chicago: University of Chicago Press.

Archer, J., & Lloyd, B. (1985). *Sex and gender.* Cambridge: University of Cambridge Press.

Atkeson, B. M., Calhoun, K. S., Resick, P. A., & Ellis, E. M. (1982). Victims of rape: Repeated assessment of depressive symptoms. *Journal of Consulting and Clinical Psychology, 50,* 96–102.

Bart, P. B., & O'Brien, P. H. (1985). *Stopping rape.* New York: Pergamon.

Becker, J. V., Skinner, L. J., Abel, G. G., Howell, J., & Bruce, K. (1982). The effects of sexual assault on rape and attempted rape victims. *Victimology: An International Journal, 7,* 106–113.

Bidwell, L., & White, P. (1986). The family context of marital rape. *Journal of Family Violence, 1,* 277–287.

Bowker, L. H. (1983). Marital rape: A distinct syndrome? *The Journal of Contemporary Social Work, 64,* 347–352.

Brownmiller, S. (1975). *Against our will: Men, women, and rape.* New York: Simon & Schuster.

Burgess, A. W., & Holmstrom, L. (1974). Rape trauma syndrome. *American Journal of Psychiatry, 131,* 981–986.

Burnam, M. A., Stein, J. A., Golding, J. M., Siegel, J. M., Sorenson, S. B., Forsythe, A. B., & Telles, C. A. (1988). Sexual assault and mental disorders in a community population. *Journal of Consulting and Clinical Psychology, 56,* 843–850.

Cowan, G., Lee, C., Levy, D., & Snyder, D. (1988). Dominance and inequality in X-rated videocassettes. *Psychology of Women Quarterly, 12,* 299–311.

Davis, G. E., & Leitenberg, H. (1987). Adolescent sex offenders. *Psychological Bulletin, 101,* 417–427.

DiIorio, J. A. (1989). Being and becoming coupled: The emergence of female subordination in heterosexual relationships. In B. J. Risman & P. Schwartz (Eds.), *Gender in intimate relationships: A microstructural approach* (pp. 94–107). Belmont, CA: Wadsworth.

Dworkin, A. (1987). *Intercourse.* New York: Free Press.

Ehrhart, J. K., & Sandler, B. R. (1985). *Campus gang rape: Party games?* Washington, DC: Project on the Status and Education of Women, Association of American Colleges.

Ellis, E. M., Atkeson, B. M., & Calhoun, K. S. (1981). An assessment of long-term reaction to rape. *Journal of Abnormal Psychology, 90,* 263–266.

Estrich, S. (1987). *Real rape.* Cambridge, MA: Harvard University Press.

Feldman-Summers, S., Gordon, P. E., & Meagher, J. R. (1979). The impact of rape on sexual satisfaction. *Journal of Abnormal Psychology, 88,* 101–105.

Finkelhor, D., & Yllo, K. (1985). *License to rape.* New York: Holt, Rinehart & Winston.

Forman, B. (1982). Reported male rape. *Victimology: An International Journal, 7,* 235–236.

Frieze, I. H. (1983). Investigating the causes and consequences of marital rape. *Signs: Journal of Women in Culture and Society, 8,* 532–553.

Gelles, R. J., & Straus, M. A. (1988). *Intimate violence.* New York: Simon & Schuster.

Goodchilds, J. D., & Zellman, G. L. (1984). Sexual signaling and sexual aggression in adolescent relationships. In N. M. Malamuth & E. Donnerstein (Eds.), *Pornography and sexual aggression* (pp. 233–243). Orlando, FL: Academic Press.

Gordon, M. T., & Riger, S. (1989). *The female fear.* New York: Free Press.

Hanneke, C. R., & Shields, N. A. (1985). Marital rape: Implications for the helping professions. *Journal of Contemporary Social Work, 66,* 451–458.

Harney, P. A., & Muehlenhard, C. L. (1991). Rape. In E. Grauerholz & M. A. Koralewski (Eds.), *Sexual coercion: A source book on its nature, causes, and prevention* (pp. 3–15). Lexington, MA: Lexington Books.

Hart, B. (1986). Lesbian battering: An examination. In K. Lobel (Ed.), *Naming the violence: Speaking out about lesbian battering* (pp. 173–189). Seattle: Seal Press.

Hewlett, S. A. (1986). *A lesser life: The myth of women's liberation in America.* New York: William Morris.

Hull, J. G., & Bond, C. F. (1986). Social and behavioral consequences of alcohol consumption and expectancy: A meta-analysis. *Psychological Bulletin, 99,* 347–360.

Jeffords, C. R. (1984). The impact of sex-role and religious attitudes upon forced marital intercourse norms. *Sex Roles, 11,* 543–553.

Kanin, E. J. (1967). An examination of sexual aggression as a response to sexual frustration. *Journal of Marriage and the Family, 29,* 428–433.

Kaufman, A., DiVasto, P., Jackson, R., Voorhees, D., & Christy, J. (1980). Male rape victims: Noninstitutionalized assault. *American Journal of Psychiatry, 137,* 221–223.

Kilpatrick, D. G., Resick, P. A., & Veronen, L. J. (1981). Effects of a rape experience: A longitudinal study. *Journal of Social Issues, 37,* 105–122.

King, H. E., & Webb, C. (1981). Rape crisis centers: Progress and problems. *Journal of Social Issues, 37,* 93–104.

Koss, M. P., & Dinero, T. E. (1988). Predictors of sexual aggression among a national sample of male college students. In R. A. Prentky & V. L. Quinsey (Eds.), *Human sexual aggression: Current perspectives* (pp. 133–147). New York: New York Academy of Sciences.

Koss, M. P., & Dinero, T. E. (1989). Discriminant analysis of risk factors for sexual victimization among a national sample of college women. *Journal of Consulting and Counseling Psychology, 57,* 242–250.

Koss, M. P., Dinero, T. E., Seibel, C. A., & Cox, S. L. (1988). Stranger and acquaintance rape: Are there differences in the victim's experience? *Psychology of Women Quarterly, 12,* 1–24.

Koss, M. P., Gidycz, C. A., & Wisniewski, N. (1987). The scope of rape: Incidence and prevalence of sexual aggression and victimization in a national sample of higher education students. *Journal of Consulting and Clinical Psychology, 55,* 162–170.

Koss, M. P., Leonard, K. E., Beezley, D. A., & Oros, C. J. (1985). Nonstranger sexual aggression: A discriminant analysis of the psychological characteristics of undetected offenders. *Sex Roles, 12,* 981–992.

Levine, E. M., & Kanin, E. J. (1987). Sexual violence among dates and acquaintances: Trends and their implications for marriage and family. *Journal of Family Violence, 2,* 55–65.

Lobel, K. (1986). *Naming the violence: Speaking out about lesbian battering.* Seattle: Seal Press.

Malamuth, N. M., & Check, J. V. (1981). The effects of mass media exposure on acceptance of violence against women: A field experiment. *Journal of Research in Personality, 15,* 436–446.

Muehlenhard, C. L. (1988). Misinterpreted dating behaviors and the risk of date rape. *Journal of Social and Clinical Psychology, 6,* 20–37.

Muehlenhard, C. L., & Calvin, S. (1989, November). *The impact of gender role socialization on women's reactions to unwanted sexual advances.* Presented at the annual meeting of the Society for the Scientific Study of Sex, Toronto.

Muehlenhard, C. L., & Cook, S. W. (1988). Men's reports of unwanted sexual activity. *Journal of Sex Research, 24,* 58–72.

Muehlenhard, C. L., & Falcon, P. L. (1990). Men's heterosocial skill and attitudes toward women as predictors of verbal sexual coercion and forceful rape. *Sex Roles, 23,* 241–259.

Muehlenhard, C. L., & Hollabaugh, L. C. (1988). Do women sometimes say no when they mean yes? The prevalence and correlates of women's token resistance to sex. *Journal of Personality and Social Psychology, 54,* 872–879.

Muehlenhard, C. L., & Linton, M. A. (1987). Date rape and sexual aggression in dating situations: Incidence and risk factors. *Journal of Consulting Psychology, 34,* 186–196.

Muehlenhard, C. L., Linton, M. A., Felts, A. S., & Andrews, S. L. (1985, June). Men's attitudes toward the justifiability of date rape: Intervening variables and possible solutions. In E. Allgeier (Chair), *Sexual coercion: Political issues and empirical findings.* Symposium conducted at the Annual Midcontinent meeting of the Society for the Scientific Study of Sex, Chicago.

Muehlenhard, C. L., & MacNaughton, J. S. (1988). Women's attitudes toward women who "lead men on." *Journal of Social and Clinical Psychology, 7,* 65–79.

Muehlenhard, C. L., & McCoy, M. L. (in press). Double standard/Double bind: The sexual double standard and women's communication about sex. *Psychology of Women Quarterly.*

Muehlenhard, C. L., & Quackenbush, D. M. (1988, November). *Can the sexual double standard put women at risk for sexually transmitted disease? The role of the double standard in condom use among women.* Presented at the annual meeting of the Society for the Scientific Study of Sex, San Francisco.

Muehlenhard, C. L., & Schrag, J. (1991). Nonviolent sexual coercion. In A. Parrot & L. Bechhofer (Eds.), *Acquaintance rape: The hidden crime* (pp. 115–128). New York: Wiley.

Murnen, S. K., Perot, A., & Byrne, D. (1989). Coping with unwanted sexual activity: Normative responses, situational determinants, and individual differences. *Journal of Sex Research, 26,* 85–106.

National Coalition Against Domestic Violence. (1990). *Break the silence around lesbian battering.* Washington, DC: Author.

Reynolds, L. (1984). Rape: A social perspective. *Journal of Offender Counseling and Rehabilitative Services, 9,* 149–160.

Rich, A. (1980). Compulsory heterosexuality and lesbian existence. *Signs: Journal of Women in Culture and Society, 5,* 631–660.

Richardson, D., & Campbell, J. L. (1982). The effect of alcohol on attributions of blame for rape. *Personality and Social Psychology Bulletin, 8,* 468–476.

Rubin, G. (1984). The traffic in women: Notes on the "political economy" of sex. In A. M. Jagger & P. S. Rothenberg (Eds.), *Feminist frameworks* (pp. 155–171). New York: McGraw-Hill.

Russell, D. E. H. (1982). *Rape in marriage.* New York: Macmillan.

Russell, D. E. H. (1984). *Sexual exploitation: Rape, child sexual abuse, and workplace harassment.* Beverly Hills, CA: Sage.

Sarrel, P. M., & Masters, W. H. (1982). Sexual molestation of men by women. *Archives of Sexual Behavior, 11,* 117–131.

Shotland, R. L. (1989). A model of the causes of date rape in developing and close relationships. In C. Hendrick (Ed.), *Close relationships* (pp. 247–270). Newbury Park, CA: Sage.

Shotland, R. L., & Goodstein, L. (1983). Just because she doesn't want to doesn't mean it's rape: An experimentally based causal model of the perception of rape in a dating situation. *Social Psychology Quarterly, 46,* 220–232.

Shotland, R. L., & Straw, M. K. (1976). Bystander response to an assault: When a man attacks a woman. *Journal of Personality and Social Psychology, 34,* 990–999.

Smith, D. D. (1976). The social content of pornography. *Journal of Communication, 26,* 16–24.

Sprecher, S., McKinney, K., & Orbuch, T. L. (1987). Has the double standard disappeared?: An experimental test. *Social Psychology Quarterly, 50,* 24–31.

Stanko, E. A. (1988). Fear of crime and the myth of the safe home: A feminist critique of criminology. In K. Yllo & M. Bograd (Eds.), *Feminist perspectives on wife abuse* (pp. 75–88). Newbury Park, CA: Sage.

Struckman-Johnson, C. (1988). Forced sex on dates: It happens to men, too. *Journal of Sex Research, 24,* 234–241.

Sutherland, S., & Scherl, D. J. (1970). Patterns of response among victims of rape. *American Journal of Orthopsychiatry, 40,* 503–511.

Waggett, G. J. (1989, May 27). A plea to the soaps: Let's stop turning rapists into heroes. *TV Guide,* pp. 10–11.

Warshaw, R. (1988). *I never called it rape.* New York: Harper & Row.

Waterman, C., K., Dawson, L. J., & Bologna, M. J. (1989). Sexual coercion in gay male and lesbian relationships: Predictions and implications for support services. *Journal of Sex Research, 26,* 118–124.

Weingourt, R. (1985). Wife rape: Barriers to identification and treatment. *American Journal of Psychotherapy, 39,*187–192.

Weitz, R. (1989). What price independence? Social reactions to lesbians, spinsters, widows, and nuns. In J. Freeman (Ed.), *Women: A feminist perspective* (4th ed., pp. 446–456). Mountain View, CA: Mayfield.

Weitzman, L. J. (1979). *Sex role socialization: A focus on women.* Palo Alto, CA: Mayfield.

Wolfe, J., & Baker, V. (1980). Characteristics of imprisoned rapists and circumstances of the rape. In C. G. Warner (Ed.), *Rape and sexual assault* (pp. 265–278). Germantown, MD: Aspen Systems.

Zilbergeld, B. (1978). *Male sexuality: A guide to sexual fulfillment.* New York: Bantam.

9 Sexuality in Homosexual and Heterosexual Couples

Lawrence A. Kurdek
Wright State University

In view of findings that personal well-being is closely related to experiencing a satisfying relationship (Diener, 1984), researchers from various disciplines have attempted to understand how relationships begin, develop, and terminate. However, most of our information regarding relationships—including sexuality—comes from the study of heterosexual couples. The purpose of this chapter is to review information regarding sexuality in homosexual relationships. Because relevant information is limited, this chapter also presents findings from a study of sexuality in homosexual and heterosexual couples.

JUSTIFICATION FOR A SCIENTIFIC INTEREST IN HOMOSEXUAL COUPLES

There are several reasons for a scientific interest in homosexual couples and in their differences from heterosexual couples. First, homosexual couples exist in the absence of socialized role models. When children play house, the roles are almost always assigned on the basis of gender. One person plays the mommy-wife, and the other person plays the daddy-husband. However, a recurrent theme in the small empirical literature on gay and lesbian relationships is that partners in these relationships eschew traditional male and female roles in favor of an ethic of equality and reciprocity (Peplau & Gordon, 1983). Thus, the study of gay and lesbian relationships provides some insight into how relationships evolve without the strictures imposed by gender-related roles.

Second, gay and lesbian relationships develop without institutional support. Although there are current movements to legalize homosexual relationships and to extend spousal benefits to gay and lesbian partners, gay and lesbian relationships are not legally sanctioned. To the contrary, sexual activity in these relationships is illegal in some states. This deficit in institutional support results in partners in gay and lesbian relationships lacking the external benefits of marriage as a legal institution (e.g., tax reductions, insurance and health benefits); having few external barriers to ending the relationship (e.g., fear of the social stigma associated with being divorced, fear of losing support from family members); and relying heavily on friends for support (Kurdek, 1988a; Kurdek & Schmitt, 1986). Thus, the study of gay and lesbian relationships affords an opportunity to examine how interpersonal dynamics play themselves out without the support typically provided by society at large or by family members in particular.

Third, sexual activity in gay and lesbian relationships occurs without procreative intent. Thus, sexual activity in these relationships can be viewed almost exclusively as an end in itself rather than as a means to reproduction. A focus on sexuality as personal pleasure raises issues regarding monogamy and fidelity. Relative to heterosexual couples, homosexual couples—especially gay couples—often negotiate rules regarding sex outside of the relationship (McWhirter & Mattison, 1984), although this may be occurring less frequently due to health concerns regarding AIDS. Nonetheless, gay and lesbian relationships can be studied to see how nontraditional attitudes regarding monogamy and fidelity affect relationship quality and relationship stability.

Fourth, because the number of gays and lesbians is limited, partner selection is fairly restricted. This restriction enables an examination of how mate selection occurs among homosexuals in the absence of concerns regarding reproductive resources (Buss, 1988) and tests the generalizability of the similarity-attraction paradigm as one basis for the development and stability of romantic relationships (Byrne, 1971).

Finally, gay and lesbian relationships exist in a context of homophobia. Despite documentation that homosexuality is not associated with psychopathology (Kurdek, 1987), that homosexuality is not a matter of personal choice (Ellis & Ames, 1987), and that homosexual cohabiting couples and heterosexual married couples are indistinguishable in their appraisals of relationship quality (Kurdek & Schmitt, 1986), negative attitudes and violence toward gays and lesbians are at epidemic proportions, perhaps spurred in part by the current AIDS health crisis (Herek, 1989). This homophobic context raises the issue of how internalized homophobia affects relationship functioning.

SEXUALITY IN HOMOSEXUAL VERSUS HETEROSEXUAL COUPLES

Given the differences between homosexual and heterosexual couples noted above, one might expect to find differences in their sexual behavior. Indeed, the most extensive and comprehensive study to date of these types of couples supports this expectation. Blumstein and Schwartz (1983) received mailed questionnaires from 969 gay, 788 lesbian, 3,574 married, and 642 heterosexual cohabiting couples from across the nation. Subjects were predominantly white and well educated and lived together an average of 6.0, 3.7, 13.9, and 2.5 years, respectively. The couples were found to differ on several dimensions of sexual behavior. Relative to other couples, gay couples had sex most often in the early part of their relationship and engaged in the greatest variety of sexual activity. After 10 years, however, gay couples had sex less frequently with each other than did married couples, but were more likely than other couples to have sex outside of the relationship with the consent and even participation of both partners.

Relative to the other couples, lesbian couples had sex least frequently, engaged in sexual activity outside of the relationship least often, and were most likely to kiss during sex. The authors speculated that because lesbians grow up learning society's restrictive guidelines regarding female sexuality, their sexual behavior may be negatively affected in unconscious ways. However, they also noted that lesbians were less inhibited about oral sex and more positive about their bodies and genitalia than were heterosexual women.

Despite these differences in sexual behavior between homosexual and heterosexual couples, some similarities have also been reported. Blumstein and Schwartz (1983) found that the quantity and quality of sex were related to overall satisfaction with the relationship in each of the four types of couples they studied. Further, in each type of couple the emotionally expressive partner was the one more likely to initiate sexual activity. Peplau and Gordon (1983) also noted that, regardless of sexual orientation, people want affection and companionship from their relationships.

More detailed information regarding the sexual activities of gay couples comes from McWhirter and Mattison's (1984) interview study of 156 gay couples. Like Blumstein and Schwartz (1983), these authors found that gays were very versatile in their sexual behavior, and did not assume male and female roles. Rather, reciprocity in doing and receiving was the norm. In the year prior to the study, over 90% of the men reported having engaged in kissing and hugging, body rubbing, tongue kissing, fellatio, being fellated, mutual masturbation, and mutual fellatio. A smaller percentage (71%) reported penetrating or being penetrated anally, and a smaller percentage yet (42%) did or received analingus. Finally, of the 95 couples together more than 5 years, in *none* were partners sexually exclusive with each other.

It is important to note, however, that interviews were conducted in 1979, a pre-AIDS era, and that the sample was geographically restricted to the San Diego area. Other studies using samples from more geographically diverse areas have not found such an absolute relation between relationship longevity and sexual nonexclusivity. For example, with a sample of 65 gay couples from 22 states, Kurdek (1988b) found that of 19 couples together more than 10 years, 26% were sexually exclusive. It is also of note that gay partners in sexually exclusive and sexually nonexclusive relationships reported equivalent levels of relationship quality (Blasband & Peplau, 1985; Kurdek, 1988b).

In-depth descriptions of the types of sexual activity engaged in by lesbian couples could not be found. However, Bell and Weinberg (1978) reported that, in a sample of 228 white and 64 black lesbians from the San Francisco Bay area, some form of masturbation with the partner was the most common sexual activity, followed by cunnilingus. In a geographically diverse sample of 286 lesbians, Califia (1979) found that the preferred technique to reaching orgasm was, in order, oral sex, manual stimulation, vaginal stimulation, masturbation, tribadism (genital appositioning), and anal stimulation.

A STUDY OF SEXUALITY IN HOMOSEXUAL AND HETEROSEXUAL COUPLES

It is clear from the data reviewed so far that we currently know little about sexual behavior in homosexual couples and how their behavior might differ from heterosexual couples'. In an effort to address these limitations, the rest of this chapter describes a study in which the sexual behavior of gay, lesbian, heterosexual unmarried, and heterosexual married cohabiting couples was compared. Data come from a larger study of relationship quality (Kurdek & Schmitt, 1986, 1987). Unlike previous studies in this area, the different types of couples were compared with controls for demographic factors that included length of time the couple lived together. Although the original focus of the study was not exclusively on sexuality, four aspects of sexual behavior in the relationship were assessed: sexual satisfaction, attitudes regarding fidelity, attitudes regarding new sexual techniques, and dysfunctional beliefs regarding sexual perfection.

Specific Questions of Interest in the Study

This study provides answers to five questions: (a) Do sexually exclusive and sexually nonexclusive couples differ in the four aspects of sexuality of interest? (b) For each of the four types of couples, how similar were partners' sexuality scores within each type of couple? (c) Do the four types of couples differ in their sexuality scores? (d) What is the relation between the sexuality scores and global satisfaction with the relationship for each type of couple? and (e) What is the relation between discrepancies between partners' sexuality scores and global satisfaction with the relationship for each type of couple? Predictions regarding the answers to each question are discussed later.

Participants in the Study

Participants were both partners of 77 gay, 58 lesbian, 36 heterosexual unmarried, and 49 heterosexual married couples. Partners in each couple lived together and had no children living with them. Participants were recruited through responses to a description of the study published in national gay and lesbian periodicals and through personal contacts. Although participants resided in 25 states, the majority of the gay, lesbian, heterosexual cohabiting, and married couples were from the Midwest (66%, 64%, 63%, and 93%, respectively).

The four types of couples were equivalent in age and highest level of education. The mean age for the entire sample was 31.05 years, and the majority of subjects had either some college (31%) or were college graduates (30%). However, the couples were not equivalent on income and number of months living together. Married couples had higher joint incomes (average of more than $50,000) than each of the other couples (combined range of $40,000–$44,999). Married couples and gay couples lived together more months than heterosexual cohabiting couples (respective mean values = 54.59, 49.96, and 24.65), while lesbian couples did not differ on this variable from any other couple (mean = 41.99 months).

Description of the Study Questionnaire and How Data Were Collected

Each couple interested in the study received by mail a pair of identical questionnaires. In order to ensure honesty in responding, data were collected anonymously, participants were directed not to discuss their responses with each other until the questionnaires had been completed and returned, and partners were asked to respond honestly. Completed questionnaires were returned in two separate postage-paid envelopes. Because questionnaires were frequently distributed by second parties, the actual return rate is unknown. However, the proportion of the number of questionnaires completed and returned by both partners to the number of distributed questionnaires was .32. Because the number of questionnaires distributed is not known, this proportion is an underestimate of the actual return rate. Nonetheless, the low response rate dictates that the findings be viewed with caution because the sample cannot be claimed to be representative. The measures of interest in this study were part of a larger assessment battery.

Demographic and background information.   Participants provided information regarding age, income, education, number of months living together, and the sexually exclusive/sexually nonexclusive status of the relationship. The last was assessed by having respondents check which one of the following two statements (derived from Bell & Weinberg, 1978) better described their relationship: (a) We are closely bound to each other. We look to each other rather than to outsiders for interpersonal and sexual satisfaction. We spend most of our leisure time together. (b) While attached to each other, we have an open relationship. We receive interpersonal and sexual satisfaction not only from each other but from others outside the relationship as well.

Global relationship satisfaction. Global appraisals of relationship quality were assessed in order to avoid an overlap in item content between assessments of relationship quality and sexuality (cf. Fincham & Bradbury, 1987). Here, such a global appraisal of relationship satisfaction was derived from four items from the relationship satisfaction subscore of Spanier's (1976) Dyadic Adjustment Scale. No item specifically assessed sexuality. The items included global assessments (1 = Never, 6 = All the time) of the frequency of discussing or considering separation; thoughts about things between partners going well; and ever regretting having lived together. Subjects also provided a rating of the overall degree of happiness in the relationship (1 = Extremely Unhappy, 7 = Perfect). Cronbach's alpha (a numerical index of the internal consistency of a summed composite score) based on the total sample was .80.

Sexual satisfaction. Sexual satisfaction was assessed by four items. Two were derived from the Marital Satisfaction Scale (Roach, Frazier, & Bowden, 1981) ("An unhappy sexual relationship is a drawback in my relationship" and "I look forward to sexual activity with my partner with pleasant anticipation"), which required ratings of agreement from 1 (Strongly Disagree) to 5 (Strongly Agree). The third item was derived from Spanier's (1976) Dyadic Adjustment Scale, and involved rating how frequently partners agreed (0 = Always Disagree, 5 = Always Agree) with sexual relations. The final item was derived from the Attractions, Barriers, and Alternatives measure developed for this study (see Kurdek & Schmitt, 1986). It involved rating the extent of agreement (1 = Strongly Disagree, 5 = Strongly Disagree) with the item "I enjoy my sexual relationship with my partner." The four scores were standardized to *z*-scores and summed for a composite score. Cronbach's alpha for this score based on the total sample was .88.

Importance of sexual fidelity. The importance of sexual fidelity was assessed by three items. Two came from Peplau and Cochran's (1981) Survey of Relationship Values, which involved rating the importance (1 = Not Important, 9 = Very Important) of the items "Sexual fidelity in the relationship" and "Being able to have sexual relations with people other than my partner." The third came from the Attractions, Barriers, and Alternatives measure mentioned above, and required rating the extent of agreement (1 = Strongly Disagree, 5 = Strongly Agree) with the item "If my relationship with my partner were to end, I would enjoy being with another sexual partner." Items were standardized to *z*-scores and were summed to create a composite score. Cronbach's alpha for this score based on the total sample was .64.

Importance of new sexual techniques. The importance of new sexual techniques was assessed by one item derived from Peplau and Cochran's (1981) Survey of Relationship Values. It involved rating the importance (1 = Not

Important, 9 = Very Important) of the item "Trying new sexual activities and techniques with my partner."

Beliefs regarding sexual perfection. Dysfunctional beliefs regarding sexual perfection were derived from the Relationship Beliefs Inventory (Eidelson & Epstein, 1982), which required subjects to indicate how true (0 = Very False, 5 = Very True) each of eight items was. Sample items were "I get upset if I think I have not completely satisfied my partner sexually" and "If I cannot perform well sexually whenever my partner is in the mood, I would consider that I had a problem." Cronbach's alpha for the summed composite score based on total sample was .74.

In order to assess the degree of overlap among the sexuality scores, their intercorrelations were examined. The Pearson correlations among the four sexuality scores were not very high, rs ranging from $-.26$ to $.21$. Given the low degree of shared variability, the four scores were retained as separate dimensions of sexuality.

ANSWERS TO THE QUESTIONS OF INTEREST

Do Sexually Exclusive and Sexually Nonexclusive Couples Differ on the Sexuality Scores?

In order to answer this question, only gay couples were considered because the percentage of sexually nonexclusive couples was greatest for these couples relative to lesbian, heterosexual cohabiting, and married couples (respective values = 31%, 1%, 0% and 4%). By definition, sexually nonexclusive couples were expected to value fidelity less than sexually exclusive couples. However, no differences were expected on the other sexuality scores, consistent with the theme that sexually exclusive and sexually nonexclusive gay couples do not differ in relationship quality (Kurdek, 1988b).

In order to see if there was reason to maintain the distinction between sexually exclusive and sexually nonexclusive gay couples for the other analyses conducted, these two groups of couples were compared on the four sexuality scores with a one-way (type of couple) multivariate analysis of variance (MANOVA). The single effect was significant, $F(4, 72) = 16.55, p < .0001$. (Here and below, all multivariate Fs are based on Pillai's trace statistic.) Subsequent univariate analyses of variance (ANOVAs) indicated that this effect was due to differences on only the fidelity score, $F(1, 75) = 67.58, p < .00001$. As expected, sexually exclusive couples valued fidelity more than did sexually nonexclusive couples. Given the equivalence of the two groups on the other sexuality scores, they were combined into a single gay group.

How Similar Were Sexuality Scores for Partners Within Each Type of Couple?

While previous studies have revealed a general pattern of partner similarity in appraisals of relationship quality, evidence suggests that partner similarity may be greater for homosexual couples, especially lesbian couples (Kurdek & Schmitt, 1987). Consistent with the trend that gay and lesbian partners subscribe to an ethic of reciprocity, especially with regard to sexual behavior (Blumstein & Schwartz, 1983; Peplau & Gordon, 1983), partner scores were expected to be more similar for homosexual couples than for heterosexual couples.

Intraclass correlations between partners' sexuality scores are presented by type of couple in Table 9.1. Although most of the correlations were not significantly different from each other, two patterns are of note. First, sexual satisfaction scores were significantly positively related for each type of couple. Second, only for lesbian couples were partners' scores significantly related for each score.

Did the Sexuality Scores Differ by Type of Couple?

It was expected that homosexual couples would value fidelity less than heterosexual couples, and that gay couples in particular would place more importance on new sexual techniques than the other couples (Blumstein & Schwartz, 1983; McWhirter & Mattison, 1984; Peplau & Gordon, 1983). Differences among couples were not expected on the other two sexuality scores.

Mean scores for each sexuality score, adjusted for the effects of income and months living together, are presented by type of couple in Table 9.2. A one-way (type of couple) multivariate analysis of covariance (MANCOVA) yielded a significant effect, $F(12, 639) = 4.97, p < .0001$. Univariate effects were significant for fidelity and new sexual techniques. As shown in Table 9.2, gay couples valued fidelity less than each of the other three couples and placed a higher importance on new sexual techniques than did lesbian couples.

TABLE 9.1
Intraclass Correlations Between Partners' Sexuality Scores by Type of Couple

| | Type of Couple | | | |
	Gay	Lesbian	Cohabiting	Married
Sexual satisfaction	.56*	.64*	.59*	.51*
Importance of fidelity	.61*	.30*	.07	.16
Importance of new sexual techniques	.39*	.48*	.15	.15
Beliefs about sexual perfection	.16	.54*	.02	.34*
n	77	58	36	49

*p < .01.

TABLE 9.2
Adjusted Mean Sexuality Scores by Type of Couple

	Type of couple				
	Gay	Lesbian	Cohabiting	Married	F (3, 214)
Sexual satisfaction	0.10	0.03	-0.13	-0.06	1.12
Importance of fidelity	-0.32[a]	0.25[b]	0.00[b]	0.23[b]	13.85**
Importance of new sexual techniques	6.46[a]	5.15[b]	5.74	5.74	6.10**
Beliefs about sexual perfection	15.02	14.43	14.43	15.54	0.74
n	77	58	36	49	

Note. Means with the same superscript do not differ from each other, $p < .05$. Means are adjusted for the effects of income and months living together.

Were the Sexuality Scores Related to Global Relationship Satisfaction?

Based on Blumstein and Schwartz's (1983) finding that the quantity and quality of sex were positively related to overall satisfaction with the relationship, sexual satisfaction was expected to be positively related to relationship quality for each couple. Because gay couples in particular place a low value on fidelity, the importance of fidelity was expected to be positively related to relationship quality for all but this type of couple. Many dysfunctional beliefs regarding sexual performance were expected to be negatively related to relationship quality for each type of couple (Kurdek & Schmitt, 1986). Because there are no previous data on the relation between the importance of new sexual techniques and relationship quality, this relation was explored here.

Partial correlations, controlling for income and months living together, between the four sexuality scores and the global relationship satisfaction score are presented for each type of couple in Table 9.3. Entries are provided for each partner, the couple, and the absolute value of partners' discrepancy scores. For gay and lesbian couples, Partner 1 and Partner 2 status was randomly determined; in the heterosexual couples it was assigned to males and females, respectively.

Few of the correlations among the four groups were significantly different from each other, but several patterns of relations are of note. Sexual satisfaction was positively related to relationship satisfaction for each partner within each type of couple. Generally, fidelity was positively related to relationship satisfaction for all but gay couples. The importance of new sexual techniques was generally unrelated to relationship satisfaction for each couple. Finally, beliefs regarding sexual perfection were negatively related to relationship satisfaction for gay and heterosexual cohabiting couples.

TABLE 9.3
Partial Correlations Between Sexuality Scores and Global Relationship Satisfaction Score by Type
of Couple

	Type of Couple			
	Gay	Lesbian	Cohabiting	Married
Sexual satisfaction				
Partner 1/male	.43**	.53**	.54**	.40**
Partner 2/female	.40**	.57**	.76**	.51**
Couple	.44**	.59**	.69**	.47**
Discrepancy	-.11	-.43**	-.40**	-.26*
Importance of fidelity				
Partner 1/male	.16	.45**	.37*	.03
Partner 2/female	.02	.24*	.34*	.47**
Couple	.09	.37**	.52**	.43**
Discrepancy	-.01	-.21*	-.28	-.33**
Importance of new sexual techniques				
Partner 1/male	.10	-.17	.27	-.12
Partner 2/female	-.03	-.15	-.07	-.13
Couple	.05	-.26*	.12	-.29*
Discrepancy	-.16	.00	-.18	-.02
Beliefs about sexual perfection				
Partner 1/male	-.28**	-.20	-.23	.04
Partner 2/female	-.06	-.11	-.30*	.23
Couple	-.31**	-.16	-.46**	.17
Discrepancy	-.25**	-.10	-.19	.00
n	77	58	36	49

Note. Correlations are computed with the effects of income and months living together removed.
*p < .05.
**p < .01.

Were Discrepancies Between Partners' Scores Related to Global Relationship Satisfaction?

In view of findings that discrepancies in married partners' self-report scores on relationship-oriented variables are negatively related to relationship quality (Cowan & Cowan, in press), differences between partners' sexuality scores were expected to be negatively related to the couples' assessment of relationship quality.

As can be seen from the "discrepancy" rows of Table 9.3, the general pattern of findings was for large discrepancies to be associated with low relationship quality. However, findings were not entirely consistent across each sexuality score. Relationship quality was negatively related to partner discrepancies on both sexual satisfaction and fidelity for all but the gay couples and to partner discrepancies on sexual perfection for only gay couples.

Partner discrepancies on new sexual techniques were unrelated to relationship quality.

RELEVANCE OF FINDINGS AND SUGGESTIONS
FOR FUTURE RESEARCH

Although this study is limited by the exclusive use of self-report measures and the absence of in-depth assessments of sexual behavior, the current findings fit in well with previous studies and extend previous findings to new areas.

Sexual Nonexclusivity Among Gay Couples

Perhaps the most salient difference between homosexual and heterosexual couples revealed by previous studies is that homosexual partners—especially gay partners—often engage in sex outside of the relationship with each other's knowledge. Gay couples in this study were indeed more likely than the other three couples to be sexually nonexclusive. Also, as expected, sexually nonexclusive gay couples valued fidelity less than sexually exclusive gay couples. However, this was the only area in which differences between the two groups were found. Sexually exclusive and sexually nonexclusive gay couples were equivalent on ratings of sexual satisfaction, the value placed on new sexual techniques, and beliefs regarding sexual perfection. These findings are consistent with reports by Blasband and Peplau (1985) and Kurdek (1988b) that sexually exclusive and sexually nonexclusive gay couples are identical in their assessment of relationship quality.

Sexually nonexclusive gay couples have lived together longer than sexually exclusive gay couples (Kurdek, 1988b; McWhirter & Mattison, 1984). In the absence of longitudinal data, however, it is unknown whether the sexually nonexclusive couples began their relationships on a sexually exclusive basis and then changed to a sexually nonexclusive agreement or whether their relationship was nonexclusive from the beginning.

Given health concerns related to AIDS, the frequency of sex outside of existing primary relationships is likely to decrease or to cease altogether (Stall, Coates, & Hoff, 1988). Because long-lasting gay relationships are often sexually nonexclusive, the shift to sexual exclusivity may introduce new stressors to long-term gay relationships regarding issues of decreased sexual attraction, possessiveness, and autonomy (Barrows & Halgin, 1988). AIDS also presents issues for single gays. Foremost to dating and sexual activity are concerns regarding each partner's human immunodeficiency virus (HIV) status and the ease with which safe-sex techniques can be discussed and practiced (Barrows & Halgin, 1988).

Partner Similarity on Reports of Sexuality

Because gay and lesbian couples are more likely than heterosexual couples to base their relationship on an ethic of equality and reciprocity (Kurdek & Schmitt,

187

1987), the similarity between partners' scores was expected to be stronger in gay and lesbian couples than in heterosexual couples. There was some support for this prediction. Although the sexual satisfaction scores were moderately correlated for partners in each of the four types of couples, partner scores for gay and lesbian couples were also related on the fidelity and new sexual techniques variables. Further, partner scores were correlated for each of the four sexuality scores for only lesbian couples.

Although this pattern of enhanced similarity between partners in homosexual relationships provides additional evidence that same-sex partners are similar to each other (Kurdek & Schmitt, 1987), such similarity may complicate communication between partners regarding the negotiation of roles and workloads within the relationship. Most married couples rely on gender-related socialization expectations to allocate role and workload responsibilities (Hardesty & Bokemeier, 1989), but these are not relevant to same-sex couples. An exciting area of future study is examining how partners in gay and lesbian couples work out these concerns.

Differences Between Homosexual and Heterosexual Couples on Sexuality

In accord with previous findings that gay couples more frequently than other types of couples engage in sex outside of the relationship and experience a greater variety of sexual behaviors (Blumstein & Schwartz, 1983; McWhirter & Mattison, 1984; Peplau & Gordon, 1983), gay couples in this study valued fidelity the least and placed the greatest importance on new sexual techniques. However, it is perhaps even more important to note that the four types of couples were equivalent in their assessments of sexual satisfaction and in their endorsements of dysfunctional beliefs regarding sexual perfection. It is clear that blanket statements cannot be made regarding similarities and differences in sexual behavior between homosexual and heterosexual couples. Rather, such statements must be anchored to a particular dimension of sexual behavior. Further, because concerns regarding AIDS are giving gay couples reasons to be sexually exclusive, differences between homosexual and heterosexual couples on monogamy may diminish. Overall, then, homosexual and heterosexual couples will be more alike than different from each other on the aspects of sexuality studied here.

The Relation Between Satisfaction with Sex and Relationship Satisfaction

Consistent with the findings of Blumstein and Schwartz (1983), satisfaction with sex was positively related to global appraisals of the quality of the relationship. This finding is of note because it occurred for both partners within each type of couple on measures that did not overlap in content. Also, as expected, ratings of the importance of fidelity were positively related to global relationship quality for all but gay couples. Because fidelity and relationship quality were related for both partners in lesbian couples and for wives in married couples, fidelity may be a more critical aspect of relationship quality for women in committed relationship than for men (Blumstein & Schwartz, 1983).

There was little evidence that placing an importance on new sexual techniques was related to relationship quality. The only finding of note here was that couple scores on this variable for lesbian and married couples were *negatively* related. The finding for lesbians is concordant with previous reports that lesbians do not engage in sex frequently and do not experience great variety in the sexual activity they do have, possibly due to the internalization of negative messages regarding female sexuality (Bell & Weinberg, 1978; Blumstein & Schwartz, 1983). This finding should be viewed with caution, however, because the correlations for each lesbian partner were nonsignificant and the assessment of new sexual techniques consisted of a single item. Future studies are needed to assess attitudes toward sexuality among women in particular, and to do so with multi-item measures with demonstrated reliability and validity.

The link between dysfunctional beliefs regarding sexual perfection and relationship quality was significant for only gay and cohabiting couples. What is most interesting about this finding is that these two groups have been noted for their high levels of sexual activity (Blumstein & Schwartz, 1983; Newcomb, 1986). This suggests that couples who prize sexual activity may nonetheless experience relationship distress because of their underlying dysfunctional beliefs regarding sexual perfection. Without a change in these beliefs, frequent sexual activity may only serve to increase relationship distress.

The Relation Between Partner Discrepancies on Sexuality Scores and Relationship Satisfaction

As predicted, discrepancies between partners' sexuality scores were generally negatively related to couples' overall appraisal of relationship quality. This finding extends Cowan and Cowan's (in press) results to the specific domain of sexuality in both homosexual and heterosexual couples. The general pattern of this finding was most evident for the sexual satisfaction score, but not for gay couples. Rather, for these couples, discrepancies on sexual perfection scores were negatively related to global relationship quality. As suggested above, dysfunctional beliefs regarding sexual perfection may be especially problematic in gay relationships. Future studies need to explore the processes underlying the development of such dysfunctional beliefs in order to design interventions on how to change them.

CONCLUSIONS

Relative to heterosexual couples, homosexual couples develop without socialized role models, with no formal social-cultural support, without the biological potential for raising children, and with restrictions in partner selection. Despite these differences, the overall picture that emerges from the study reported here is that homosexual couples are more like heterosexual couples than they are different from them. On the aspects of sexuality examined here, and in agreement with most extant research, evidence showed that partners from the four types of couples were similar to one another on the sexuality scores; that satisfaction with affection and sex is reliably positively related to global relationship satisfaction; and that discrepancies between partners' sexuality scores are negatively related to global relationship satisfaction. The only major difference between homosexual and heterosexual couples was that gay couples placed a lower value on fidelity. However, as the current AIDS crisis has underscored the health risks associated with multiple sex partners, gays may be placing greater importance on monogamy. Therefore, differences between homosexual and heterosexual couples on this dimension of sexuality may diminish in time.

The anatomy of partners in same-sex or opposite-sex couples obviously influences the kind of sexual activity engaged in by homosexual couples and heterosexual couples. These anatomical differences, however, do not prevent sexuality in homosexual and heterosexual couples from serving very similar functions and from operating by very similar psychological processes.

REFERENCES

Barrows, P. A., & Halgin, R. P. (1988). Current issues in psychotherapy with gay men: Impact of the AIDS phenomenon. *Professional Psychology: Research and Practice, 19,* 395–402.

Bell, A. P., & Weinberg, M. S. (1978). *Homosexualities: A study of diversity among men and women.* New York: Simon & Schuster.

Blasband, D., & Peplau, L. A. (1985). Sexual exclusivity versus openness in gay male couples. *Archives of Sexual Behavior, 14,* 395–412.

Blumstein, P., & Schwartz, P. (1983). *American couples.* New York: Morrow.

Buss, D. M. (1988). The evolution of human intrasexual competition: Tactics of mate attraction. *Journal of Personality and Social Psychology, 54,* 616–628.

Byrne, D. (1971). *The attraction paradigm.* New York: Academic Press.

Califia, P. (1979). Lesbian sexuality. *Journal of Homosexuality, 4,* 255–266.

Cowan, P. A., & Cowan, C. P. (in press). Becoming a family: Research and intervention. In I. Sigel & E. Brody (Eds.), *Family research* (Vol. 2). Hillsdale, NJ: Erlbaum.

Diener, E. (1984). Subjective well-being. *Psychological Bulletin, 95,* 542–575.

Eidelson, R. J., & Epstein, N. (1982). Cognition and relationship maladjustment: Development of a measure of relationship beliefs. *Journal of Consulting and Clinical Psychology, 50,* 715–720.

Ellis, L., & Ames, M. A. (1987). Neurohormonal functioning and sexual orientation: A theory of homosexuality–heterosexuality. *Psychological Bulletin, 101,* 233–258.

Fincham, F. D., & Bradbury, T. N. (1987). The assessment of marital quality: A reevaluation. *Journal of Marriage and the Family, 49,* 797–810.

Hardesty, C., & Bokemeier, J. (1989). Finding time and making do: Distribution of household labor in nonmetropolitan marriages. *Journal of Marriage and the Family, 51,* 253–267.

Herek, G. M. (1989). Hate crimes against lesbians and gay men. *American Psychologist, 44,* 948–955.

Kurdek, L. A. (1987). Sex role self schema and psychological adjustment in coupled homosexual and heterosexual men and women. *Sex Roles, 17,* 549–562.

Kurdek, L. A. (1988a). Perceived social support in gays and lesbians in cohabiting relationships. *Journal of Personality and Social Psychology, 54,* 504–509.

Kurdek, L. A. (1988b). Relationship quality of gay and lesbian cohabiting couples. *Journal of Homosexuality, 15,* 93–118.

Kurdek, L. A., & Schmitt, J. P. (1986). Relationship quality of partners in heterosexual married, heterosexual cohabiting, gay, and lesbian relationships. *Journal of Personality and Social Psychology, 51,* 711–720.

Kurdek, L. A., & Schmitt, J. P. (1987). Partner homogamy in married, heterosexual cohabiting, gay, and lesbian couples. *Journal of Sex Research, 23,* 212–232.

McWhirter, D. P., & Mattison, A. M. (1984). *The male couple: How relationships develop.* Englewood Cliffs, NJ: Prentice Hall.

Newcomb, M. D. (1986). Sexual behavior of cohabitors: A comparison of three independent samples. *Journal of Sex Research, 22,* 492–513.

Peplau, L. A., & Cochran, S. D. (1981). Value orientations in the intimate relationships of gay men. *Journal of Homosexuality, 6,* 1–9.

Peplau, L. A., & Gordon, S. L. (1983). The intimate relationships of lesbians and gay men. In E. R. Allgeier & N. B. McCormick (Eds.), *Changing boundaries: Gender roles and sexual behavior* (pp. 226–244). Palo Alto, CA: Mayfield.

Roach, A. J., Frazier, L. P., & Bowden, S. R. (1981). The Marital Satisfaction Scale. *Journal of Marriage and the Family, 40,* 537–546.

Spanier, G. B. (1976). Measuring dyadic adjustment. *Journal of Marriage and the Family, 38,* 15–28.

Stall, R. D., Coates, T. J., & Hoff, C. (1988). Behavioral risk reduction for HIV infection among gay and bisexual men. *American Psychologist, 43,* 878–885.

Afterword: Couples and Coupling

Steve Duck
University of Iowa

My first reaction when the editors invited me to write the afterword was panic: "What is sex and why am I here?" were my first thoughts. I have done work on relationships, but not on sexuality, so why me? Now that I have had a chance to reflect and to read the chapters and rereflect, I see my first thoughts as essentially honest but misplaced. This book is, so far as I am aware, the first to try to focus explicitly and directly on research on sexuality in the context of processes of close personal relationships. Clearly, in compiling this book, enlisting these particular authors, and shaping the book the way it has been shaped, the editors are stating their mission and making the claim that research on sexuality needs to explore more usefully the dynamic role of sexuality in relationship processes and vice versa. It comes across clearly as one of the authors' messages in most chapters, either as theme or subtheme. However, as I argue below, the parallels between the two fields are greater than may have been realized before, and the editors are to be commended for opening up this possibility in the pioneering mission of this volume.

Clearly the processes of sexuality, whatever they are conceived to be, must emerge from somewhere and most often come in to being from the background of a close personal relationship between the relevant partners. At least that is what happens most often in our society. For seemingly obvious reasons, therefore, the link between the existing relationship and the emergence of sexual activity can be tied to a number of relational issues. My purpose in this chapter is to dwell briefly on these issues and then to explore the parallels between work on personal relationships and sexuality. I see development in the two fields following from development of similar themes and concepts.

193

WHAT IS SEX AND WHY AM I HERE?

As Orbuch and Harvey rightly pointed out in their chapter, sexuality can, and perhaps should, be seen as a social process that is different from, but clearly intertwined with, the study of personal relationships in general. There are parallels between growth of sexuality and relationships (both as fields of study and as phenomena for individual members), but I think that this parallelism is problematic and insufficiently clarified at present. Partly this is because research has not yet elucidated and connected three ways in which sexuality and relationships could be interrelated (cf., Duck & Pond, 1989, on the roles of talk in relationships):

1. *Instrumental role (to achieve specific goals).* Sex could be used to develop relationships and relationships could be use to develop sexual involvement. Gigolos who argue that the relationship has reached a stage where sexual intercourse is appropriate are acting instrumentally, as are those who offer sex as a bargain for commitment.

2. *Indexical role (to indicate and "publish" features of the relationship).* The degree of sexual involvement could be tied indexically to the stage of development of a relationship, such that the sexual behavior indexes and manifests, rather than creates instrumentally, the degree of commitment. Those who see sexual intercourse as appropriate only after the marriage ceremony are implicitly seeing it as having at least an indexical role, as were formal witnesses to deflowering in ancient marriage ceremonies.

3. *Essential role (as the essence of things).* The nature of sexuality has some intrinsic quality that is quintessential to the essence of relationships. An individual who claims to be unable to relate to someone fully until after sexual intercourse is making this claim.

The exact nature of the interconnection between sexuality and relationships is complicated by the fact that sexuality is represented in this book as a term embracing different things. According to the contributors to this book, we can view sexuality in one of several ways. In their chapter, Aron and Aron pointed out that some treat it as equivalent to sexual arousal measured at the physiological level, while others view it as an outgrowth of love; Simpson and Gangestad treated it as a consequential result of certain interior psychological structures; Cupach and Metts regarded it as a negotiative task; Bringle and Buunk treated it as a socially complex set of feelings having socially complex results for interpersonal management of relationships; Kurdek and DeLamater in their respective chapters and in different ways discussed its emergence partly from "cold" or distant social structure; for Christopher and Roosa—and to some extent Muehlenhard et al.—it is the result of complex decision making that can be influenced by the "hot" immediate network in which it occurs.

At one level the creation of sexual opportunities is clearly a persuasive task: At least one lustful person persuades another to indulge the lustfulness. At another level, the form that is taken by the expression of sexuality is a clear instance of the acculturating influence of society and its systems upon its individual members, who proceed to exercise their muscular spasms innocently but inexorably in tune to the orchestration of social prescription. Somewhere in between is the argument that sexuality is a consequence and a parallel of the emergence of dyadic commitment, although the correlation speaks to no particular direction of causal influence.

However one comes down on the issue of sex and relationships, there are clearly several components to sexuality that are relevant in relationships, and vice versa. Both have an attitudinal and personality component in that the individuals in the relationship have attitudes about each other, about the nature of sexuality, about specific sorts of sexual activity, and about its role in relationships. This may be honed by personality from the raw lumber of attitudes transmitted culturally through socialization and the media, but we can be sure that the hierarchy of sexual preferences and preferred behaviors is not innocently and immediately identical in all pairs of individuals that could be constructed, a situation that presents couples with a need to negotiate and discover. Sex and relationships can be construed as persuasive tasks (encouraging someone else to engage in a relationship or in sexual interaction, or in specific sorts of sexual activity), and both have been seen that way in the scholarly literature (e.g., Christopher & Roosa, this volume; Cupach & Metts, this volume; Miller & Boster, 1988). Both can develop and change with time. Both are thought to depend to some extent in most cases on personal commitment, personal involvement, and personal wishes, but the role of these in the trajectory taken by a couple is clearly not self-evident and seems likely to be mediated by mechanisms to which no chapter here speaks directly (but cf. Cupach & Metts), namely the role of *everyday talk* and mundane daily relational communications through which both the relationship and sexual activity are predominantly and inevitably (but not exclusively) negotiated.

Such a point is important, I believe, because whether sexuality is viewed as primarily a physiological, psychological, or sociological investment, the meaning attached to particular activities is clearly a symbolic feature of the enterprise; when we talk of sexuality in personal relationships, we are implicitly focusing on personal and dyadic meaning. In fact, we are doing that in at least two ways. First, if the graduation or development of sexual behavior is tied to the development of relationships, then it means something in that context in the sense that people would not do it if they were not seeing it as relevant to the relational context. Second, if sexuality is in any way tied to expression of self or of emotion or as a signal of commitment (i.e., to the *existence* of a relationship), then its signaling function is based on the meaning that certain types of behavior are felt to convey to others.

Davis (1983) took a similar but more expansive view when he argued that sex is closely tied to ideology and conveys to most thinkers a representation of social structure and influence. As Davis (1983) asked: First, not why does sexual behavior occur, but why does it occur *in private?* Second, why do people want to do it, and why do other people want to stop them or to regulate it? In other words, why does society devote such energy to restricting the expression of sexual desire and to regulating its form of expression? For such authors as Davis, sex is a symbol for people and carries important and powerful messages that ultimately relate to the society's views of free will, individuality, morality, and the fabric in which society is woven. As I argue here, the role of sex in relationships comes down to a similar symbolic function based on the meaning of certain behavior in the context of relationships. Davis would perhaps argue that even the tying of sex to relationships, as in this volume, and attempts to explain its role in relationships are subtle ways for us to accept socialization forces that require us to make respectable the animal side of life and to bond it closely to other, more acceptable, social institutions such as relationships. There is after all no a priori or physical reason why sex and personal relationships should be linked, as relationships between customers and prostitutes seem to show. The reasons are clearly socially more than physically necessary. Thus, the very juxtaposing of sexuality in the context of relationships makes some assumptions, which we all tend to accept because they seem obvious. However, it is not obvious, and it is a testament to our socialization that we see it so. What faces us are the issues of deciding why romantic relationships do not emerge from a social vacuum and of accounting for the vastly complex ideational and attitudinal environment from which two individual personalities negotiate the sexual activity in their relationship.

Given these considerations, let me now turn to the field of personal relationships and what it can teach us about the processes of relationship development in the context of sexuality.

SEXUALITY AND RELATIONSHIPS

I believe that present trends in the personal relationship field have great relevance to this book's concerns and mission, even though they stem from the discourse of another research domain. But, more than this, I believe that some of the emphases identified by the editors and authors, and other emphases that can be drawn from their work, are deep reflections of parallel concerns in the new wave of research on personal relationships that is beginning to turn the tide of older thinking in that field.

What's New in the Study of Relationships?

I have spent all of my scholarly life attempting to promote interdisciplinary work on personal relationships and trying to show how the everyday conduct of relationships influences and is influenced by the activities that occur in the routine and mundane behaviors of life (Duck, 1973, 1986, 1988, 1990). In the course of this involvement with the field, I have seen its main character and emphasis slowly change. When I began my pilgrimage, the hot topic was interpersonal attraction and the scientific study of its elusiveness. The classic work by Berscheid and Walster (1969) was published, auspiciously, the year after I began my doctorate.

The early work on interpersonal attraction was largely concerned with the stimulus properties of individuals as perceived by one another. It explored the cognitive and judgmental results of being presented with stimuli that had known value (whether physical attractiveness levels rated by outsiders, descriptive trait judgments established by reliable tests, or attitude similarity manipulated precisely by the experimenters). Although such work took us into some new corners in the academic storehouse, it was fundamentally a "three-eyed" model: individualistic, internalized, and inert. Attraction was in the individual's head; it was a standardized global response to cues of known (and therefore not idiosyncratically valued) worth, so that everyone else's reaction to them ought to be the same. It was essentially something that just happened, almost without the partner having anything to do with it except present his or her external appearance or cognitive structure for evaluation and judgment. Such an emphasis somewhat disembodies cognitive processes and presents them not as forces in a living interactive world but rather like a calculating machine that is, like an elderly relative, benevolently trundled from place to place, stimulus to stimulus, and interaction to interaction. The interactions that it observes, but does not really participate in, are not emotionally involving, are never problematic for the participants, do not require to be managed, do not have moral and personal consequences in the here and now, present no instant dilemmas for facework, and do not stir the loins, except insofar as these are hard-wired into judgmental processes. Incidentally, for all of these reasons, we know more about initial liking than long-term relationships and more about sexually attractive stimuli than how sex works in real life.

I do not reject this work out of hand, as some do (Levinger, 1972). It has its place and tells us something useful about parts of an extremely complex process, whose complexity became clearer only after researchers were stimulated by this work to explore further. Obviously, social judgment occurs (and not altogether in ways that are self-evident). Such processes also obviously affect social interaction and need to be understood. But they also need to be contextualized and redintegrated with what else we have learned about the enactments of social and sexual life, the dilemmas, problems, and issues faced there in the everyday conduct of social interaction. Two new and recent directions stemming from this beginning are toward negotiation of the form and content of the relationship, and toward an emphasis on personal meaning of behavior, although logical extensions of the earlier work also persist.

The field of personal relationships now evidences strong interests in the ways in which people negotiate and develop their working relationships from initial desires and preferences for a partner (Huston, Surra, Fitzgerald, & Cate, 1981). The emphasis is now on relationships as processes, involving the long-term management, maintenance, development, and, in some cases, decline of relationships rather than their straightforward and optimistic initiation (Cate & Lloyd, 1988; Dindia & Baxter, 1987; Duck, 1982; Duck & Sants, 1983). In the course of making such a change of emphasis, the field has inevitably moved from its overwhelming concern with the interior world of social judgment and internal social-psychological cognitive processes. In their place is now a view of such factors balanced against the realities of everyday life communication and everyday pressures that occur in the context of relationships, interaction with the society in which the relationship occurs, and a range of issues having to do with life-course development (Hay, 1988; Montgomery, 1988).

To put this another way, from a growing understanding of the role of attitudes and cognitions in the birth and formation of relationships there has developed an equally strong desire to understand the ways in which partners conduct those relationships, shape them, are shaped by them, influence their pathways, and enact them in and into the rest of their lives. Long rejected now is the old notion, still vigorously advocated by the dating agencies, popular magazines, and some of our own unconscious ways of thinking and behaving, that people are destined for each other on the basis of their individual characteristics alone. On that model, relationships succeed because of the individual qualities that partners bring to them, for instance their attitudes, their personalities, their socio-demographic characteristics, or their physical attractiveness. Now the concern is with the ways in which these qualities and characteristics translate into behavior and interpersonal communication (Duck & Sants, 1983), with the ways in which the two persons negotiate a working relationship out of such qualities, and with the processes that are set in train by the operation and even the clashing of these separate things (Baxter, in press).

To draw a moral for the present concerns, we can see that likewise the area of sex research has not only been interested in the attitudes toward sex that are held by partners individually or the emotions that they feel toward one another, or the beliefs that they have about sex, but has also tended to try to predict success of the sexual relationship or sexual satisfaction on the basis of such information (see Simpson & Gangestad, this volume). I will argue that future work on sex should follow the developing trend in this field, as in personal relationships, toward a more strongly communicative emphasis that explores the *interaction* of minds rather than the *contents* of minds, an emphasis upon process, in other words (cf, Cupach & Metts, this volume; Christopher & Roosa, this volume).

This can be taken further. We do need to understand the ways in which well-explored cognitive structures influence the actual behavior, communication, interaction, and, dare I say it, social intercourse of partners—and to do this we must *explore* influence rather than assume we know how it works. In brief, we need to incorporate some explicit model of the way in which cognitive structures lead to specific behavioral and explicitly communicative output—a topic long studied in both communication studies and rhetoric from different points of view but sadly neglected by cognitive social psychology. To do this we need to step back and learn what is the *meaning* to partners of such things, what they symbolize, and what they convey communicatively as signs of the relationship (cf, DeLamater, this volume).

Thus, the second new concern that I noted above (i.e., *meaning*) is relevant here and inextricably connected with a move to study *process* and *communication,* three factors identified by Mead (1934) as related. Important here are the creation of personal and dyadic meanings as relationships develop and a sense of uniqueness or specialness or identification derived from talk and interpersonal interaction, joint action, planning, daydreaming, hoping, and all the other activity that is involved in relating or focusing two minds on the relationship or on sex, if it comes to that (Duck & Pond, 1989). This is both a parallel and a consequent development with the first. On the one hand, a relationship clearly involves some sort of accommodation of the two individuals to each other, to their needs and their preferences. Thus, their attitudes, behaviors, plans, nonverbal communication, styles of behavior, communication, talk, time together, leisure, discourse, beliefs, performances and microbehaviors need to be adapted, accommodated, and coordinated. Such coordinations are not natural, inevitable, and inexorable consequences of the expression of some ethereal cognitive content. In the real world beyond the laboratory they actually have to be *done,* and they are done not by abstract negotiation but by specific talk.

Equally, the meanings of behavior, of the other person as a partner, and of the relationship, are clearly not absolute but are decided by persons according to their own individual frames of reference. Partners will develop cute linguistic and behavioral signs of their cognitively felt connection, such as tie signs (Goffman, 1959) or personal idioms of speech (Hopper, Knapp, & Scott, 1981), especially about sexual matters (Bell, Buerkel-Rothfuss, & Gore, 1987). Thus, the negotiation of relationships is also essentially a negotiation of meaning as well as of behavior, preferences, styles, and other things and one that is influenced by the personal and cultural meanings that the individuals themselves bring to the experience. For instance, a relationship is satisfying not simply because the individuals enjoy the profit–loss ratio but because that whole equation is something that this culture teaches us to calculate and for which, by various means and media, it establishes reference points (McCall, 1988). This is because the culture has evolved expectations about the way in which relationships develop (e.g., their speed of development, the timing of certain behaviors, the direction of growth, the ways in which development should be manifested) and because the individuals in that relationship know about all of that to some degree and accept it. By contrast, other cultures, such as those based on Buddhist principles, see the causation and development of relationships as less to do with personal agency in the Western, Aristotelian, teleological terms, and more to do with the correct disposition of contextual forces that come together in auspicious ways that promote the relationship.

Translating some of this into the terms of this book, we can see that much of the above also applies equally well to research on sexuality and sexual behavior in close personal relationships. Sexual behavior involves not only negotiation by means of a behavioral and communicative translation of beliefs, attitudes, and emotions, but also the evocation, development, and sharing of sets of meanings that, although personal, are also firmly embedded in the cultural contexts where the sexual behavior takes place. Some sexual practices are generally regarded, as unacceptably perverse (e.g., pedophilia), and others (e.g., masturbation), once condemned wholesale, are now enjoyed more widely than they were even in Kinsey's time (and perhaps partly because of Kinsey's demonstration that they are more widely practiced than had been realized). Pedophilia was, however, a widespread and commonly accepted practice in ancient Greece, the cradle of modern civilization, and as reported by Herdt (1981), is still practiced in some cultures as part of magic rituals to bring boys to manhood. Thus, we can be sure that in any society, the negotiation of acceptable sexual practices within a given dyad is something that can have variability and individualistic interpretation (Reiss, 1989) but that nevertheless does need to be sorted out by the dyad in terms of its own meaning system within the culture in which it is embedded. To some extent the relationship takes its own character from its resolution of such issues, and this is not predetermined. Christopher and Cate (1985) were quite right to alert us to the fact that there are different ways to do this, the miracle being that they found as few as four basic means of doing this.

In the field of personal relationships, one could level the criticism that the social-psychological reapers and sowers have often and for too long acted as if interaction is of little relevance to relationships. In its concern over cognitive variables whose interactive effects are simply presumed without test, the field has only slowly come to attend to such matters as the strategies that people adopt to express their cognitive contents or the behavioral means through which strategies are actually enacted, decoded, and expressed in real living behavior. For example, one major and extremely productive methodological development in the past 15 years, the Rochester Interaction Record (RIR) (Wheeler & Nezlek, 1977; Wheeler, Reis, & Nezlek, 1983) has allowed researchers to study subjects' reports of their social participation and to discover how these relate to relationally impactful variables such as physical attractiveness or loneliness (Wheeler, Reis, & Nezlek, 1980; Wheeler, et al., 1983). However, although the RIR has created a fertile atmosphere for the conduct of studies of social participation in many different disciplines, which is all to the good, it contains not one single item, question, or scale about talk, which it thus implicitly represents as irrelevant to the study of interaction. Yet what is interaction if talk is taken out of it?

A further odd assumption is to act as if the future is a certainty for partners and as if the present form and shape of a relationship essentially determine its future form and shape. In essence, the personal relationships field, as has the sexuality field to judge from the present chapters, has assumed that relationships are constants once defined/achieved: A courtship or a dating relationship or a sexual partnership is treated as a little constant moving forward through the world. But we miss the point here about the way in which human beings experience their relationships or their sexual partnership, because we have focused on the mean, as it were, rather than the variance. An alternative, advocated in the broad case by Billig (1987), is to see life as unfinished business, of which relationships are also an unfinished part, as I have argued at length elsewhere (Duck, 1990). Partners in relationships, whether sexual ones or not, are never able to state with absolute certainty that the future of the relationship will be as it has been in the past and sex in the future in the relationship may not be as it has been in the past. In addition, their daily involvement with it is often uncertain and replete with dilemmas and new experiences and circumstances.

We have paid too little attention to the transformations and variations that can occur in attitudes and behaviors, including sexual attitudes and behaviors, day by day or the variation brought about by, for example, mood, daily stress, circumstances, daily events, recent experiences in the relationship, boredom, other tasks, the influence of outsiders, and the recency or success/failure of previous attempts at intimacy or sexual activity or intercourse. Thus, although several chapters here reported on patterns of sexual behavior in the general case, none (and incidentally, almost none in the field of personal relationships either) explored the specific conduct of individual sexual relationships over periods of time, day by day, as a way of understanding how they work. Such work could, of course, be relatively tedious and somewhat intrusive, but not really much more of either of these things than some previous work such as that by Blumstein and Schwartz (1983), which amounted to their massive qualitative and quantitative survey *American Couples: Money, Work, Sex*. It requires merely systematic attention to the real lives of individuals, which is essentially the mundane reality that all our scholarship and experimental attempts to achieve mundane realism are ultimately attempting to explicate.

In underresearching such things as mundane activities and talk, the field has so far paid too little attention to the ways in which relationships are created and embodied in the talk, daily routines, and mundane interactions of partners with each other not only about the relationship but also about other things in their experiences day by day. In brief, day-to-day experiences of relationships have essentially been presented as functionally irrelevant to scholarly understanding of them. I believe that in both close personal relationships and sexuality research this is a faulty assumption because the variation in many relationships is quite as much a cause for discussion and relationship negotiation as is the average. Indeed, I am convinced that variation and difference are their very essence. Rates of sexual involvement, as well as sexual desire, sexual satisfaction, sexual motivation, and so on, are not perpetually constant and invariant in relationships any more than anything else is, and this variation may be a cause for relationship problems (cf. Bringle & Buunk, this volume). In any case, variety and variation promote talk, discussion, and the need to resolve and regularize things, given the human tendency to seek and create order, consistency, and stability.

This generally curious state of affairs exists in many forms of social scientific research, namely, the undervaluing of the roles of talk in social settings especially about everyday occurrences and events or problems. It is apparent here also. In the sexuality research in this volume, the variables of communication (such as topic control, synchrony of talk, the way talk is organized, dominance in discourse, communicator style, strategies of message production) seem to be largely omitted or perhaps assumed to operate in known ways and have known effects. Authors such as Simpson and Gangestad argued essentially that, if we know someone's personality, we can make clear predictions about the ways in which these personality characteristics are expressed and we can essentially take for granted the ways in which they operate in day-to-day talk with a partner. The Cupach and Metts chapter is a notable and exemplary exception here in that they focused, for the first time, I believe, on issues of face management in enacting decisions that appear from other chapters to be such easy and uncomplicated products of a rational, disembodied, cognitive process. Their view of communication denies the often-implicit view of "communication as mail delivery" rather than as sharing and *coordination* of systems of meaning, many of them personally created within the couple itself.

Yet if sex is not intimately interactive, then what is it? Davis' (1983) book *SMUT* clearly discusses the role of talk and other forms of communication in sexual settings especially as a manipulator of symbols in ways that speed the transition from normal to erotic reality—a transition that Davis sees as a fundamental part of sexual experience. Yet we find that the types of variables (such as attitudes, parental beliefs, estrogen levels and physiology, or personality style) used to explain sexual behavior are essentially static and individually centered.

To judge from the chapters here, then, one could level the criticism against research on sex that the styles of interaction between partners are too little studied, that the future is treated as something that is essentially certain and as if the present shape and form of relationships have certain built-in assumptions about sexual relationships; it has paid too little attention to microscopic change in relationships and sexual activity day by day, and has covered very little of the day-by-day talk and conversation that partners use to embody their relationships and set the scene for whatever sexual activity takes place.

For us to develop from this point, I believe that the personal relationships field, the field of study of sexuality in close relationships, and the sexuality field need to converge upon the theme that I have developed here: the way in which separate personalities come together to create a system of shared meaning in which their feelings for each other and their sexual behaviors are each a part. We need therefore to study everyday life talk.

I believe that we need more work on the direct strategies with which people operate with their cognitive processes in talk, but more than this we need maps of talk in everyday settings. We really know far too little about the sorts of things that people say to each other in relationships, whether they are discussing sex or not. A focus on specific sorts of talk or negotiation, such as decision making or conflict, gives only a glimpse of the total distribution of talk in the typical day; even in respect of such a well-studied topic as self-disclosure a number of independent everyday talk studies now show that its incidence in real life has been seriously overestimated (Fitzpatrick, Dindia, & Kenny, 1990; Duck, Rutt, Hurst, & Strejc, in press).

We need to clarify the ways in which people propose sexual activity (Christopher & Roosa, and Muehlenhard, Goggins, Satterfield, & Jones, this volume), eroticise their discussions with each other, just say no to sexual advances, actually verbalize the problem of asking about safe sex, talk to others in the peer group about sex, and so on. In addition, we need an understanding of the ways in which sex talk arises from the normal interaction of relationships, as partners get ideas and desires, make suggestions to each other, react to the other's suggestions, and generally fit sex into their ordinary lives (cf. Davis, 1983). Furthermore, we need to understand the role of talk, not just as an unexplored or taken-for-granted medium for the conveyance of personality traits into the outside world, but as a real dynamic force in the conduct of relationships and sexual interaction.

To meet such a prescription, I have been vigorously developing a research instrument to assess daily experience of relationship talk in a systematic way. The Iowa Communication Record (ICR) is a form on which subjects report their conversations and the circumstances surrounding them in a structured fashion (see Duck et al., in press; Leatham & Duck, 1990). The ICR produces details about the talk that people carry on in daily interaction, the situation and context for the talk, and its relational consequences. Modeled on the Rochester Interaction Record but extended to talk and communication, it offers a rich harvest of raw data about the everyday interactions and conversations upon which people build their relationships and their sexual interactions. Such raw data, although of interest in themselves (e.g., we have found that Wednesday is the day most likely to generate stressful discussion in normal relationships; Duck et al., in press), can also be tied to other events and circumstances in the relationship.

Although such a technique has not yet been applied to work on sexuality or sexual talk, it is clearly a potential means of relating recall of talk to personality variables, to issues of jealousy origin and management, to adolescent discussions with peers about sex, to the sexual scenarios that lead to violence, and to the issue of face management in sexual negotiations. It is also possibly useful in exploring sexual decision making, comparing conversational management of sexual relations in heterosexual and homosexual couples, and clarifying the role of sex in the talk of individuals seeking self-expansion, perhaps even to elucidate why there exists the poor correspondence between parent–child communication and the sexual behavior of adolescents noted by Christopher and Roosa (this volume). It is not a panacea, but I do think that it helps to focus us on the key issue that makes couples and coupling two parallel domains of study: talk as the dynamic for relationships.

In conclusion, and whether or not the reader is persuaded to consider such a technique, it is clear that the role of talk in relationships is fundamental, and it is also important in sexuality. Where sexual behavior takes place in the context of a close relationship, I simply cannot see why or how talk (and all the communicative stuff that goes with it, in terms of strategies, style, and organization) can be omitted from our studies. Perhaps one of the many benefits of this volume will be that it stimulates other researchers to ask that very question.

REFERENCES

Baxter, L. A. (in press). *Relationships and culture.* New York: Guilford.

Bell, R. A., Buerkel-Rothfuss, N., & Gore, K. (1987). "Did you bring the yarmulke for the cabbage patch kid?" The idiomatic communication of young lovers *Human Communication Research, 14,* 47–67.

Berscheid, E., & Walster, E. H. (1969). *Interpersonal attraction.* Reading, MA: Addison-Wesley.

Billig, M. (1987). *Arguing and thinking: A rhetorical approach to social psychology.* Cambridge, UK: Cambridge University Press.

Blumstein, P., & Schwartz, P. (1983). *American couples: Money, work and sex.* New York: Morrow.

Cate, R. M., & Lloyd, S. A. (1988). Courtship. In S. W. Duck (Ed.), with D. F. Hay, S. E. Hobfoll, W. Ickes, & B. Montgomery, *Handbook of personal relationships* (pp. 409–427) Chichester, UK: Wiley.

Christopher, F. S., & Cate, R. M. (1985). Premarital sexual pathways and relationship development. *Journal of Social and Personal Relationships, 2,* 271–288.

Davis, M. S. (1983). *SMUT: Erotic reality/obscene ideology.* Chicago: University of Chicago Press.

Dindia, K., & Baxter, L. A. (1987). Strategies for maintaining and repairing marital relationships. *Journal of Social and Personal Relationships, 4,* 143–158.

Duck, S. W. (1973). *Personal relationships and personal constructs: A study of friendship formation.* Chichester, UK: Wiley.

Duck, S. W. (1982). A topography of relationship disengagement and dissolution. In S. W. Duck (Ed.), *Personal relationships 4: Dissolving personal relationships* (pp. 1–32). London: Academic Press.

Duck, S. W. (1986). *Human relationships.* London: Sage.

Duck, S. W. (1988). *Relating to others.* London: Open University Press; Monterey, CA: Dorsey/Brooks/Cole/Wadsworth.

Duck, S. W. (1990). Relationships as unfinished business: Out of the frying pan into the 1990s. *Journal of Social and Personal Relationships, 7,* 5–28.

Duck, S. W., & Pond, K. (1989). Friends, Romans, countrymen, Lend me your retrospective data: Rhetoric and reality in personal relationships. In C. Hendrick (Ed), *Review of Social Psychology and Personality (10): Close Relationships* (pp. 1–27). Newbury Park, CA: Sage.

Duck, S. W., Rutt, D. J., Hurst, M., & Strejc, H. (in press). Some evident truths about communication in everyday relationships: All communication is not created equal. *Human Communication Research* (under revision).

Duck, S. W., & Sants, H. K. A. (1983). On the origin of the specious: Are personal relationships really interpersonal states? *Journal of Social and Clinical Psychology, 1,* 27–41.

Fitzpatrick, M. A., Dindia, K., & Kenny, D. (1990). Personal communication.

Goffman, E. (1959). *Behaviour in public places.* Harmondsworth: Penguin.

Hay, D. F. (1988). Section overview. In S. W. Duck (Ed.), with D. F. Hay, S. E. Hobfoll, W. Ickes, & B. Montgomery, *Handbook of personal relationships* (pp. 117–120). Chichester, UK: Wiley.

Herdt, G. (1981). *Guardians of the flute: Idioms of masculinity.* New York: McGraw-Hill.

Hopper, R., Knapp, M. L., & Scott, L. (1981). Couples personal idioms: Exploring intimate talk. *Journal of Communication, 31,* 23–33.

Huston, T. L., Surra, C. A., Fitzgerald, N. M., & Cate, R. M. (1981). From courtship to marriage: Mate selection as an interpersonal process. In S. W. Duck & R. Gilmour (Eds.), *Personal relationships 2: Developing personal relationships* (pp. 53–87) London & New York: Academic Press.

Leatham, G., & Duck, S. W. (1990). Conversations with friends and the dynamics of social support. In S. W. Duck (Ed.), *Personal relationships and social support.* (pp. 1–29). London: Sage.

Levinger, G. (1972). Little sandbox/big quarry. *Journal of Unpublishable Results, 1,* 10–11.

McCall, G. J. (1988). The organizational life cycle of relationships. In S. W. Duck, (Ed.) with D. F. Hay, S. E. Hobfoll, W. J. Ickes, & B. M. Montgomery, *Handbook of personal relationships* (pp. 467–489), Chichester, UK: Wiley.

Mead, G. H. (1934). *Mind self and society.* Chicago: University of Chicago Press.

Miller, G. R., & Boster, F. (1988). Persuasion in personal relationships. In S. W. Duck (Ed.) with D. F. Hay, S. E. Hobfoll, W. Ickes, & B. Montgomery, *Handbook of Personal Relationships* (pp. 275–288). Wiley: Chichester, UK.

Montgomery, B. M. (1988). Quality communication in personal relationships. In S. W. Duck, (Ed.) with D. F. Hay, S. E. Hobfoll, W. Ickes, & B. Montgomery, *Handbook of personal relationships* (pp. 343–359). Chichester, UK: Wiley.

Reiss, I. L. (1989). Society and sexuality: A sociological explanation. In K. McKinney & S. Sprecher (Eds.), *Human sexuality: The societal and interpersonal context* (pp. 3–29). New York: Ablex.

Wheeler, L., & Nezlek, J. (1977). Sex difference in social participation. *Journal of Personality and Social Psychology, 45,* 943–953.

Wheeler, L., Reis, H. T., & Nezlek, J. (1980). Physical attractiveness and social interaction. *Journal of Personality and Social Psychology, 38,* 604–617.

Wheeler, L., Reis, H. T., & Nezlek, J. (1983). Loneliness, social interaction, and sex roles. *Journal of Personality and Social Psychology, 35,* 742–754.

Author index

Subject Index